Technology
Economic Growth
and Public Policy

RICHARD R. NELSON

MERTON J. PECK

EDWARD D. KALACHEK

Technology
Economic Growth
and Public Policy

A RAND Corporation and Brookings Institution Study

THE BROOKINGS INSTITUTION

WASHINGTON, D.C.

© 1967
THE RAND CORPORATION
Santa Monica, California

Published January 1967 by
THE BROOKINGS INSTITUTION
1775 Massachusetts Avenue, N.W.
Washington, D.C.

Library of Congress Catalogue Card Number 67-14973

THE BROOKINGS INSTITUTION is an independent organization devoted to nonpartisan research, education, and publication in
economics, government, foreign policy, and the social sciences
generally. Its principal purposes are to aid in the development of sound public policies and to promote public understanding of issues of national importance.

The Institution was founded December 8, 1927, to merge the activities
of the Institute for Government Research, founded in 1916, the Institute of
Economics, founded in 1922 and the Robert Brookings Graduate School
of Economics and Government, founded in 1924.

The general administration of the Institution is the responsibility of a
self-perpetuating Board of Trustees. The trustees are likewise charged with
maintaining the independence of the staff and fostering the most favorable
conditions for creative research and education. The immediate direction of
the policies, program, and staff of the Institution is vested in the President,
assisted by the division directors and an advisory council, chosen from the
professional staff of the Institution.

In publishing a study, the Institution presents it as a competent treatment of a subject worthy of public consideration. The interpretations and
conclusions in such publications are those of the author or authors and do
not purport to represent the views of the other staff members, officers, or
trustees of the Brookings Institution.

THE RAND CORPORATION is an independent nonprofit organization engaged primarily in research on problems related to national security. A major portion of the Corporation's work is under contract with the United States Air Force. Research is also done for other agencies, such as the Office of the Secretary of Defense, the United States Atomic Energy Commission, and the National Aeronautics and Space Administration. In addition, the Corporation does research under grants from the National Institutes of Health and from private foundations, and with its own funds.

A Board of Trustees representing science, industry, and the public governs the Corporation. Some 600 members of the RAND staff are directly engaged in research, which is conducted in eleven technical departments: Aero-Astronautics, Computer Sciences, Cost Analysis, Economics, Electronics, Geophysics and Astronomy, Logistics, Mathematics, Physics, Social Science, and System Operations. Each department undertakes research in its special field, but major studies cross administrative lines and draw upon all the requisite professional skills in the organization.

RAND Corporation-sponsored research deals with nonmilitary aspects of national security and the public welfare.

RAND research is published in reports, memoranda, papers, and books. Classified publications are distributed to the Department of Defense and its contractors, and to other governmental agencies. Unclassified publications are made available to the public. The interpretations and conclusions of RAND research are the authors' and should not be considered as reflecting the views of the Corporation or any of its governmental or private research sponsors.

Foreword

The contribution of technological change to economic growth and the problem of adjusting to technical progress have commanded increasing public attention in the 1960's. This book explores the relations among research, development, innovation, and economic growth; considers the manner in which the economy adapts to technical change and the problems encountered in the processes of adaptation; and recommends several policy changes designed to encourage technological change consistent with other public policy objectives. Since they address policy makers as well as scholars, the authors have tried to avoid scholarly jargon without sacrificing scholarly rigor.

Richard R. Nelson of the RAND Corporation, Merton J. Peck of Yale University and the Brookings Institution, and Edward D. Kalachek of Washington University at St. Louis completed this study as a joint project of the Brookings Institution and the RAND Corporation. The project was financed by the Ford Foundation, the RAND Corporation, and the Brookings Institution.

The authors acknowledge with gratitude the incisive comments of the Brookings reading committee consisting of Carl Kaysen, William Capron, Edwin Mills, Edwin Mansfield, and Zvi Griliches. At RAND, James Schlesinger, Bruce Smith, and George Hall commented extensively on various drafts. Burton Klein and Joseph A. Pechman were helpful advisers throughout. The authors are also strongly indebted to Jacob Schmookler for his basic contributions to this field of study. The manuscript was edited by Patricia B. Natirbov, and the index was prepared by Helen B. Eisenhart.

The views expressed in this book are those of the authors and are not presented as the views of the Ford Foundation, the RAND Corporation, or the staff members, officers, or trustees of the Brookings Institution.

Robert D. Calkins
President

Washington, D.C.
December 1966

Contents

xi

Tables

Contents

Charts

Introduction

Technological advance has generally mystified layman and economist alike. In the popular literature technological advance tends to be viewed as the result of the insight of a hero inventor, or as the automatic by-product of a great scientific discovery—in any case, an unpredictable and uncontrollable force. With few exceptions, until recently the economist's treatment of technological advance did little better in facilitating understanding of the subject. In most of the literature on economic growth, technological advance tended to float in the air as a factor which increased the productivity of capital and labor, its contribution being estimated sometimes by the residual in the growth rate after allowance for growth explained by other factors, sometimes by a time trend in productivity.[1]

In recent years economists and other social scientists have begun to deal more explicitly with technological change. Research has been undertaken on the relationship between productivity growth and research and development spending and other activities directed towards advancing technology. Other studies have examined the factors influencing the allocation of resources to advancing technology among the various sectors of the economy. Still other work has focused on the factors influencing the rate at which new technology is absorbed into the economy.[2] Part I of this

[1] Edward F. Denison, *The Sources of Economic Growth in the United States and the Alternatives Before Us* (New York: Committee for Economic Development, 1962), is an example of the first; Robert Solow, "Technical Progress, Capital Formation, and Economic Growth," *American Economic Review,* Vol. 52, No. 2 (May 1962), is an example of the second.

[2] See, for example, Zvi Griliches, "Research Expenditures, Education, and the Aggregate Agricultural Production Function," *American Economic Review,* Vol. 54 (December 1964); Edwin Mansfield, *Econometric Studies of Industrial Research and Technological Innovation* (New York: W. W. Norton & Co., 1967); Jacob

1

book draws together much of this work, and attempts to further develop understanding of the relationship between technological advance and the economy.

Central to the analyses in Part I is an operational concept of technological knowledge. The discussion centers on the different kinds of pertinent knowledge, the various stages in its creation and application, the diverse inputs required in these stages, and the factors affecting the allocation of these inputs. Also examined is the interdependency between technological advance and other important factors in the process of economic growth, such as expansion and updating of capital stock, increases in educational attainment, and shifts in the allocation of resources from low to high productivity uses.

Part II deals with the ways the economy adjusts to technical change. It addresses the laymen's fears that the existing economic and social structures are not capable of adjusting to the consequences of technical change. In the past, technological change has destroyed the social and economic framework of traditional rural pursuits and small-scale craft production and brought job and income insecurity in its wake. Many people see this problem intensifying in the future, as a wave of automation inundates existing economic institutions.[3]

Professional economists generally take a more sanguine view of the future regarding job security. After three decades of revolutionary change in social policy, society seems on the verge of reconciling rapid technological advance with continuing high employment and a high degree of personal economic security. There remains, however, a serious reluctance to deal with other costs of technological advance and rapid economic growth, such as smog, water pollution, noise, congestion, and other hazards to health and safety which have become blights on the physical and psychological landscape. Indeed, society is still so lethargic in dealing with these problems that it often accepts them fatalistically as the "costs of progress."

Schmookler, *Invention and Economic Growth* (Cambridge: Harvard University Press, 1966), and Everett Rogers, *The Diffusion of Innovations* (New York: The Free Press of Glencoe, 1962).

[3] Perhaps the most striking example of the panic literature is Donald N. Michael, *Cybernation: The Silent Conquest* (Santa Barbara: Center for Study of Democratic Institutions, 1962). The report of the National Commission on Technology, Automation, and Economic Progress, *Technology and the American Economy*, Vol. 1 (Washington: Government Printing Office, 1966), takes a more balanced view.

Clearly, the net benefit that society reaps from technological progress depends in considerable degree on the costs of adjusting to change, and the costs of inadequately adjusting. The extent to which society should foster technological advance therefore depends on the strengths and weaknesses of existing adjustment mechanisms, a matter examined in Part II.

Part III is more directly oriented toward public policy concerning technical advance. Certainly this area is no longer ignored. Rather, there is considerable interest in federal policies to stimulate technical advance and channel it in more socially productive directions. Research and development (R&D) programs on supersonic civilian transport aircraft and inter-urban ground transport have been initiated. A program of support of textile research has begun, and a Presidential Commission has been formed to examine the patent system. Proposals have been made for a vast expansion of R&D for the nondefense public sector, and for support of civilian technology generally.[4] Since this volume was substantially completed, the Presidential Commission an Automation has reported, but its report became available after this manuscript was completed.[5]

Despite the ferment, and a considerable amount of action, policy making in this field has suffered from an inability to delineate the proper role of private and public financing and institutions, and from the lack of agreement on criteria for determining when government programs are justified. Part III of this book outlines a suitable framework for establishing such criteria. It suggests both a set of broad problem areas where new governmental programs might have positive results, and a general strategy for policy making in this area.

[4] For an example, see *Report of the Committee on the Economic Impact of Defense and Disarmament,* July 1965 (Washington: Government Printing Office, 1965), particularly pp. 51-55; U. S. Department of Commerce, U. S. National Bureau of Standards, "Improving the National Climate for Invention and Innovation" (Washington: The Bureau, mimeo, 1965); and Council of Economic Advisers, *Economic Report of the President Together with the Annual Report of the Council of Economic Advisers* (Washington: Government Printing Office, 1962), pp. 123-27. See also the report of the National Commission on Technology, Automation, and Economic Progress, *op. cit.,* Chaps. 6 and 7.

[5] The report of the Automation Commission concerns many issues discussed in this book. At various places reference to the report is made in footnotes. While the report material would not alter the authors' approaches or conclusions, had it been available earlier, it would have been given more extensive reference in the text itself. The various monographs sponsored by the Automation Commission were not available at the time of printing.

PART I

Technology and Growth

1

Technological Advance and Growth of Potential Output

Most contemporary analyses of economic growth focus on the relationship between output and inputs of various factors of production. Technological advance is treated as one factor shifting that functional relationship so as to increase productivity. Several recent studies have attempted to relate technological advances to research and development expenditures.[1] This approach, however, has the disadvantage of treating technological change implicitly. An effect is measured—an increase in the productivity of inputs. A possible cause is examined—R&D expenditure. But technological advance itself, which would seem to demand definition in terms of an increase in knowledge relevant to economic activity, is not treated explicitly.

Instead of emphasizing inputs and treating technological knowledge as a key factor determining their productivity, the authors have focused on technological knowledge with physical inputs as determinants of the extent to which knowledge is applied.

In a strict formal sense, it makes no difference whether an analysis of the determinants of output centers on technology or on physical inputs. In the broader context of growth theory, the set of simultaneous equa-

[1] Edwin Mansfield, "Rates of Return from Industrial Research and Development," *American Economic Review*, Vol. 55, No. 2 (May 1965) and Zvi Griliches, "Research Expenditures, Education, and the Aggregate Agricultural Production Function," *American Economic Review*, Vol. 54 (December 1964), pp. 961-74.

tions is the same, although they are ordered and expressed somewhat differently. The restructuring is a matter of convenience, permitting a sharper focus on the principal topic of this book. The different focus, however, brings out more clearly the critical role of technological advance in economic growth.

Knowledge and Potential Output

Knowledge is a protean concept. Although there have been many attempts to define and classify it, whenever a specific case of any complexity is examined the definitions and classifications do not quite apply. This is a problem that plagues any discussion of the general concept of knowledge.

The following discussion will be limited to technological knowledge which pertains predominantly to the production of goods and services in organized economic activity. The operational part of the body of technological knowledge is a set of techniques, each defined as a set of actions and decision rules guiding their sequential application that man has learned will generally lead to a predictable (and sometimes desirable) outcome under certain specified circumstances.[2]

The Stock of Technological Knowledge

The stock of known technique for achieving practical results is only part of the richer and deeper body of human knowledge which includes, as well, a comprehension of the properties of things under various conditions, relationships among and between objects and properties, and broad frameworks of interpretation. Much of this rich general background of understanding is called science, but part of it cannot be dignified by that term. Rather it simply is the result of experience and its rather straightforward generalization.[3]

[2] Some technique, like that of turning the doorknob to open a door, is almost completely unintellectual and can only be dignified by the term knowledge because it is learned and can be taught—key attributes of anyone's definition of knowledge.

The stock of human techniques comprises a vast and heterogeneous lot. While almost all of it is applied in the production of economic goods and services—like the technique of opening doors, or of writing with a pencil—most of it is not what people have in mind when they discuss technology and technological advance in the process of economic growth.

[3] This treatment of the distinction between understanding and technique has much in common with the distinction between science and technology made by James B. Conant in his *Science and Common Sense* (New Haven: Yale University Press, 1951).

In many cases technique can be derived from the general body of understanding. Thus, building and use of a ramp to extricate a car from a ditch is a technique. A person may be able to figure out how to build an adequate ramp and use it properly from his knowledge of the weight of a car, the strength of wood, and his grasp of the simple physics of inclined planes, even if he had no prior experience with or knowledge of ramps per se. A technique that can be derived in fine detail from more basic understanding can be called perfectly understood. Few techniques are perfectly understood in this sense. Generally there are at least a few fine points which go beyond understanding, and these significantly influence effectiveness. Indeed, in some cases understanding may even fall short of the rough outlines of known effective technique; the technique is almost completely empirical.[4] It is known through experience that something works in a predictable way, but it is not known why.[5]

The fact that technique can often be largely or partially derived from the more general body of human knowledge crucially affects the way many new techniques get discovered or invented, and has important implications for the way people learn to master known techniques. But while technique blends into the rest of human knowledge, it is a body of knowledge in its own right.

In theory any technique can be described by and communicated as a set of instructions—as a cookbook recipe or a computer program[6]—whether or not the technology is understood in terms of more fundamental knowledge.

Technology is the operational part of a production function. If used with the inputs it specifies, the result will be an output of specified characteristics.[7] Generally a technique or technology is not completely

---

[4] For many years this was so for many chemical processes: thus iron was reduced from ore years before anyone really understood oxidation and reduction. For a general discussion see Rupert Hall, "The Scholar and the Craftsman in the Scientific Revolution," in M. Clagett (ed.), *Critical Problems in the History of Science* (Madison: University of Wisconsin Press, 1959).

[5] In terms of decision theory the distinction made is between knowledge required to structure the choice problem and knowledge of a good strategy. While good strategies often can be derived from logical manipulation of the general problem formulation, this is often hard to do. Further, good strategy may sometimes be discovered by trial and error.

[6] For a more general discussion of the use of the concept of a computer program to model human activity see H. A. Simon and Allen Newell, "The Simulation of Human Thought" (Santa Monica: The RAND Corporation, P-1734, June 1959).

[7] In the main line of economic theory the concept of a technology and the concept of a production function tend to be used synonomously; thus Tjalling Koop-

describable by a unique routine; usually there are options in the program. These options permit some choice of inputs and input proportions (a recipe may work with either whole or powdered eggs) and some flexibility with respect to operations (the eggs may be added before or after the sugar). The operations may be performed in different ways; for example, different degrees of mechanization may be employed (the mix may be beaten with a spoon, a hand beater, or an electric beater). Some variation in output specification may be possible (such as the shape of the cake or the kind of frosting).[8] These variations in processes or output determine the degree to which economic efficiency can be maintained in the face of varying circumstances (such as changing supplies of different primary inputs and of labor and machinery, and changing demand for different product variants).

The flexibility built into a technology also provides scope for errors without catastrophic results. (A recipe may produce a roughly adequate product if the cook puts in a little more, or a little less milk than is called for, although the cake may not have as good a texture, and if more milk is added than is optimal, there will be needless expense.) Thus a relative novice sometimes can operate the technology, but not as well as an expert, and his grasp of the technology may include only a small subset of the possible variations.

At any given time the stock of known technique defines the set of products which may be produced, and the known broad processes (and the range of variation within these processes) for making them.

The Embodiment of Technological Knowledge in the Labor Force

The use of technological knowledge in economic activity requires a labor force in whom that knowledge is embodied through education, training and experience. There is no unique relationship between the technologies used by a society and the specific pattern of labor force embodiment. Rather there are a wide range of alternatives, both for dividing up

---

mans defines technology as the vector of inputs and outputs resulting from use of an activity at a unit level. See his "Analysis of Production as an Efficient Combination of Activities," in Tjalling Koopmans (ed.), *Activity Analysis of Production and Allocation* (New York: John Wiley and Sons, 1951). What is suggested here is that a vector of inputs, *plus* a vector of actions or operations, leads to an output. The vector of operations can be defined as the technology used in the production function which creates the output from the inputs.

[8] The lines between variability within a technology and different technologies are blurred, but appear meaningful.

the knowledge requirements among the labor force, and for imparting that knowledge.

On the requirements side, the technology used in a particular activity is broken down into a set of subtechniques, plus a hierarchal set of coordinating programs. Correspondingly, activities are decomposed into a set of sub-activities which can be conducted largely independently, plus a set of management functions. Furthermore, for each of the sub-activities it is often possible to build a portion of the operations and their control into machines, making a further division of knowledge, between machine builders and machine operators. Thus to run an activity effectively it is not necessary that every, or even any, person know the full technology. Rather the operation of a technology is essentially a team or group problem.[9]

Such a decomposition of activities into sub-activities permits a vast reduction in the amount any person must know in order to be an effective worker. All a single worker needs is the technique relevant to his job.

On the impartation side, there are a range of possible systems by which technology can be embodied in the labor force. It would be possible, of course, to have a specific self-contained training program for each job. However, if activities are appropriately divided, many jobs in different activities will have a great deal in common. A system of knowledge embodiment has been designed to capitalize on these common elements.

The techniques relevant to most jobs have a large common set of elemental building blocks. It greatly simplifies the teaching and learning of techniques if these more primitive elements are already learned—if a cake recipe can simply state "pour in a cup of milk" and not explain what milk is or describe how to measure and pour. General education imparts these general purpose skills, relations, data, and language.

In addition to these elemental building blocks, there are certain sets of higher order techniques and categories of general knowledge which are

---

[9] The embodiment of technological knowledge in the minds of men has been stressed by Theodore Schultz, particularly in his *Transforming Traditional Agriculture* (New Haven: Yale University Press, 1964). Robert Solow, in contrast, has stressed the embodiment of technology in machinery in his "Investment and Technical Progress," in *Mathematical Methods in the Social Sciences, 1959* (Stanford: Stanford University Press, 1960). Of course, knowledge must be in the minds of men before it is in the design of machines.

useful in mastering certain complex jobs common to a wide range of activities. Technique and knowledge tend to become associated with occupations and professions, and their impartation institutionalized in occupational and professional training.

Skillful decomposition of activities, and an education and occupational training system well tuned to the pattern of decomposition, permit a great reduction in the amount of knowledge that must be specific to any particular activity.[10] However, almost every job will have a few nuances, and most activities will require at least a few people with a considerable amount of specialized knowledge. This may be the case for certain operating jobs; thus a machinist involved in producing aircraft engines must have his general training as machinist, supplemented by special knowledge and instructions relevant to the parts of an aircraft engine with which he is concerned. And it almost always is true that the higher order coordinating programs are quite specialized; to manage the machinery operation of engine production requires considerable knowledge about aircraft engines in general, as well as the specific aircraft engine, beyond that which a production engineer or manager learns in his general professional training.

Therefore general and vocational education must be supplemented by specific job training.[11] A considerable part of this training, like more general education and training, is formal. But in many cases the special knowledge required to operate a technique effectively cannot be taught fully in a formal training program. Often formal training and education provides enough knowledge to enable a person to perform the job or manage the operation crudely, but not enough to achieve the highest quality or the lowest cost. Formal training and education must be complemented by experience—the self-training and education that comes from doing.[12]

[10] Mary Jean Bowman, in several essays in C. A. Anderson and M. J. Bowman (eds.), *Education and Economic Development* (Chicago: Aldine Publishing Company, 1965), has presented a model of the education system and the returns to education very similar to the one presented here.

[11] George R. Hall and Robert E. Johnson of the Rand Corporation make a related distinction—between general knowledge and activity specific knowledge—in their "Aircraft-Co Production and U. S. Procurement Policy." Unpublished manuscript.

[12] The relationship between what has already been learned in general and occupational education, and what remains to be learned in job specific training, has been discussed and analyzed by Gary S. Becker in *Human Capital,* National Bureau of Economic Research (New York: Columbia University Press, 1964).

To acquire knowledge relevant to a specific technique, a considerable amount of redundant knowledge is picked up which may not pay off on a particular job. It may, however, facilitate the understanding and mastery of new jobs and techniques. Redundant knowledge pays off in terms of flexibility.[13]

Determinants of Potential Output

For a technology to be applied to economic activity, three things are needed: workers possessing the relevant knowledge; organization capable of effectively putting this knowledge into action; the required material inputs.

Economic activities differ intrinsically in their complexity. However, the fact that a technology is complex does not necessarily mean that a considerable amount of specialized training and experience is required of the work force. This depends largely on the nature of the sub-jobs into which the activity is decomposed. Jobs can require considerable specialized knowledge, or they can be automated or otherwise structured so as to demand only the kinds of knowledge imparted in general and occupational education programs.[14] When much specialized knowledge is required to perform a job satisfactorily, special training and experience may be the key to work force competence. However, when a technology is automated or reduced to a set of sub-techniques matched to existing professional and occupational training, or when a technology is so new that specialized experience is scarce and special training programs have not been worked out, but is at least partially understandable within existing professional knowledge, the strength of the overall education sys-

[13] The other side of the coin is that knowledge specific to any job generally is picked up in pieces. Consider the self-education and training that a person would have to experience to build a television set. If this were his first attempt he would be likely to make some mistakes, but he would probably be able to muddle through, following published instructions. However, if he did not know how to solder a connection, for example, he would have to consult another source. If he did not know how to read and understand diagrams or understand the symbols describing the various components, he would have to study a more general electronics handbook, which in turn might well require that he know at least high school algebra. Further, he might find a knowledge of elementary physics essential to the instructions and certainly helpful in enabling him to decide how closely he must follow the details.

[14] Alternative decompositions are the points along an isoquant of different possible sets of actions, and different possible mixes of required labor training.

tem may be far more important in determining the supply of competent labor.

The effective operation of a technology also requires competent organization. If the activity involves a considerable division of labor and expertise, it may be no trivial matter to coordinate and organize the work. A decision making and control mechanism generally must be tailored to that particular technology.

Effective organization requires more than managerial knowledge, since the requirements for coordinating are beyond the scope of any one activity and the control of any particular manager. There must be effective links to organizations that provide the necessary equipment and other inputs, as well as links to customers. These links involve technical assistance (reflecting the division of knowledge) and the flow of physical products. The effectiveness of this wider organization depends in large part upon the laws and institutions that determine the kinds of communication, incentives, and constraints which can be used to inform or influence people and other organizations.

Finally, the material inputs must be available. If basic raw materials are ignored the availability of the necessary inputs—machinery, components, and materials—depends ultimately on whether organization and knowledge can be acquired to produce them. The rapid recovery of Germany and Japan from the damage to their physical capital inflicted during World War II, and the inability of many of today's underdeveloped economies to use equipment effectively, provide dramatic evidence of the primacy of technological knowledge and the organizational capabilities to bring this knowledge to fruition. These are the key factors determining the long run productive potential of an economy.[15] Considerable time and resources may be needed to produce machinery and equipment in sizeable quantities, however. In the short run, the existing stock of physical plant and equipment obviously is an important factor in determining the extent to which a technology can be applied.

There are four principal constraints, then, to the kinds and quantities of goods that an economy can produce per worker:

(1) The stock of technological knowledge, which limits the kinds of products man knows how to produce, and the various processes he knows for producing them.

[15] See K. C. Yeh's discussion of this point for Chinese industrialization in his "Soviet and Communist Chinese Industrialization Strategies" (Santa Monica: The RAND Corporation, P-3150, May 1965).

(2) The education, training, and experience of the work force, which determines the extent to which this knowledge is embodied in people.

(3) The organization of firms and of the economy as a whole, which determines the effectiveness with which this knowledge can be used.

(4) The stock of physical capital and the availability of natural resources.[16]

Within these limits—and given time to permit human and material resources to be reallocated—there is a considerable range for private and public choice concerning what and how much can be produced. Society can choose how much of its productive potential it will allocate to meet defense needs, produce automobiles, produce food, build hospitals, houses or roads, add to blast furnace capacity, teach children, or undertake research and development. Society has a choice between more production and more leisure. If voluntary leisure is considered a good, then potential output can be described by the outer boundary of the set of output possibilities open to a society over a period of time.[17]

Dynamics of Growth

Economic growth is the shifting outward of this frontier of possibilities. Growth may occur fortuitously. A new and rich source of oil may be discovered accidentally, for example, but this happens only occasionally. Sometimes growth results from improved economic organization, but in a reasonably well organized economy the opportunities through this route are limited. The principal source of growth is investment—the employment of resources in building plants and equipment, roads and dams, and other physical capital; in providing training and education; in research and development, and in other activities which advance technology.

[16] This list of factors resembles most conventional analyses of growth process. See for example *The Annual Report of the Council of Economic Advisors*, January 1962 (Washington: Government Printing Office, 1962).

[17] Potential output has been defined as the possibilities open over a period of time, not at a specific moment. Along the production possibility frontier, choices of output composition reflect various choices in the allocation of resources. Time and often the utilization of resources are required to effect a change in allocation. Another way of defining the potential output frontier is in terms of the alternative output combinations the economy can be producing at some specific time in the future. In either case, the production possibility concept inherently involves future adjustments and reallocations over a period of time, not different allocations of resources at any one moment.

Catalytic Role of Technological Advance

Any analysis of economic growth must identify the functional relationships between growth of potential output and the quantities of different forms of investment, and discover how the magnitude and kind of investment are determined. The problem is made especially difficult because of the complexity of interaction among the many variables.[18]

The contribution of additional capital equipment and education, for instance, is strongly dependent upon the rate at which technological knowledge is advancing. At a constant level of technological knowledge, output per worker can be increased through more equipment, or through better training, but only to a certain extent. Equipping a worker with an even bigger shovel will be pointless. Giving him more training in the use of a shovel will yield little return, for there will be little left to learn. The rate at which returns diminish can be retarded by switching to known techniques that were unprofitable when capital was scarcer or the worker less educated, such as using a bulldozer. But in the absence of new technological knowledge, sooner or later these possibilities would be exhausted. As returns to additional capital and education declined, not only would their contribution to further expansion diminish; their rate of expansion probably would decline as well.[19]

With technological knowledge improving over time, new and more productive techniques will become available (for example, a radically new ditch digging machine). New physical capital will be needed to apply the new technology. Further, technological advance probably will permit growing quantities of capital per laborer to be compatible with high rates of return on capital. Thus, the growth of physical capital can proceed with high returns.

The contribution of and the returns to educated people also will be enhanced. With technology changing, the advantage to workers (and their employers) of an education beyond that which is needed for a particular job will be significantly greater. This is so not because the new technology is inherently more complex than the old, but because it is

[18] An earlier discussion of these interactions is contained in Richard R. Nelson's "Aggregate Production Functions and Medium-Range Growth Projections," *American Economic Review*, Vol. 54 (September 1964).

[19] It is assumed that the interest rate and the relative wages of educated workers tend to fall as capital and education become more plentiful.

different. Consequently, there is a premium on the ability to learn new techniques rapidly and, sometimes, to work with those as yet unroutinized. The demand for well educated workers reflects the fact that they are relatively easy to train for a variety of jobs, and thus are particularly valuable when the composition of jobs changes. The assignment of a highly paid chemical engineer to a production job during the installation of a new chemical process is made because the process is not routinized sufficiently to permit rapid training of workers without the relevant background understanding.

The effect is not just on the production work force. Technological advance changes the whole pattern of information that must flow between economic units. High remuneration of technically trained sales people in the electronics industry, for example, relates to their ability to communicate new developments to the potential market. Returns to trained management reflects their ability to assess new alternatives and to deal expertly and imaginatively with the problems created by new techniques. The economic advantage of education here extends far beyond the imparting of specific skills to deal with specific problems. It lies in the added flexibility to learn new things and understand new kinds of opportunities and problems that some types of education impart, and which rapid technical change make important.[20]

Rapid technological advance not only enhances the contribution of physical capital and education, but also spurs their expansion.

The interactions also exist in the other direction. If current technical advance creates high levels of demand for educated personnel, current investment in education affects the future cost of generating and diffusing technical change. The rate of advance of technical understanding in recent years has probably been closely related to the number of educated personnel engaged in R&D. And the speed of the diffusion process depends on the availability of people capable of evaluating and perceiving potential markets, communicating technical information, and dealing with the problems which invariably arise in the early stages of production before techniques become routinized.

While the development of new products and processes stimulates investment booms and permits capital-labor ratios to rise without depressing the profitability of new investment, at the same time new

[20] Naturally this depends on the kind of education. Certain kinds of education, and attitudes toward education, can make a person less, not more, flexible.

technology often needs new capital. It is also true that the extent to which average technique in use lags behind the most advanced technique depends on the rate of gross investment.[21] Further, rapid growth of and updating of the capital stock stimulates the advance of the frontier. Improvement and perfection is a sequential learning process. The rate of learning is dependent not only on the length of experience with a particular version of the technology, but also on the ability to try suggested improvements. If these improvements require embodiment, the rate of learning will be strongly affected by the rate of new physical investment.[22]

While an advance in any key element in the growth process tends to raise the productivity of and spur the advance of the others, technological advance is the key catalytic factor. If technology continues to advance, but the size and average age of the capital stock and the average level of education remain constant, per capita economic growth would slacken—but the slackening might well be moderate. Old workers die and new workers graduate from M.I.T., Michigan, and Central High. Old machines wear out and are replaced by new. Design improvements consequently could be embodied in new machinery and generalized advances in knowledge in new textbooks. Economic growth might be more closely bounded, but still vigorous. If technological advance dries up, however, the system soon would reach a limit in terms of per capita income.[23] It may be a different matter for those underdeveloped countries which can borrow technology; for them capital formation and education alone may have a more powerful independent thrust. But, as Schumpeter stated,[24] in advanced nations economic growth is best understood with technological advance playing the leading role, and capital formation and education providing the necessary support.[25]

[21] The embodiment effect has been stressed by Robert Solow, *op. cit.*, and W.E.G. Salter, *Productivity and Technical Change* (Cambridge: Cambridge University Department of Applied Economics, 1960).

[22] Learning by doing has been stressed by Kenneth J. Arrow in his "The Economic Implications of Learning by Doing," *Review of Economic Studies*, Vol. 29 (June 1962). There is a large literature on learning curves which we shall discuss subsequently.

[23] This is an implication of almost all growth models, not just the one proposed by the authors.

[24] Joseph Schumpeter, *The Theory of Economic Development* (Cambridge: Harvard University Press, 1934).

[25] Recent studies which have attempted to estimate the contribution of techno-

New Products

Technical change is emphasized here not only because of its role as a catalyst, but also because it endows economic growth with much of its capacity for satisfying human wants. This latter point is generally not fully appreciated, since the unique contribution of many new products is not adequately captured by the Gross National Product measure.

Certain technological advances, like the automatic loom and improved catalytic process equipment for producing gasoline, increased the ability of the economy to produce established private or public consumption goods, but did not introduce any new dimension to the available goods which determine the welfare of consumers. Similarly, from the viewpoint of the final consumer, hybrid corn (fed to livestock, not people) is not a new consumer good, but a more efficient way to produce beef and pork. Other technical changes create the possibility of producing substantially new or improved consumer goods. The airplane, penicillin, and television expanded the range of final goods and services, and permitted the satisfaction of wants which had not been satisfied before.[26]

---

logical advance to growth of GNP have yielded significant underestimates. There are several sources of underestimation.

First, many of the studies have assumed a Cobb-Douglas production function. If, as is strongly suspected, the elasticity of substitution is significantly less than one for large increases in the capital-labor ratio (for a given technology), this should result in an overestimate of the contribution of growing capital per worker and, hence, an underattribution to other factors, including technological advance.

Second, to the extent that the returns to a particular factor are dependent on the rate of technological progress and this is not explicitly taken into account, some of the credit which should go to technological advance is attributed to these other factors. This is probably the case regarding the high returns to education—these returns would have been far less if technological advance had been slower. As another example, some authors have credited significant increases in output to reallocation of labor from low to high productivity jobs. Surely a large part of this reflects the exploitation of new technological knowledge which created the new jobs, and is the lagged effect of technological advance (and of education which permits labor to learn the new techniques) rather than an independent factor.

Third, the studies generally ignore the effect of an increase in one factor on the supply of the others. Supply interactions reduce the significance of attribution, but do not necessarily lead to bias. However, if technological advance is strongly catalytic, as suggested, one of its major effects is inducing increases in other factors. See Nelson, *op.cit.*

[26] Introduction of a new final good means the introduction of a new good for which no combination of older goods provides a perfect substitute.

The differentiation between new and established final products is not razor sharp. Final products are, after all, merely ways of satisfying consumer wants. New final goods are often simply more efficient processes—less costly ways of meeting needs that were met before.[27] While in some situations the airplane is simply a less costly way to travel (counting time) than a train, it made cross-country travel possible in a few hours—something which was previously impossible. Penicillin has made it possible—not just less costly—to save the lives of many people with certain infections.

When technological advance increases the productivity of existing goods and services, its contribution is not essentially different from that of any other investment. In terms of potential output, it makes no difference whether steel capacity is increased by providing more blast furnaces of existing design or by discovering how to make existing equipment more productive.

For enlarging the spectrum of choice, however, there is no substitute for technological advance. The dramatic increase in modern health standards could not have been achieved simply by allocating more men and equipment to meeting health needs. While this also has happened, the main improvements have been the advances in the quality of medicines and in medical knowledge. Improvements in transportation and communications likewise would have been impossible but for the invention and development of the radio and the airplane. These and other advancements represent the most treasured prizes of economic growth.

Stated another way, growth of economic potential has a direction as well as a rate. If production possibilities shifted outward uniformly, there would be little difficulty in providing a scalar measure of growth, and indeed potential GNP as it is calculated would provide a good measure. However, a better process for making aluminum will not shift outward beyond the frontier uniformly; rather it will primarily shift those productive possibilities which involve a large aluminum output. Creation of a new final product will actually introduce a new dimension to production possibilities.

Without new products, Americans still would have achieved a significant improvement in their standards of living, but the kinds of de-

[27] Kelvin Lancaster, "Change and Innovation in the Technology of Consumption," *American Economic Review,* Vol. 56 (May 1966), p. 22, presents a useful model.

velopments would have been different. The fourfold increase in measured GNP which has occurred since 1900 would have meant far less in terms of potential to meet needs. New products are measured in the GNP calculations by the amount people spend on them, but for many people the value of obtaining the new product far exceeds the total price. If airplane service were eliminated from the spectrum of final products, many consumers would require a significant increment of income to achieve comparable levels of satisfaction. For those who owe their lives to penicillin, the value of the new product is not measurable.[28]

The most prized aspects of increasing affluence are largely attributable to technological advance rather than to generalized economic growth. Real GNP per person is more than twice as large as in 1900, but technological change has so altered the nature of society and the quality of life that GNP comparisons over such long periods of time are meaningless. Man today has a life expectancy of 70 years, is much better protected from a wide range of devastating diseases, has teeth extracted with little pain, and has his view of the world expanded by cheap and rapid travel. Even without these developments, the growth of GNP would have helped to eradicate poverty and increase the enjoyment of life. But it would have been far less powerful a liberating force in a society restricted to the consumption possibilities of 1900—wider carriages, more coal for the kitchen stove, and more kerosene for the oil lamp.

---

[28] It is not argued here that, because of the introduction of new products, growth of GNP underestimates growth of welfare: rather, that a given growth of measured GNP means more in terms of consumer satisfaction if it is accompanied by the availability of new products. It is clear that if a person is unable to buy a particular product he presently is purchasing, he is made worse off even if he can purchase other products at existing prices. The argument is reversible. People with a specific income and facing a set of product prices will be made better off if a new product is introduced—provided the product and its price are sufficiently attractive that they buy it.

Put another way, the consumer price index suggests that the prices of consumer goods and services in 1960 were approximately three times the 1900 level. Most people would probably be willing to settle for far less than three dollars to spend on goods available in 1960 at 1960 prices rather than one dollar to spend on goods available in 1900 at 1900 prices. But it is impossible to say how much less.

Of course, some people would not agree that the 1960 range of choice is better than that of 1900. A 1960 dollar buys far less personal service and housing space than did a 1900 dollar. For those whose tastes stress these things, it is possible that they would be willing to trade much more than three 1960 dollars for one 1900 dollar and the accompanying prices. This problem of values is the heart of the measurement problem.

2

Factors Determining Technological Advance

This chapter examines the process that creates technological advances—advances in knowledge which, when put to work, result in an increase or improvement in output. The kinds and quantities of inputs required to achieve technological advance are also discussed.

Technological advances take the form of new product designs or new process routines. Examples of the first are the jet engine and penicillin; of the second—the oxygen process for steel making and the arc welding technique. Technological advances in the broader sense also include improved management techniques, such as statistical quality control or production programming, and new concepts for organizing economic activity like the supermarkets and the linear assembly line. Although this book concentrates on technological advances in the form of new product designs and process routines, these are only part of the advances in knowledge which enrich the production capabilities of an economy.

The Production Function for Technological Advances

At any given time technological knowledge exists to produce a considerably wider range of products or use a larger set of processes than, in fact, are being supplied or employed. Some of these have been well tested, but have been made obsolete by newer technologies. Others have not been operationally tested but are sufficiently close to those that have so that, given the extent of understanding, a satisfactory recipe or program could easily be specified were there incentive to do so; the job would be considered routine engineering. Like the obsolete technologies, these are not in use because they are not economic under existing conditions of demand and supply.

In addition to the stock of presently operational techniques, at any time there is a considerable store of ideas reasonably well worked out, but still short of operational, and an almost infinite stock of partial or embryonic ideas which are not even close to operational. Technology advances as these ideas are developed into operational form. The conscious application of resources to this objective may be defined as applied research and development. As pointed out earlier, several recent economic models have attempted to relate the pace of technological progress to the volume of resources applied to R&D. Implicity or explicitly it is assumed that there is a "production function" relating input of these resources to the output of technological advance.

The following discussion presents a more disaggregated theory than contained in these papers of the production function for technological progress, examining the kinds and quantities of R&D inputs needed to make a design idea operational. The quantity of resources required depends on three key variables: (1) the magnitude of the advance sought over existing comparable products; (2) the nature of the product field, in particular the size and complexity of the system; and (3) the stock of relevant knowledge that permits new techniques to be derived or deduced, as well as the stock of available materials and components with which designers can work.[1] These factors can be illustrated by the tasks

[1] Some of these variables have analogues in production function theory relating to physical output. The magnitude of the advance sought is analogous to the number of units of physical output produced. The stock of knowledge and supply of components variable plays a role similar to the state of technology variable in physical production theory; it determines the resources required to achieve a given advance or output. But it also has some attributes in common with external economies or free inputs created by other economic units in production theory. The size and complexity of the system variable does not appear to have been dealt with as a special variable in production theory. To be sure, there are different "natural" units of physical output in different fields which intrinsically require different quantities of output per unit of input (small cars versus big trucks), but because the problem is so obvious no one seems to have commented on it. However, differences in the "natural" physical units of output appear to carry implications for the resources involved in improving that product's design, which have not been widely noted.

involved in developing a new transport aircraft for unusually demanding use in remote areas.[2]

Magnitude of the Advances Sought[3]

Assume that the Air Force desired a transport aircraft especially suited for use and maintenance in remote areas, and especially rugged so as not to be vulnerable to small arms fire. Advances in other performance parameters are not important; compared with existing transports the new aircraft need not be especially fast nor have a particularly long range.

The design and development task probably would be relatively easy, well within the capabilities of present understanding. A group of engineers, drawing on their knowledge of existing aircraft design and on their scientific and engineering background, could quickly sketch out a broadly adequate concept. Indeed, many aspects of the design could be identical to those of existing aircraft. Others, however, would have to be designed to meet special objectives; thus a research and development effort is required. The new aspects might require only a few new components, but these might be major ones: the required ruggedness might call for an airframe quite different from that in existing vehicles, and the need for easy maintenance might require a new engine. However, literature on how to make a more durable aircraft would undoubtedly be available, and could be a basis for research.

Although the broad design concept might come easily, considerable effort and time might still be involved in developing it—filling in details by analyzing different approaches to sub-design problems, and compar-

---

[2] The ideas contained in the following section are similar to those found in Thomas Glennan, "Issues in the Choice of Development Policies" (Santa Monica: The RAND Corporation, P-3153, October 1965).

[3] The problems of "measuring" a technological advance were touched on in the preceding chapter. If all advances were input saving (but did not affect the attributes of the final product) and all technological advances were neutral, the magnitude of the advance could be measured, as in the Mansfield, Griliches, and Denison papers mentioned earlier. This asserts the other side of Mansfield's proposition that the rate of advance of technology is dependent upon the quantity of R&D input—that the greater the advance, the greater the inputs that are required. However, when it is acknowledged that much of technological advance results in changes in product performance in various dimensions—faster planes, or devices that receive and show visual images as well as receive and reproduce sound signals—the question of just how to measure a technological advance becomes very difficult.

ing alternative materials, components, and sub-systems to find those best suited to performance and production cost objectives. Much of this work would involve standard engineering references and catalogues of components. Some of it might involve finding out how similar problems were solved in other aircraft. Some might involve small-scale applied research projects. While each of these tasks might be simple, the development of even a small aircraft requires decisions regarding thousands of design details.

Sooner or later, equipment would have to be built and tests run on various parts of the system, and on the system as a whole. The tests probably would lead to several changes in components and various other design modifications. While the revisions might not be radical, they could be quite necessary.

Once the design of the aircraft and its new components was specified, production methods might be obvious, using existing techniques and sub-techniques modified only slightly to meet the new specifications. On the other hand, certain rather special production techniques might be required; an improved way of joining parts to give greater strength might be an example.

After the design and any special production techniques were developed, considerable work still would be involved in preparing production blueprints, drawings, and instructions to provide the communications link between the designers, producers, and users.

Thus, even small advances in performance may require large inputs, which increase as greater advances are sought. If, in the case above, the Air Force added the requirement of significantly higher speed than in existing vehicles, more time and effort would be required. Since fewer aspects of design could be borrowed from existing aircraft, development success would be less dependent on accumulated design experience and more critically dependent on general scientific and engineering understanding, plus theoretical and piecemeal empirical literature on the problems and ideas for faster aircraft. Problems of detailed design would be much more difficult—and much less likely to be close analogs to those previously solved. Thus, both achievement of the design concept and the development of details might require a significant research program to clarify key uncertainties.

In addition, the design group might be forced to design a significant proportion of the components of the system—catalogue items would not be satisfactory to meet the more far-reaching objective. Probably the amount of required testing also would be much greater, and so would the modifications made as a result of testing experience. A considerable number of special production techniques, and equipment for them, might have to be developed. Even the blueprints and instructions would be more numerous and detailed, reflecting both the original nature of many of the components and techniques and the fact that, due to the newness of the design and some of the techniques, much less background knowledge could be assumed of producers and users.

As the magnitude of the sought-for advance increases, expected required inputs probably increase disproportionately. The number of specially designed components will tend to mount sharply as the reach of the design and development effort extends. Initial uncertainties regarding major problems and how they can be solved will be far greater. While prior research can reduce some of these uncertainties, misjudgments and mistakes are almost sure to be made if the advance sought is ambitious. Many jobs will have to be redone, and redone again. In the end it is quite possible that the original objectives will prove unachievable, requiring that the project be scaled down or possibly abandoned as a costly failure.

Size and Complexity

Most R&D projects aim for rather marginal improvements in a product or item of equipment, and usually the effort is directed toward improving a few dimensions of performance. As a result, the effort generally can focus on several components and take the rest as given. Thus, automobile economy can be improved by an effort to improve carburetor design without changing the design of the rest of the engine or the automobile. However, many development efforts aim to achieve at least some improvement in a wide variety of performance dimensions, and some aim to achieve major advances in a particular dimension; either objective may require significant redesign of the total system. For such efforts, the resources required may depend on certain physical attributes of the product class—specifically on the number of diverse components and their interdependence.

While generally it takes more resources to redesign a product with a large number of components than one with a smaller number, the number of diverse elements is significant mainly through their interdependency.[4] For example, a television set has more components than a radio; indeed all the elements of a radio are contained in a television set. Assume that it is desired to improve the television's audio performance by creating a design which incorporates a new speaker system that requires more power. This will involve a new speaker feed-in and the redesign of certain other components. If the audio and visual parts of the television circuitry are basically two different systems, the work may require little more than redesigning a radio to incorporate the new speaker system; the introduction of a new transformer may be the only difference. However, if the audio and visual circuitry of the TV are closely integrated it may be necessary to redesign the entire system.

The problem with trying to achieve major advances in large and complex systems—products with a large number of tightly interdependent components—is that to change any one item causes reverberations throughout the system. Even small changes in performance in just one or two dimensions may require a vast amount of redesign. For smaller or less complex systems involving fewer or less interdependent components, one aspect of design can be changed with relatively little overall redesign.

Stock of Knowledge and Components

The amount of effort also will depend on the designer's background knowledge. The task of creating the Air Force plane could be considerably reduced by stronger aerodynamic theory permitting significantly better prediction of the performance of various shapes and of skin frictions. Prior research that explored ideas for and problems involved in increasing aircraft durability and speed, perhaps including the articulation of certain design concepts, or experience in developing and testing an experimental aircraft, or a past development effort which failed, could facilitate design. The needed research integral to the design effort would be less, the stock of design ideas richer, and early judgments of promising and unpromising approaches could be made with greater confidence and accuracy. The stock of components and materials available from a catalogue will also affect the amount of effort required. If a better all weather navigation system were available there would be no need to de-

---

[4] Needless to say, the size and complexity of the system is a difficult variable to measure. Nonetheless, many partial orderings are possible—as the television-radio example illustrates.

sign one especially for the aircraft. If a significantly better engine were available, it might be possible to dispense with especially designed afterburners, and the constraints on airframe weight might be much less.

Factors Influencing the Direction of Technological Advance

At any particular moment, in almost all fields, a number of efforts are in progress aimed at creating new or improved products and processes. Some are aimed at various dimensions of product performance, others at reducing cost. Some reach for major advances, some for minor improvements. As a result, technology seldom is stagnant in any field. However, the pace of technological advance varies strikingly from one product field to another, and from time to time.

This section examines the factors that lie behind the differing and changing rates of technological progress. Two broad factors are at work. First, there are differences and changes in the rewards from particular kinds of technological advance—demand factors that stimulate or repress efforts aimed at achieving them. Second, there are differences and changes in the stock of relevant components and materials, and of knowledge, and in the number of people who possess the relevant knowledge—supply factors which permit or restrict certain kinds of advances.

In short, the output of technological advances is sensitive to the same economic factors that influence the output of more pedestrian products and services. It is true that many of the advances that have been achieved stemmed, at least in part, from the work of a single man or a small group of men with zeal for an idea and only limited concern for profit, social value, or cost. Even for these, however, the need for outside financing brings the effort increasingly within the orbit of economic calculation as work proceeds and costs rise.

In the following sections the discussion will focus on changes in certain variables which tend to induce changes in the distribution of technological advances. The distribution of technological advances is largely the result of the accumulated impact of past changes in the determining variables. However, explanation of the existing distribution is much more difficult than explanation of directional changes in the distribution of technological advances, due to possible special factors innate to certain fields, and differences among fields in the quantitative impact of changes in the key variables.

Demand

The effects of changing patterns of demand on invention is illustrated by the sequence of major textile inventions in England during the late eighteenth and early nineteenth centuries. During the early eighteenth century the invention of the flying shuttle and the silk throwing machine greatly increased the amount of cloth and knit goods that could be produced per worker. The result was a fall in the price of cloth, more cloth output, and more demand for yarn to make cloth, thus raising economic returns to technical advances in the spinning processes. The profit prospects for successful invention were further enhanced by labor shortages and rising wages since the supply of spinners increased slowly. The work which led to the water frame, the spinning jenny and, later on, the spinning mule (which combined aspects of the water frame and the jenny) was directly stimulated by this increase in demand for yarn and in wages of spinners. This spurt of induced invention in spinning eventually overshot, and shortages of weavers began to materialize. These new shortages were met in part by a shift of labor into weaving, and in part by the shift of attention of inventors from spinning to weaving resulting in the development of the power loom.[5]

A more modern example is provided by the TH microwave relay system at the Bell Telephone Laboratories. Marschak's study indicates that the development of that system, designed to relay telephone and television signals at very high frequencies, was motivated in large part by a rising demand for communications and a growing scarcity of low frequency channels.[6]

In both of these examples, two factors lay behind the changes in the demand for particular advances. First, there was an increase in the demand for the product to which the advance was applicable. Second,

[5] For a history of this series of inventions see T. S. Ashton, *The Industrial Revolution, 1760-1830* (London: Oxford University Press, 1964).

[6] See Thomas A. Marschak, "Strategy and Organization in a System Development Project," *The Rate and Direction of Inventive Activity: Economic and Social Factors,* a Report of the National Bureau of Economic Research (Princeton: Princeton University Press, 1962), henceforth denoted as *The Rate and Direction of Inventive Activity.*

there was a growing shortage of a factor of production (reflected either in rising factor costs or growing difficulty of procurement) which led to effort aimed at mitigating the effect of that shortage. While these two factors often go together, they can shift independently. Therefore it is useful to consider them for the moment as separate factors.

An expansion of demand for a good can be reflected in increased demand for advances which reduce the cost of existing products, or for advances which permit higher performance, or both. The reflection of growing demand generally is an increase in the scale of output of a particular industry. An expansion of industry output clearly provides stimulus to both cost reducing and quality improving advances.[7] The larger the overall market, the greater the potential profit a firm can make from an improvement in efficiency which permits it both to cut costs and to shade prices, and the larger the absolute expansion in sales to be expected from any product improvement.[8]

The stimulus will affect not only firms in the industry experiencing the initial expansion of demand, but also will extend back to material and equipment suppliers in the form of an enlarged overall market for their products. Schmookler has found that the number of patents taken out on capital equipment for a particular industry was strongly correlated with the volume of sales of capital equipment to that industry.[9] The same

[7] Jacob Schmookler has, in a number of articles, stressed the importance of demand. See, for example, his "Changes in Industry and in the State of Knowledge as Determinants of Industrial Invention" in *The Rate and Direction of Inventive Activity, op. cit.;* "Economic Sources of Inventive Activity," *Journal of Economic History,* Vol. 22 (March 1962); with Oswald Brownlee, "Determinants of Inventive Activity," *American Economic Review,* Vol. 52 (May 1962); and his most recent *Invention and Economic Growth* (Cambridge: Harvard University Press, 1966).

[8] There are some difficult theoretical issues in linking an expansion of overall demand for the product of an industry to increased profits for a firm which experiences a given decrease in unit costs, or a given improvement in differential product attractiveness. Indeed, under conditions of perfect competition or imperfect competition in a Chamberlain sense there is no connection between the long run profitability of a firm, or the returns to an innovation by a firm, and overall demand for the industry's product. For this relationship to hold, the firm's demand curve must be a finite fraction of the industry's demand curve, the fraction depending on the relative attractiveness of its products and its demand curve shifting out as overall demand for the industry's product increases. Naturally the possession of a patent on its products or processes tends to move a firm into a position where it sells more than an infinitesimal share of total output, where expansion in overall demand does shift out its demand curve, and where it can achieve a finite monopoly rent from its own innovation.

[9] See Jacob Schmookler, *op.cit.*

type of relationship also holds over a period of time. Thus, for the railroad industry the number of patent applications relating to rails and passenger cars tended to increase with a slight lag during periods when sales of passenger cars and rails were growing, and to fall during periods when such sales were declining. A similar relationship existed between output of equipment for petroleum refining and paper making and patents relating to such equipment. (See Charts II-1 and II-2, pages 36 and 38.)

Shifts in latent demand—demand for goods not yet existing—have the same effect upon the incentives for invention as changes in the demand for existing products. As income, taste and circumstances shift, human wants change. Thus, during the nineteenth century there was a growing potential market for an efficient and rapid long range communication system and for a more rapid means of personal travel. This was reflected not only in expansion of pony express and the railroads, but also in an increase in the returns an inventor could expect if he could develop a product significantly more satisfactory than existing ones, like the telegraph or automobile.

The examples also suggest that growing scarcity or rising cost or a particular input (labor in the case of spinning, low frequency channel capacity in the case of the TH system) can also stimulate changes in the nature of technological advance. As in the cases above, the factor shortages are reflected in an increase in the latent demand for a new product; namely the equipment which conserves the use of the scarce factor. Thus the effect of changing factor prices is analytically identical to changes in demand. Most R&D done by firms in an industry is on the industries' products, not its processes. The relative prices or costs of different factors used by an industry determine the savings it achieves by various kinds of new machines or materials, and thus determines the pattern of demand for new products facing the firms supplying the industry, which conduct most of the R&D influencing its processes. However, the principle is the same whether or not the invention is embodied in a machine. An increase in the price of a factor increases the profitability of technological advances which reduce the requirements for that factor relative to others.

It is hard to obtain quantitative evidence on the effect of changing relative factor prices on invention, but the effect seems to be strong. In addition to the examples above, Habakkuk has argued that in England, where fuel was scarce and expensive, a much larger percentage of technological advances was aimed at saving fuel than in the United States.

Watt's steam engine and Bessemer's hot blast process are instances where the record shows clearly that the inventors were interested in saving fuel. Habakkuk suggests that, in contrast, a much larger percentage of effort in the United States than in England was specifically aimed at saving labor.[10]

The tendency toward laborsaving inventions may be a continuing phenomenon in countries like the United States.[11] As a result of general technological advance, including that in the capital goods industries, together with a high percentage of GNP allocated to physical investment, the cost of new machinery has tended to fall relative to the wage rate.[12] This has raised substantially the profitability of technological advances which improve the terms at which machinery can be substituted for labor. The effect should have been to increase incentive for laborsaving inventions.[13]

[10] H. J. Habakkuk, *American and British Technology in the Nineteenth Century* (New York: Cambridge University Press, 1962).

[11] For a discussion of the various definitions of what laborsaving innovation means see M. Blaug, "A Survey of the Theory of Process-Innovations," *Economica*, Vol. 30 (February 1963).

The concept of a laborsaving invention can be illustrated by the example of the invention of an attachment to a loom which eliminates the need for a laborer to feed in yarn, and which stimulates a reduction in the number of laborers per machine, given the going wage rate. For a capital saving innovation, consider an improvement in machine construction which eliminates down time, and hence which stimulates a reduction in the number of machines that business firms find it profitable to have on stock, for a given labor force.

[12] This has mostly been reflected in a decline in the price of a new machine relative to the wage rate, and to a lesser degree a decline in the interest rate.

[13] A considerable literature has developed on the question of whether *high* labor cost relative to the rental on capital should induce laborsaving innovation. This is not the topic under discussion here. As W.E.G. Salter has pointed out in his *Productivity and Technical Change* (Cambridge: Cambridge University Department of Applied Economics, 1960), without some kind of benchwork it is not clear what high relative labor cost means. William Fellner, in his "Two Propositions in the Theory of Induced Innovations," *Economic Journal*, Vol. 71 (June 1961), presents a similar analysis.

The discussion here relates to whether a *rise* in the price of labor relative to the rental on machines influences incentives for different kinds of inventions; the concern is with the impact of changes, not level. Charles Kennedy's analysis is suited to dealing with this question although he, as Fellner, is principally concerned with the effect of the ratio of factor costs. See his article, "Induced Bias in Innovation and the Theory of Distribution," *Economic Journal*, Vol. 74 (September 1964). Three recent papers have, in different ways, presented roughly the model implicit in the analysis above. See E. M. Drandakis and E. S. Phelps, "A Model of Induced Innovation, Growth, and Distribution" (Cowles Foundation Discussion

Assuming that the static elasticity of substitution is quite low, the fact that the relative share of capital in national income has not fallen precipitously despite the large and rapid increases in capital per laborer is convincing indirect evidence that technological advance has been quite laborsaving or, put another way, quite capital using.[14]

Thus efforts to advance technology will tend to be drawn toward reducing cost and increasing product performance in industries and classes of products where demand is rising, and toward saving on factors whose relative cost is rising. Since the costs of different kinds of advance may differ this does not necessarily mean that technological advance will be more rapid in large industries, or that factor saving innovation will always be sufficiently strong to offset the growing scarcity of a particular factor—only that allocation of inventive effort will tend to move in these directions.[15] However, Schmookler's convincing evidence that the relative number of patents awarded for capital equipment for different industries is closely related to the lagged expenditures on capital equipment by these industries suggests that the simple demand-pull model described

Paper No. 186, 1965); P. A. Samuelson, "A Theory of Induced Innovation Along Kennedy-Weisäcker Lines," *Review of Economics and Statistics,* Vol. 47 (November 1965); and M. I. Kamien and N. L. Schwartz, "Optimal Induced Technical Change" (Pittsburgh: Carnegie Institute of Technology, mimeo., 1966). However, none of these papers recognize the similarity of the mechanism by which changes in factor prices and changes in the demand for a final product induce increased demand for certain kinds of inventions.

The analysis here represents a throwback to the first statement of the question, that of John R. Hicks in *The Theory of Wages* (London: Macmillan & Co., 1932), modified to stress that *changing* relative factor prices provide an *increase* in relative incentives to invent to save on the factor growing in relative scarcity, recognizing that there may be cost of invention biases that pull the other way.

[14] An interesting technical side point is that, if the elasticity of substitution is greater than one, and technical advance is factor augmenting, then growth of one factor relative to the other, although decreasing its relative price, will also increase its relative share of national income. The fall in its relative price, by inducing changes that tend to facilitate substitution of that factor for the other, will further tend to increase its relative income share. (Again no cost of invention biases are assumed in the other direction—if there are, the effect will be technological change which is less saving of the other factor than would have been the case had relative prices not changed.) Technological advance which tends to reduce relative requirements for the factor growing in relative price tends to stabilize relative shares only when the elasticity of substitution is less than one. See Drandakis and Phelps, and Samuelson, *op. cit.*

[15] This is a question relating to the shape of the invention possibility frontier, to use Kennedy's language.

above explains much of the existing pattern of allocation of inventive effort, as well as changes in that pattern.[16]

Changes in Capability

The fact that a strong demand exists for a particular technological advance—that the payoff would be great if it could be achieved—is not sufficient to call forth a significant amount of effort. Whether or not people try to solve a problem depends on whether they think it can be solved, and at what cost, as well as on the gross returns from solving it. The pace of technological advance in a field depends not only on the number of people trying to achieve advances there, but also on their productivity. Capability is important as well as demand.[17]

The capability to achieve technological advances in a particular field depends on the number of people possessing the knowledge needed to invent in that field. It also depends on the stock of materials and components with which these people can work, and the stock of knowledge that they can apply—factors stressed earlier as key determinants of inventive productivity. These are the variables which lie behind the supply curve of inventions. Changes in these variables, which cause a shift in the supply curve, as well as changes in demand, tend to result in changes in the kinds and quantities of advances experienced.[18]

In turn, three broad factors lie behind changes in these variables: industry size and growth; advances in science and education; the development of a scientific base under the technology of an industry.

[16] See Jacob Schmookler, *Invention and Economic Growth* (Cambridge: Harvard University Press, 1966).

[17] This whole section relates to the shape of, and factors which can change the shape of, the invention possibility frontier. However, while Kennedy has aimed his analysis at examining the possibilities for capital and labor saving invention, the possibilities for invention in different industries and fields are the principal subject here. If the bulk of process invention is done by equipment and material suppliers, as would appear to be the case, this analysis is relevant to changes in factor saving.

[18] Unlike increases in the demand for a kind of invention, which should increase both the quantity of resources aimed at achieving it and, if the efforts are successful, the output of inventions (or the pace of technological progress), increases in the capability to achieve certain advances, while almost certainly increasing the rate at which those advances occur, may or may not increase the total resources employed in making them. It will if the increase in capability is an increase in the supply of people capable of inventing in the field, but if the increase in capability is the result of increased productivity of inventors the quantity of resources will increase or decrease depending on whether the demand for inventions is elastic or inelastic.

Industry Size and Growth

Probably the vast majority of efforts aimed at advancing technology seek modest improvements in a product or process, rather than revolutionary advances. The size of the effort is relatively small, the design concept relatively simple, and its development relatively easy. Gilfillan[19] describes technological advance in ships and shipbuilding as occurring largely through these kinds of efforts—the accretion of small and piecemeal improvements—spiced by an occasional major advance.

The key inputs to the modest design improvement work would appear to be knowledge won through practical experience, people possessing this kind of knowledge, and a flow of new materials and components from the supplying industries. In Gilfillan's description, as ships of various designs were used people involved in operating and designing them became aware of the ways in which design was unsatisfactory or could be improved, and how various innovations could be made. These were built into the next round of designs. While old and established aspects of designs continued to be gradually improved, the greatest improvements were made on the more recently incorporated aspects of design and components. This would appear to be a typical phenomenon. Learning through experience was complemented by new materials and components—better and lower cost metals, and more powerful engines, which opened up previously closed design possibilities.[20]

For this kind of design improvement work the size of an industry and its growth clearly play an important role in determining the supply of technological advances. The expansion of an industry increases both the amount of experience with a product or technology (a key factor in expanding knowledge relevant to improvement) and the number of people with this knowledge. In addition, by stimulating technological progress in the industries supplying materials and components, industrial expan-

[19] S. C. Gilfillan, *The Sociology of Invention* (Chicago: Follett Publishing Co., 1935) and *Inventing the Ship* (Follett, 1935).

[20] The A. D. Little, Inc., description of technological advances in machine tools and in textile machinery (*Patterns and Problems of Technical Innovation in American Industry*, Report to the National Science Foundation, September 1963) and the Ronald Miller-David Sawers study of the development of civil aircraft (*The Development of Civil Aircraft*, forthcoming) contain many aspects in common with Gilfillan's description of advances in ship building—in particular the important role played by steady, but piecemeal improvements in design based on experience and the exploitation of new materials and components.

Chart II-1

Capital Formation and Patents in the Railroad Industry, 1840-1950 [a]

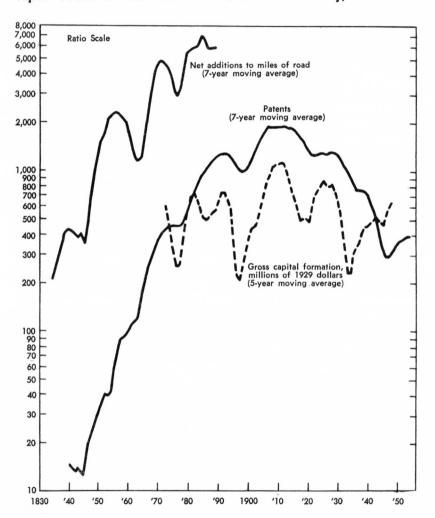

Source: Adapted from Jacob Schmookler, "Changes in Industry and in the State of Knowledge as Determinan of Industrial Invention," in The Rate and Direction of Inventive Activity, National Bureau of Economic Resear (Princeton: Princeton University Press, 1962).
a Patents cover equipment and structures. Net additions to road are taken as representative of capit formation during the early years when a more suitable index is not available.

sion tends to enrich the set of basic elements with which inventors and improvers within the industry can work. Thus, railroad expansion increased the demand for metals and played a large role in stimulating improvements in that field. These advances, in turn, permitted subsequent major advances in the design of rails, engines, and other railroad equipment. Thus, we would argue that the patterns shown on Charts II-1 and II-2 reflect capability increases as well as demand expansion.

Indeed, when the demand for the product of an industry is relatively responsive to price reductions or improved quality, the linkage of incentive for and capability of technological advance to industry size provides a very powerful dynamic thrust. An initial increase in demand or a key invention leads to industrial expansion, heightening the gross returns to and increasing the capabilities for achieving advances. Advances result in better or lower cost products, stimulating further expansion of the industry, providing greater spur and more capability for further advances. As the industry grows and absorbs a larger share of the economy's resources and consumers' incomes, demand becomes less elastic and less responsive to further advances and the dynamic thrust is dampened. This is the classic pattern of industrial growth observed by such writers as Kuznets and Merton.[21]

Advance of Science and Education

When only marginal modifications in a product or process are sought, the knowledge required need not extend much beyond existing technology. When the advances sought are greater, the inventor must see existing technique within a significantly larger and perhaps a quite different context. Often scientific knowledge has been the key to that larger context.[22]

At least over the last century and a half, advances in scientific knowledge have had a profound effect on kinds of technological advances, both attempted and achieved. For example, there was strong demand for products such as antiseptics and the telephone long before their inven-

---

[21] Simon Kuznets, *Secular Movements in Production and Prices* (Boston: Houghton Mifflin Company, 1930); R. K. Merton, "Fluctuations in the Rate of Industrial Invention," *Quarterly Journal of Economics,* Vol. 49 (May, 1935). It is not clear whether these authors had in mind the declining demand elasticity as the key initial factor, but they pinpointed the general pattern.

[22] See for example Donald A. Schon, *Displacement of Concepts* (New York: Humanities Press, 1964).

Chart II-2

Capital Formation, Patents, and Important Inventions in the Petroleum Refining Industry, 1840-1950

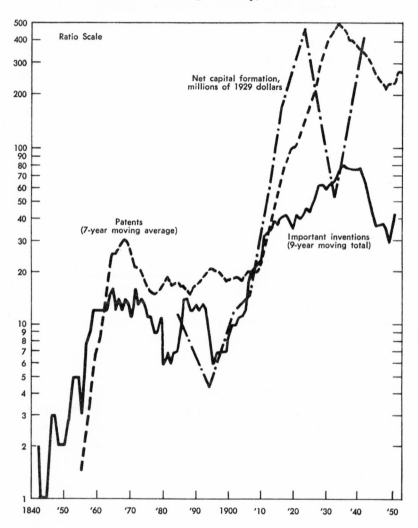

Source: Reproduced from Jacob Schmookler, op. cit., p. 217.

tion. Had they been invented years before, there is little doubt that they would have been profitable. In both cases there is no question but that practical experience played a role in posing the problem and in suggesting certain aspects of the solution. But in each, an essential part of the thinking which triggered the efforts at invention and was applied to solve the problem involved scientific understanding which did not exist before; the germ theory of infection in the one case, the theory of electromagnetism in the other.

Turning to the present, the great postwar increase in research and development in the field of health and medicine reflects not only the increased value society places on health, but also the advances in knowledge which have increased expectation that further research and development will yield significant results.[23]

The growing relevance of science to invention has had four major consequences. First, the creation of technology that is in large part derived from more general knowledge has greatly raised the importance of formal education as a factor in invention. When the technology of an industry is not well understood (in the sense that it cannot be or is not described in books and articles, and cannot be or is not explained in terms of general scientific or engineering concepts) the engineer or scientist is at a disadvantage relative to the experienced industry technician. However, when aspects of the technology are formally understood, the scientist or engineer can apply an entire stock of accumulated knowledge that even the most experienced workman does not have if he lacks formal training. Germany's large role in the major advances in chemical technology during the nineteenth century is largely due to the fact that she was training more chemists than other countries. The prominent role of the United States in the post World War II era is in part due to its great supply of trained scientists and engineers. The rising importance of formal education is suggested in a study by Schmookler, showing a steady and dramatic rise between 1900 and 1950 in the correlation between patents taken out by state residents and scientists and engineers in that state. In 1900 the correlation was .08. In 1950 it was .83.[24]

[23] This appears to be a case where increased productivity of inventing in a field led to increased resources applied, thus multiplying the effect. Increases in productivity of invention, however, need not make it profitable to employ more resources.

[24] Jacob Schmookler, "Inventors Past and Present," *Review of Economics and Statistics,* Vol. 39 (August 1957).

Second, invention has become more of a separate activity, rather than one carried out on the shop floor as a joint product with current production. In contrast with those technologies which are largely empirical, the inventor and the applier of new technology in the science-based sectors are often quite different kinds of people, with different kinds of education and training.

Third, inventive efforts have significantly increased in those fields and on those problems which most fruitfully could exploit scientific knowledge. Stafford shows a much more rapid growth of patents (perhaps an index of manpower applied to invention) in the chemical and electrical fields than in mechanical fields.[25] While the effect on industries and classes of products has not been sharp (there are chemical processes and electronics equipment applicable to the textile industry, as well as to the chemical and electrical equipment industries), it has not been even among industries.

Finally, by providing a context of knowledge far transcending the details of existing technology, advances in sciences have led to a succession of radical technological advances. This is not to say that major advances in technology follow recent advances in science closely and directly. The principle that expanding gases absorb heat was known long before the gas refrigerator was invented. Marconi's bringing to practice of improved understanding of electromagnetism followed many years after the theoretical experiments of Maxwell and Hertz. Lack of close proximity in time, however, should not obscure the point that the earlier advances were pivotal. Indeed, science-based inventions have been the major factor differentiating the products and processes of the twentieth from the nineteenth centuries. Without advances in understanding many important technological advances undoubtedly would have been made, but it is unlikely that the vast scope of modern medicine or modern communications would have been achieved.

The Development of a Scientific Base

Compare Watt's utlization of the theory of latent heat in his invention of the separate condensing chamber for steam engines, or Marconi's exploitation of developments in electromagnetism with Carothers' work which led to nylon, Shockley's work which led to the transistor, or

[25] A. B. Stafford, "Is the Rate of Invention Declining?" *American Journal of Sociology*, May 1952.

recent technological advances in drugs and military aircraft. In the earlier cases the scientific research that created the breakthrough was completely autonomous to the inventive effort. In the later cases, much of the underlying scientific knowledge was won in the course of efforts specifically aimed at providing the basic understanding and data needed to achieve further technological advances. Carothers' basic research at Du Pont which led to nylon was financed by management in the hope that improvements in the understanding of long polymers would lead to important new or improved chemical products. Shockley's Bell Telephone Laboratories project was undertaken in the belief that improved knowledge of semiconductors would lead to better electrical devices.[26]

Undertaking scientific research with the explicit objective (on the part of the financier) of practical payoff is far from a recent phenomenon. Yet the early large-scale support of research with the aim of practical payoff was primarily governmental, rather than private. The Army arsenals, and the early maritime and military medical services conducted a considerable amount of research. Later the Department of Agriculture— both with its own facilities and through the federally-subsidized experimentation stations—supported much of the research upon which the scientific underpinnings of agricultural technology were based.[27]

Government agencies were not alone in supporting research in hopes of practical payoff. Many famous scientists did at least part of their work with exactly this in mind; Pasteur's work and the germ theory is one illustration of a long tradition of basic research aimed at facilitating practical advances in the field of medicine. There are several examples in the United States and in Germany of nineteenth century companies putting chemists to work on various problems.[28] Generally, however, the large private companies with the basic research laboratories are late comers.

Establishing a science base is not the same thing as exploring the feasibility of a particular design concept before deciding to initiate a de-

[26] For a detailed examination of basic research at Bell Telephone Laboratories and of the transistor project, see Richard R. Nelson's "The Link Between Science and Invention: The Case of the Transistor," in *The Rate and Direction of Inventive Activity, op. cit.*

[27] A. Hunter Dupree, *Science in the Federal Government* (Cambridge: Belknap Press of Harvard University Press, 1957).

[28] C. E. Mees and J. A. Leermakers, *The Organization of Industrial Scientific Research* (New York: McGraw-Hill Book Co., 1950).

velopment effort, or conducting research on a specific, well-defined, practical problem. The objectives generally are far broader. Often the type of research involved is the sort that scientists would undertake simply to advance their disciplines. Carothers' work on long polymers and Shockley's work on semi-conductors were of major academic interest. But consciously laying a science base is not the same thing as generalized support of basic scientific research.

When sponsored by organizations such as Du Pont, General Electric, the National Institutes of Health (NIH), and the Department of Defense (DOD), the distinguishing aspect of basic research is emphasis on certain key areas where improved understanding is judged particularly likely to yield solutions to practical problems and open up promising areas for development. Usually it involves a major increase in and sharp focusing of scientific talent in areas which, although of some academic interest, would not receive such attention simply out of scientific curiosity—the research support provided by the Department of Defense on properties of solid fuel combustion, or that supported by General Electric or Bell Labs on semi-conductors, for example. Sometimes the added support is so great that it almost amounts to the building of a new scientific discipline, as in government support for aerodynamics in the 1920's and 1930's.

Sometimes it will involve work of little interest to a scientific discipline. Research on materials (such as research in the properties of textile fibers) or on the characteristics of the process (such as analysis of the mechanics of lathe cutting) are a prominent part of modern industrial research. Designing, building, and experimentation with radically new product designs to learn about them or from them (rather than as a prototype of a specific planned product)—experimental development—also is an important part of the knowledge push. The X-15 rocket aircraft program has been conducted primarily to explore facets of hypersonic flight and aspects of aircraft design, rather than to provide information relevant to a particular production aircraft.

The electronics and chemical industries are particularly fortunate in the existence of a closely related scientific discipline. But even here much research and hardware experimentation is undertaken which probably would not be done by academics. In the case of aviation, an entire new discipline was developed. Some industries were, in a sense, born close to science; others formed their own science base, but in any case it takes considerable effort to remain close to science.

The science-based technologies and industries have a great advantage in achieving major advances in products and processes. Research aimed at opening up new possibilities has substituted both for chance development in the relevant sciences, and for the classical major inventive effort aimed at cracking open a problem through direct attack. The post World War II explosion of major advances in electronics, aircraft, missiles, chemicals, and medicines, reflects the maturing of the science base in these industries, as well as the large volume of resources they employ to advance technology. Many of the products of the science-based industries are the materials used by other industries and their improvement has led to rapid productivity growth in many sectors of the economy. The more important new consumer goods have come either directly from these industries or through incorporation into new products by other industries of the materials and components created by the science-based sector.

Much of economics is devoted to showing that what laymen call "new" is really a manifestation of a long-term trend. In the case of the science-based industries there is something distinctly new: science has been incorporated as a normal part of the business organization. Schumpeter partially saw this. In his *The Theory of Economic Development*[28] and his *Business Cycles*[29] the entrepreneur is shown as capitalizing on the work of the garret inventor. In his *Capitalism, Socialism, and Democracy* a vice-president of research presides over a large organization devoted to inventive activity.[30] But, while he recognized that major advances come more easily in the science-based industries, Schumpeter failed to see that the reason is not the resources of the large corporate firm, or the organized R&D laboratory, but rather the large and continuing effort toward basic and exploratory research.

[28] Joseph A. Schumpeter (Cambridge: Harvard University Press, 1934).
[29] *Business Cycles, a Theoretically Historical and Statistical Analysis of the Capitalist Process* (New York: McGraw-Hill Book Co., 1939).
[30] (New York: Harper and Row, 1950.)

3

The Invention Industry

The factors determining technological advance have their effects through the various institutions called here "The Invention Industry." While principal organizations of this industry can be grouped in various ways, the authors prefer to emphasize the distinction between industrial R&D facilities, where the output can be utilized within the organization,[1] and separate R&D facilities—principally universities, government laboratories, and other nonprofit research institutions. The other categories discussed are independent inventors, and foreign sources which have major distinctive characteristics of their own.

Industrial R&D

Industrial R&D includes all organized efforts to advance technology conducted by business firms that produce and sell goods and services.[2]

[1] The term "invention industry" is used as short hand for the group of organizations that create new or improved technology generally, not just patentable inventions which are only a subclass (if an important one) of technological advances.

[2] Years ago statistics may have distinguished between research and development, and more routine design improvements. Today any such distinction has become blurred. While the National Science Foundation definition of development explicitly excludes "routine technical services to customers," there is little question that companies certainly include as R&D the more or less routine work that goes into the yearly changes in model design. In recent NSF publications listing uses of scientists and engineers in industry, design is not listed as a separate activity nor grouped with R&D (other categories are sales, production and operations, management, etc.). Thus the figures for industrial R&D probably include almost all of the organized

44

TABLE III-1. *Flow of R&D Funds in the United States, 1961–62*[a]

(Dollar amounts in millions)

Sources of R&D Funds	Performers of R&D Work					Percent of Total
	Federal Government	Industry	Universities	Other Nonprofits	Total Funds Supplied	
Federal government	$2,090	$6,310	$1,050	$200	$9,650	*65.5*
Industry	0	4,560	55	90	4,705	*31.9*
Universities	0	0	230	0	230	*1.6*
Other nonprofits	0	0	65	90	155	*1.1*
Total cost of R&D performed	2,090	10,870	1,400	380	14,740	*100.0*
Percent of total	*14.2*	*73.7*	*9.5*	*2.6*	*100.0*	

Source: National Science Foundation, "National Trends in R&D Funds, 1953–62," *Reviews of Data on Research and Development*, NSF 63–40, No. 41 (September 1963), p. 2.
Note: Figures are rounded and may not add to totals.
[a] The hyphenated year indicates a span of one year that takes into account the various calender and fiscal years of R&D performers.

As shown in Table III-1, industrial R&D spending was about three-fourths of the $15 billion national R&D spending reported by the National Science Foundation (NSF) for 1961-62,[3] although, as Table III-1 also shows, about 60 percent of the industrial spending was financed by government funds.

The principal part of the overall effort excluded from the NSF figures is the work of individual inventors. However, in 1960 corporate patents taken out outnumbered those taken out by individual inventors six to four and undoubtedly the input of resources per corporate patent greatly exceeded the input per individual patent.[4] Thus industrial research and

effort by industry to advance technology—a considerable amount of design improvement work (of the sort which results in the yearly automobile changes), some major inventive efforts, and some technology oriented basic research.
[3] In 1960 over 800,000 people were engaged in industrial R&D: 200,000 engineers, 80,000 scientists, 170,000 technicians, and 350,000 craftsmen, administrators, clerical, and other supporting personnel. Roughly half the costs were attributable to salaries, and half to maintenance, depreciation of plant and equipment, and materials.
[4] See Jacob Schmookler, "Inventors Past and Present," *Review of Economics and Statistics*, Vol. 39 (August 1957).

TABLE III-2. *The Growth of R&D Expenditures in the American Economy, Selected Years, 1921–61*[a]

(Dollar amounts in millions)

Year	Total R&D Expenditures	Percent of GNP	Percent of R&D Expenditures Federally Financed	Federal R&D Expenditures	Nonfederal R&D Expenditures as Percent of GNP
1961	$14,740	2.8	65	$9,650	1.0
1960	13,890	2.8	65	9,010	1.0
1959	12,680	2.6	66	8,320	.9
1958	11,130	2.5	64	7,170	.9
1957	10,100	2.3	63	6,390	.8
1956	8,670	2.1	59	5,095	.9
1955	6,390	1.6	57	3,670	.7
1954	5,620	1.5	55	3,070	.7
1953	5,150	1.4	53	2,740	.7
1940	570	.6	21	120	.5
1931	300	.4	13	40	.3
1921	150	.2	17	25	.2

Sources: Computed from data in Nestor E. Terleckyj, assisted by Harriet J. Halper, *Research and Development: Its Growth and Composition* (New York: National Industrial Conference Board, 1963); National Science Foundation, "National Trends in R&D Funds, 1953–62," *Reviews of Data on Research and Development*, NSF 63-40, No. 41 (September 1963); *Economic Report of the President, January 1966* (Washington: Government Printing Office, 1966), p. 209.

[a] 1921 to 1940 estimated from partial data.

development probably accounts for significantly more than half of the total national effort to advance technological knowledge.

While the industrial R&D label covers a vast diversity of firms and kinds of work, its distinguishing overall characteristic is that it is undertaken with the objective of improving an organization's own products and process. It represents the institutional tying together of technological advances and production by a single organization, and has been one of the most rapidly growing economic activities. Corporate R&D personnel have risen from less than 20,000 in 1921 to about 80,000 in 1940, and to over 800,000 in 1960.[5] At the turn of the century the number of industrial research laboratories could be counted on the fingers; by 1920 the National Research Council listed 307; by 1960 there were more than 5,400 listed in its directory, *Industrial Research Laboratories of the U. S.*

[5] Unless otherwise noted, R&D figures cited in this chapter are from the National Science Foundation.

This rise in industrial laboratories has been part and parcel of the growing overall national R&D effort. As shown in Table III-2, the percentage of GNP devoted to R&D in 1961 was fourteen times higher than in 1921 and twice higher than in 1953, with the gains in the fifties due largely to federal spending. But corporate R&D, a major recipient of federal funds, has grown more rapidly than other kinds, rising from about 60 percent of total accounted R&D spending in 1921 to 68 percent in 1941, to about 75 percent in 1960. Patent statistics show an even greater rise relative to private inventors. In 1906, 22 percent of all patents were issued to corporations.[6] By 1946 the corporate percentage of patents was 50 percent, and by 1957, 60 percent. A good part of the rise in the corporate position is attributable to industrial R&D programs.[7]

Firm Size and R&D Spending

As pointed out earlier, the 1960 directory of industrial research laboratories listed over 5,000 laboratories. Many other firms undertake R&D without a facility large enough or specialized enough to be signified a "laboratory." In 1961 almost 12,000 firms reported that they were performing some R&D.

The vast majority of these programs were conducted by relatively small companies, with less than 1,000 employees. Roughly 40 percent of them spent less than $10,000 annually on R&D—significantly less than the full time equivalent of one scientist or engineer. For these companies, R&D is a part-time activity, and their work appears to have more in common with the work of private inventors than with the big R&D laboratories. Another 40 percent of small companies spent between $10,000 and $100,000 annually. A $100,000 budget is roughly sufficient to support four or five scientists and engineers, plus a few assistants. While such budgets do not permit the kind of R&D done by Du Pont, for example, they probably represent enough technical competence to permit small companies to utilize knowledge and components developed elsewhere, to engage in some significant design improvement work, and occasionally to come forth with some important major inventions.

---

[6] Schmookler, *op. cit.*

[7] While formal corporate laboratories are a relatively recent phenomenon, engineers and technicians working for business firms have long been a source of inventions.

TABLE III-3. *The Distribution of R&D by Firm Size in Manufacturing, 1958*

Firm Size (Employees)	5,000 or More	1,000–4,999	Less Than 1,000
Number of firms	384	1,459	260,000
Percent doing research	*89*	*50*	*4*
Percent of industry research expenditures	*85*	8	7

Source: Organisation for Economic Co-operation and Development, *Science, Economic Growth, and Government Policy* (Paris: the Organisation, 1964), p. 87.

However, the bulk of industrial R&D is conducted by a few large firms. Table III-3 shows that, in 1958, formal R&D programs were reported by 4 percent of the firms with less than 1,000 employees, 50 percent of the firms in the 1,000-5,000 range, and 89 percent of the firms with over 5,000 employees and, of course, the large firms have bigger programs. In 1961 roughly 10,500 firms with less than 1,000 employees accounted for only 5 percent of total industrial R&D spending; the 391 companies with more than 5,000 employees accounted for 86 percent. Four giant companies alone accounted for over 22 percent of total industrial R&D spending.

Industry and Product Concentration

The lion's share of industrial R&D is conducted in a few manufacturing industries. Firms in agriculture, mining, construction, and the services perform almost none. Table III-4 lists the eleven manufacturing industries that account for 95 percent of industrial R&D: the top six account for 88 percent, whereas they account for only 40 percent of the total value added and employment in the manufacturing sector.

The concentration of R&D spending is a long-standing phenomenon, as can be seen in Table III-5. Over a thirty-year period chemicals, electrical equipment, and machinery industries have consistently accounted for a large proportion. Rise of the aircraft and missiles industries has been the major recent development. As late as 1940 aircraft and missiles, together with all the other transportation equipment industries, accounted for less than 7 percent of industrial R&D employment. By 1957, aircraft and missiles alone accounted for 31 percent.

The rise of the aircraft and missile industries, and the growing relative importance of electronics, is the result of a sharp rise in government (principally DOD and the National Aeronautics and Space Agency

[NASA]) financing of industrial R&D. Prior to World War II the federal government played a relatively small role in the total, and industrial, R&D picture. By 1953 it was providing more than half of the funds; by the late 1950's it was financing roughly 65 percent of total, and about 58 percent of industrial R&D spending.

The bulk of applied research and development done by a firm is directed toward improving or expanding its line of products. A McGraw-Hill survey reports that the purpose of about half of industrial R&D spending in the companies surveyed was to create new products, about 40 percent to improve existing product lines, and about 10 percent to

TABLE III-4. *R&D Costs as Distributed by Industry, 1961*

(Dollar amounts in millions)

Industry	R&D Costs	Percent of Total Industry R&D	Industry R&D as Percent of Sales
Research Intensive Group			
Aircraft and missiles	$3,957	*36.4*	*24.2*
Electrical equipment and communication	2,404	*22.1*	*10.4*
Chemicals	1,073	*9.9*	*4.6*
Machinery, nonelectrical	896	*8.2*	*4.4*
Motor vehicles and other transportation equipment	802	*7.4*	*2.9*
Professional and scientific instruments	384	*3.5*	*7.3*
Subtotal, research intensive industries	9,516	*87.5*	
Other Industries			
Petroleum refining and extraction	294	*2.7*	*1.0*
Primary metals	160	*1.5*	*0.8*
Rubber products	126	*1.2*	*2.2*
Fabricated metal products	118	*1.1*	*1.3*
Food and kindred products	105	*1.0*	*0.3*
Other industries	553	*5.1*	*n.a.*
Total, other industries	1,356	*12.5*	
Total, all industries	10,872	*100.0*	

Source: National Science Foundation, *Research and Development in Industry 1961* (Washington: Government Printing Office, NSF 64-9, 1964), pp. 9, 40.
n.a. Not available.
Note: Figures are rounded and may not add to totals.

TABLE III-5. *Percentage Distribution of R&D Personnel by Industry, 1927–57*

	Percent of All R&D Employees			
	1927	1940	1952	1957
Research Intensive Industries				
Aircraft and parts ⎫			*21.6*	*30.8*
Motor vehicles and other ⎬	*4.3*	*6.9*		
transportation ⎭			*7.1*	*9.3*
Electrical equipment and				
communication	*31.6*	*15.6*	*26.5*	*19.9*
Chemicals and allied products	*18.1*	*20.8*	*11.8*	*9.3*
Machinery	*8.6*	*9.9*	*5.8*	*11.9*
Instruments	ᵃ	ᵃ	*5.9*	*4.0*
Professional and Scientific				
Total, Research Intensive				
Industries	*62.6*	*53.2*	*78.7*	*85.2*
Other Industries				
Food and kindred products	*2.0*	*4.0*	*1.3*	*1.2*
Paper and allied products	*1.3*	*1.8*	*0.7*	*0.7*
Petroleum refining and extraction	*4.3*	*10.2*	*5.3*	*2.8*
Rubber products	*5.9*	*3.5*	*1.4*	*1.5*
Stone, clay and glass products	*2.6*	*3.4*	*1.5*	*0.8*
Metal industriesᵇ	*6.6*	*8.1*	*4.0*	*3.1*
Other manufacturingᶜ	*3.6*	*5.1*	*2.7*	*2.2*
Nonmanufacturers, other than				
communication	*11.2*	*10.5*	*4.3*	*2.6*
Total, other industries	*37.4*	*46.8*	*21.9*	*14.8*

Source: Data from Nestor E. Terleckyj, *Research and Development: Its Growth and Composition, op. cit.*, p. 44.
ᵃ Not separately available. Included in other manufacturing.
ᵇ Includes primary metals, fabricated metal products, and ordnance, except in 1957 when ordnance is included with other manufacturing.
ᶜ 1927 and 1940 data include professional and scientific instruments; 1957 data include ordnance.
Note: Figures are rounded and may not add to totals.

improve processes.[8] It is clear that a firm's R&D is oriented to its products, even though the distinction between product and process may not be sharp because product improvement sometimes includes R&D to reduce cost and price, and the production of new products sometimes requires special production techniques. However, large firms fit awkwardly into industry boundaries; they produce a wide range of products, only

[8] See Eric Gustafson, "Research and Development, New Products, and Productivity Change," *American Economic Review,* Vol. 52 (May 1962).

some of which belong to the firm's basic industry. To examine the question of product field allocation, it is necessary then to look beyond industry categories.

Table III-6 shows the percent of R&D expenditures by the firms in an industry directed towards that industry's major products—the coefficient of specialization. The median coefficient is 58 percent. The table also shows the percent of R&D in each product field done by firms in the in-

TABLE III-6. *Coefficients of Specialization and Coverage for R&D Activities for 1960*

(In percentages)

Industry	Specialization	Coverage
Aircraft and missiles	*67.9*	*72.2*
Chemicals	*80.3*	*77.0*
Electrical equipment and communication	*48.7*	*56.9*
Fabricated metal products	*32.4*	*23.5*
Food and kindred products	*78.1*	*78.1*
Machinery	*51.4*	*50.5*
Motor vehicles and other transportation equipment	*58.1*	*87.3*
Petroleum refining and extraction	*52.6*	*93.4*
Primary metals	*58.8*	*74.3*
Professional and scientific instruments	*32.0*	*56.5*
Rubber products	*33.9*	*69.6*

Source: Computed from data from National Science Foundation, *Research and Development in Industry 1960* (Washington: Government Printing Office, NSF 63-7, 1963), pp. 80–81.

dustry which is the principal manufacturer of that product—the coefficient of coverage.[9] The median value of this coefficient is 72 percent.

On an industry by industry basis, these two coefficients are considerably higher when computed for sales rather than R&D.[10] In other words,

[9] These terms are used by economists in examining product diversification. Their meaning is indicated by looking at the research relevant to petroleum refining and extraction. Table III-6 indicates that most applied R&D on petroleum products is carried on by petroleum companies (the coefficient of coverage). Thus, petroleum companies do a great deal of R&D on other than petroleum products, but that done on petroleum products is carried on mostly by petroleum companies.

[10] Values for both the coefficients of coverage and specialization are typically in the 90 percent range in the studies of product and industry relationships—and this is for four-digit industries rather than the three- and two-digit industries used by the NSF. See *Concentration Ratios in Manufacturing Industries, 1958,* a report

TABLE III-7. *Science and Product Field Orientation of Industrial R&D, 1960*

(Dollar amounts in millions).

Science or product field	Cost of R&D Performed	Percent of Total
Applied Research & Development, Total	$10,161	*96.3*
Guided missiles	2,233	*21.2*
Communication equipment and electronic components	2,152	*20.4*
Aircraft and parts	1,132	*10.7*
Chemicals, except drugs & medicines	780	*7.4*
Industrial inorganic and organic chemicals	215	*2.0*
Plastic materials and man-made fiber, except glass	324	*3.1*
Agricultural chemicals	39	*0.4*
All other chemicals	202	*1.9*
Machinery	743	*7.0*
Engines and turbines	93	*0.9*
Farm machinery and equipment	75	*0.7*
Construction, mining, and materials-handling machinery and equipment	59	*0.6*
Metal working machinery and equipment	53	*0.5*
Office, computing, and accounting machines	314	*3.0*
Other machinery, except electrical	149	*1.4*
Motor vehicles and other transportation equipment	562	*5.3*
Motor vehicles and equipment	533	*5.1*
Other transportation equipment	29	*0.3*
Atomic energy devices	556	*5.3*
Electrical equipment, except communication	279	*2.6*
Electric transmission and distribution equipment	66	*0.6*
Electrical industrial apparatus	80	*0.8*
Other electrical equipment and supplies	133	*1.3*
Professional and scientific instruments	221	*2.1*
Drugs and medicines	175	*1.7*
Fabricated metal products	153	*1.5*
Petroleum refining and extraction	137	*1.3*
Primary metals	121	*1.1*
Primary ferrous products	70	*0.7*
Primary and secondary nonferrous metals	51	*0.5*
Other ordnance, except complete guided missiles	90	*0.9*
Stone, clay, and glass products	53	*0.5*
All other	774	*7.3*
Basic Research, Total	385	*3.7*
Physical and mathematical sciences	234	*2.2*
Engineering sciences	77	*0.7*
Life sciences	39	*0.4*
Other	35	*0.3*
All Research and Development	10,546	*100.0*

Source: Nestor E. Terleckyj, *Research and Development: Its Growth and Composition, op. cit.,* p. 50.

R&D diversification is considerably greater than product diversification. However, this has only been a minor offset to the industry concentration noted above. If R&D expenditures are arrayed by product fields, as in Table III-7, the same familiar names head the list—missiles and aircraft, electronics, chemicals, and machinery. The firms in the big R&D spending industries do diversify, but they diversify into the product lines of other such big spending industries.

The Reach of Industrial R&D

When people think of industrial R&D they tend to think of the development of the Atlas missile, or the electronic computer, or television, DDT or nylon—in short of the very major technological advances which have revolutionized the mid-twentieth century.

Efforts toward major advances probably absorb the lion's share of R&D finances in the giant firms of the aerospace complex working on defense and space contracts. Not only do many of these efforts reach far in terms of performance advances; often they aim for advances in a number of components and dimensions at once, and hence often require the design and development of many new components. In a very real sense they represent an effort to achieve, simultaneously, a number of complementary major advances.

Outside of military and space R&D, there are many privately financed corporate efforts aimed at major advances. A few of these involve complex multi-component systems or complicated chemical processes— Boeing's and Douglas' development of the civil jet transport, Bell Labs' TH system, the work of Philco and RCA on television, and Du Pont work on corfam. Many involve smaller or less complex systems. Where large complex systems or production equipment are involved, the large companies generally have been the principal undertakers. Because smaller or less complex systems generally do not require such massive inputs of resources, even to achieve major advances, a number of the important advances in electronic components have come from smaller firms. This suggests continuing relevance for the finding of Jewkes, Saw-

---

prepared by the Bureau of the Census for the Subcommittee on Antitrust and Monopoly of the Committee on the Judiciary, U.S. Senate (Washington: Government Printing Office, 1962). The fact that organized R&D is predominately carried on by large firms, which also have more diverse product lines, may explain the lower degree of specialization in R&D.

ers, and Stillerman that during the 1900-1950 period, small companies contributed a significant number of major inventions.[11]

Outside defense and space related R&D, however, and possibly some segments of the civil electronics and chemical industries, the bulk of corporate R&D is modest design improvement work not reaching very far —the type of work that results in yearly changes in automobile design, gradual improvements in refrigerators and vacuum cleaners, and steady improvements in the automaticity, speed, and capacity of machine tools, rather than radically new products and processes. The authors' interviews with executives indicate the concentration of corporate R&D activity on the more modest improvements, as does the emphasis on short pay-back periods in choosing R&D projects, for far-reaching developments typically have a long gestation. The pervasiveness of short pay-back periods is indicated by a recent McGraw-Hill study where 90 percent of the interviewed firms expected on the average to recoup all applied research expenditures within five years of the initiation of projects.[12] The A. D. Little studies of recent textile equipment and machine tools show that recent technological advance was composed of a series of piecemeal and modest improvements spiced by an occasional, but only occasional, major advance.[13] This kind of pattern would result from a modest orientation of R&D activity.[14]

[11] John Jewkes, David Sawers, and Richard Stillerman, *The Sources of Invention* (New York: St. Martin's Press, 1958), henceforth denoted as Jewkes, Sawers, and Stillerman.

[12] Dexter M. Keezer, "The Outlook for Expenditures on Research and Development During the Next Decade," *American Economic Review,* Vol. 50 (May 1960).

[13] A. D. Little, Inc., *Patterns and Problems of Technical Innovation in American Industry, op. cit.*

[14] This characterization of corporate R&D as predominantly aimed at modest "short reach" improvements is also made by Daniel Hamberg ("Invention in the Industrial Research Laboratory," *Journal of Political Economy,* Vol. 71 [April 1963]), and Jewkes, Sawers, Stillerman, *loc. cit.* It is confirmed empirically by research on the R&D practices of one large industrial corporation by Edwin Mansfield and Richard Brandenburg, published since this manuscript was completed. Since it bears so directly on our point, their paper is quoted here:

Most projects were expected to be completed in less than four years and the time interval between project completion and the application of the results was seldom expected to be more than one year. Expectations of this sort are generally optimistic; according to company officials, the elimination of this bias would increase the figures in Tables 2-3 by about 50 percent. If one follows Hamberg (as cited above) and defines short-term projects to be those taking five years or less, the bulk of the projects were short-term, even if this bias was eliminated. However, this definition of a short-term project may be too stringent. If three

TABLE III-8. *Percent Distribution of Funds for R&D by Type of Research, Selected Industries and All Industries, 1961*

(Dollar amounts in millions)

Industry	Total R&D Funds	Percent of Industrial R&D in		
		Develop- ment	Applied Research	Basic Research
Total, all industries (including those not mentioned in table)	$10,872	78	18	4
Aircraft and missiles	3,957	89	10	1
Electrical equipment and communication	2,404	84	13	3
Communication equipment and electronic components	1,183	82	13	5
Other electrical equipment	1,221	86	13	2
Machinery	896	83	14	3
Professional and scientific instruments	384	75	*	3
Fabricated metal products	118	69	30	2
Lumber, wood products, and furniture	9	*	*	0
Primary metals	160	*	*	6
Chemicals and allied products	1,073	52	37	11
Industrial chemicals	693	50	38	12
Drugs and medicines	180	31	53	17
Other chemicals	201	76	19	5
Food and kindred products	105	*	*	8
Petroleum refining and extraction	294	42	42	16

Source: National Science Foundation, *Research and Development in Industry 1961*, NSF 64-9, p. 28.
* Not separately available, but included in total.
Note: Figures are rounded and may not add to totals.

Nor do many companies undertake much in the way of basic research. Four percent of all corporate R&D expenditures are for basic research. (See Table III-8.) Many companies carry out no basic research and even

years, rather than five, were used as a cut-off point, a very substantial percentage of the projects would be long-term.

Most of the projects do not involve very great technical risks. In about three-fourths of the cases, the estimated probability of technical success exceeds .80. In part, this undoubtedly reflects the optimism so often found among professional researchers and the necessity to sell projects. But interviews with various executives of the firm indicate that, if this bias were removed, the bulk of the estimates would still be well above .50.

From Edwin Mansfield and Richard Brandenburg, "The Allocation, Characteristics, and Outcome of the Firm's R and D Portfolio: A Case Study," a paper presented at a Conference on Technological Change at the University of Pennsylvania, April 15, 1966, published in Mansfield's Economic Studies, *op. cit.*

among the giants of over 5,000 employees, only half of those who had an R&D program conducted any basic research; among firms in the 1,000-5,000 class, less than 20 percent. Further, basic research spending is localized in only a few industries; six industries account for about 83 percent. Four of these—chemicals, electrical equipment and electronics, the aerospace complex and petroleum—account for more than 70 percent. (In agriculture and several other fields, the universities and government laboratories undertake a significant amount of technology-oriented basic research.) To the extent that a major in-house basic research effort is essential to the establishment of a strong science base, only a few industries would have such a base.

A Summary Evaluation

The bulk of corporate R&D spending is done by a few large firms in a few industries, and concentrated on a few product fields. There are also a large number of companies in a wide variety of industries with small scale R&D programs. The giants, of course, play the dominant role in major and far-reaching development efforts such as in defense and space and several of them conduct sizeable basic research programs. Both large and medium sized companies engage in a considerable amount of far-reach work in fields requiring smaller and less complex systems. However, outside of the defense and space complex and the chemical and electronics industries (and to a considerable extent even within these), there is little basic research, and most applied R&D is not very far-reaching.

Independent Inventors

There are, of course, independent inventors outside formal R&D organizations. A diverse lot, their ranks include full-time free lancers, people on university staffs working on other contract or grant-financed research programs, government personnel, and non-R&D business employees, such as line executives, foremen, and salesmen trying to invent in off-hours. In addition, a small but important group of individuals working in company R&D facilities maintain considerable autonomy and at least some patent rights. Numbered here are Farnsworth (contributor to television), Thompson (automatic transmissions) and DeForest (cathode tube).[15] Some of the work of many small-scale industrial operations

---

[15] Jewkes, Sawers and Stillerman, *op.cit.*

should also be included because of the similarity of the kinds of work and the factors that motivate it.

The relative and perhaps absolute importance of this group has been declining for many years. The number of patents granted to individual inventors reached a peak in 1916 and has declined erratically since then.[16] Some of the reasons are relatively clear. On the demand side, as the typical firm grew larger it established formal R&D programs and hired the inventors who previously had been free lance. On the supply side, effective inventing in the scientifically more complex fields—and these have grown in importance—increasingly has required the use of specialized equipment beyond the resources of a free lancer. It is also possible that today's well-educated scientist or engineer inventor is less willing to go it alone.

Nonetheless, the independent inventor is far from extinct. In 1958, 40 percent of patents issued in the United States were assigned to individuals rather than corporations, and Schmookler estimates that perhaps a third of corporate patents resulted from work initiated by independents outside the formal R&D organization.[17]

Perhaps the largest part of the work of the independents appears to be the "follow on inventions" stressed by Gilfillan—those design improvements suggested by practical experience. But part of the work reaches farther. The case studies of Jewkes, *et al.* show the independent playing a large role in major machinery and consumer goods inventions, undertaking ventures which company R&D was not sufficiently imaginative or daring to undertake. Independents were responsible for the early work on the automatic cotton picker, the automatic transmission, and the self-winding watch.

While strong evidence is lacking, the allocation of efforts of independent inventors over industries and product fields appears to partially offset the industry and product field concentration of corporate R&D. Thus the A. D. Little study referred to earlier shows several important inventions being made by independents in the field of textile equipment —an area where corporate R&D is weak. But, whatever the product field or industry, independents often work on different kinds of inventions than the corporate lab—typically on small systems, or on pieces of large but not tightly connected systems, and on inventions requiring

[16] Schmookler, "Inventors Past and Present," *op.cit.*
[17] *Ibid.*

mechanical ingenuity, rather than highly sophisticated scientific understanding.[18] Thus it probably is more fruitful to view the work of the independent inventor (and the small corporate R&D program) as a complement and supplement to the work of the large corporate laboratory, rather than as a substitute.

However, there is also a small group of highly trained individuals, often faculty members with access to university facilities, which does work similar to that done in the large corporate laboratories. This group often establishes companies of its own, sometimes with financing from large corporations, sometimes by investors, and in recent years increasingly by government R&D contracts (generally defense). Inventors who fit this description include Baekeland (the inventor of the plastic Bakelite), Houdry (catalytic cracking for petroleum refining), Norman (processes for the hardening of liquid fats), Armstrong (frequency modulation radio broadcasting), Land (the Polaroid camera), and Brandenburger (cellophane).[19] As the list indicates, the contribution of this group is impressive despite its small number.

Often, the independent inventor carries out the early work on his invention on his own, and then licenses or sells his invention to an industrial R&D organization for final development and introduction to the market, or even joins the staff. This was the case, for example, with Houdry and Brandenburger.

The private inventor probably will continue to be responsible for a large share of major advances which do not involve heavy expense in areas where ingenuity and practical experience are more important than formal training. Even in more scientifically sophisticated fields, the role of the independent undoubtedly will continue to appeal to many men who desire to work on the problems they find interesting, take the risks themselves, and reap the benefits. These men prefer association with a university or working independently to fitting into the organizational matrix of a corporate R&D laboratory.

Separate R&D Facilities

Separate facilities include university laboratories, government facilities, and private nonprofit and profit contract research institutions. While this

[18] Independents account for 88 percent of mechanical inventions, 9 percent of electrical and 3 percent of chemical.

[19] Jewkes, Sawers and Stillerman, op.cit.

is indeed a heterogeneous group, its members all share characteristics sharply differentiating them from industrial R&D and independent inventors. In contrast with industrial R&D facilities, these facilities are generally not closely linked to a facility which uses their results directly. Unlike the majority of independent inventors, they carry on relatively large-scale efforts and almost always receive outside financing.

Despite the development of basic research efforts in some firms and industries, these organizations are still the principal centers of basic scientific research. While they account for only one-sixth of the applied R&D done in the United States, they account for two-thirds of the basic research.

UNIVERSITY R&D. At universities and colleges R&D amounted to $1.4 billion in 1961—9 percent of the total for the nation.[20] About 75 percent of the funds for university R&D came from the federal government, 4 percent each from industry and the nonprofit sector (primarily the private foundations), and 16 percent from the universities' own funds.

Such funds support an amazing diversity of research. One major part is expended either within the departmental structure or in research institutes closely related to academic departments. Despite the fact that the bulk of this research is funded from the outside by such organizations as the NSF, NIH, and NASA, the direction of research is largely determined by the interests of the scientific community and generally coupled to graduate instruction.

The remaining university R&D is more closely related to establishing the science base under particular technologies. The agricultural experimentation stations and research associated with medical school hospitals are prominent examples. A more significant departure from the ancient notion of the university is the postwar emergence of federally financed contract research centers such as MIT's Lincoln Laboratory or Cal Tech's Jet Propulsion Laboratory, and the growth of university affiliated organizations doing contract work for business firms. Generally such work does not involve the design and development of new products and

---

[20] These figures do not include the research and development and technical consulting done by university faculty members under private arrangements with business and government. While small in volume, this group may have a qualitative effect disproportionate to its numbers. The main users of consultants, however, are government agencies and corporations with R&D programs.

processes; usually it is more in the nature of focused basic or applied research with the final design and development stages being left to business firms. There are some exceptions to this applied research orientation; for example, the federal contract research centers in high energy physics are basic science oriented.

Universities differ strikingly in their R&D policies. Some, principally the endowed eastern universities, have generally limited their activities, to those which at least appear to support their teaching functions and their role as centers for the advancement of academic knowledge. Others, like the state universities and the engineering schools, have involved themselves in a wider range of more applied activities.

The universities have played a prominent role in many inventive efforts. Penicillin, streptomycin and electrical precipitation techniques were, until the last stages of development, largely the result of R&D at universities. University scientists and engineers have often played important roles as consultants to private companies and governments on R&D projects. The distinctive contribution of the universities, however, is as the primary source of fundamental advances in understanding that pave the way for major advances in technology in almost all fields. Universities account for 50 percent of the basic research expenditures in the United States, and even a larger share of the most fundamental work.

GOVERNMENT LABORATORIES. Government laboratories long have played an important role and in 1960 conducted $1.9 billion of R&D—about 14 percent of the nation's total. Today, two-thirds of the work is in such DOD-run facilities as the Naval Ordnance Test Center and the Fort Monmouth Signal Laboratory. However, this DOD dominance is a recent phenomenon. The National Bureau of Standards has a long tradition of research in many areas of physics. Government laboratories were, and still are, prominent in civil aviation, agriculture, and health. Outstanding examples are the Ames flight research center, the agricultural research center at Beltsville, and the National Institutes of Health. All these institutions have played a major role in establishing the science base under their respective technologies.

While government laboratories undertake considerable basic research, they typically undertake relatively more applied research and development than universities. In 1961 basic research accounted for 11 percent of their overall effort, applied research for 29 percent, and development work for 60 percent. In many cases the government laboratory has the additional role of formulating, administering, and evaluating contract research. The NASA Space Centers, for example, typically spend as much on grants to nonprofit and profit-making organizations as on their own activities. Chapter 8 will take a closer look at the role of government laboratories.

NONPROFIT R&D. The Battelle Memorial Institute and the Mellon Institute have long been internationally famous, and in recent years their ranks have been joined by such newcomers as the Midwest Research Institute and the Stanford Research Institute. The nonprofit research institutes are now a significant factor in the R&D picture. In 1961 they accounted for $380 million, or about 3 percent of the national R&D total.[21] About half of the R&D undertaken by nonprofits was financed by the federal government, about one-quarter was self-financed, or financed by other nonprofit organizations (such as foundations), and one quarter by business firms.

The nonprofits do a considerable amount of basic research. Battelle, for example, has a strong basic research program in metallurgy, and Mellon in industrial chemistry. They reported that 41 percent of their 1958 budget went for basic research, as compared with the universities' 51 percent. The universities, however, include the major figures in pure science and carry on the more basic of the basic research. The nonprofits also do much applied work aimed at providing broad solutions to particular practical problems, as well as technical consulting. Some nonprofits do extensive proprietary work for industry, as, for example, Battelle, Stanford Research Institute, and Armour. Others do research and consulting work exclusively, or almost exclusively, for the government. The RAND Corporation and Brookhaven National Laboratory are prominent examples. The major government sponsors are the Department of Defense (DOD), the National Aeronautics and Space Administration (NASA), the Atomic Energy Commission (AEC), the Department of Health, Education, and Welfare (HEW), and the National Science Foundation (NSF).

Those nonprofits conducting proprietary research, as well as the profit contract research laboratories which shall be examined later, draw most

---

[21] They employed 7,000 R&D scientists and engineers and accounted for 1.8 percent of total R&D employment.

of their business customers not from small firms without a strong R&D competence of their own, but from large firms.[22] In 1956 almost 60 percent of their business contract work was done for firms employing more than 5,000 persons. Typically, these firms had a strong R&D competence of their own, but were either fully occupied or the work required talents the company did not want to hire permanently. Thus, a chemical company working on a new petroleum refining process may contract with Battelle to examine certain interesting questions involving metallurgy. Interviews suggest that much of the work done by the nonprofits for small firms with little in-house capability is technical and managerial consulting and market research.

MISCELLANEOUS INSTITUTIONS. To date the profit-making contract research institution has played only a nominal role in the national R&D picture.[23] In this field, A. D. Little, which actually has many of the attributes of a nonprofit-making organization, looms like a giant. Clearly, as the growth of nonprofits indicate, there is a demand for research services. Indeed, much of the expansion of university contracts with business firms and much of the affluence of the professor-consultant is attributable to the absence of profit-making research firms. As the success of the aerospace firms shows, a technical staff can be quickly assembled. The nonprofits, being first on the scene, may have preempted the market. There may also be a customer preference for the nonprofit organization based on fears that profit-making firms may later go into competitive production using knowledge gained from sponsored research. There may also be a reporting bias, since much activity called elsewhere R&D is considered by profit-making firms as consulting. These are all conjectures; there are no firm answers to this question.

Still another type of institution is that which does not do R&D itself, but supports projects it considers promising, and tries to help inventors and small companies with promising ideas. The Research Corporation, now affiliated with MIT, attempts to find a market for the inventions of its clients—now largely patented inventions resulting from MIT research, but once a much broader list. Other universities have

[22] See William Baldwin, "Contracted Research and the Case for Big Business," *Journal of Political Economy,* Vol. 70 (June 1962).

[23] The NSF does not list these corporations as a separate category, but includes them with the nonmanufacturing entry in Industrial R&D. In 1960, this entry, which includes mining, construction, trade, finance, selected service industries, transportation and other public utilities, totaled only $180 million.

TABLE III-9. *Percentage Distribution of Industry R&D Expenditures in Various Countries, 1959*

(Percentages in each industry)

Industry	Country				
	United States	United Kingdom	Sweden	Japan	Canada
Research Intensive					
Aircraft	32.2	40.2		10.4	30.0
Vehicles	9.2	4.3			
Electronics	12.3	10.9	79.1	14.1	18.2
Other electrical	11.5	9.2		10.6	
Machinery	10.1	9.1		5.6	
Instruments	3.8	2.7		2.3	
Chemicals	13.0	14.2	5.3	29.4	21.0
Total research intensive	92.1	90.6	84.4	72.4	69.2
Other Industries					
Rubber	1.2	1.2	1.0	2.0	1.4
Ferrous metal	0.8	1.2	4.1	6.9	6.4
Nonferrous metal	0.7	1.3		3.8	6.6
Metal products	1.3	1.3	—	1.2	—
Stone, clay and glass	0.8	0.8	2.0	3.2	1.6
Paper	0.6	0.7	3.2	1.6	7.6
Food	0.9	1.0	1.6	3.0	2.1
Textiles and apparel	0.2	0.8	2.4	4.1	1.6
Lumber and furniture	0.1	0.1	1.0	Negl.	0.3
Other manufactures	1.3	1.0	—	1.5	3.4
Total other industries	7.9	9.4	15.3	27.3	31.0

Source: Organisation for Economic Co-operation and Development, *Science, Economic Growth and Government Policy* (Paris: 1963), p. 81.

similar organizations. The Rockefeller Brothers Company and the American Research and Development Corporation support interesting inventions and companies. However, to date the amount of funds involved has been very small.

The industrial cooperative research associations are closely analogous. Sometimes they serve as an intermediary between the small firm without strong technical competence and the contract R&D laboratory. In 1953 there were over 500 industrial associations which undertook or sponsored R&D through contributions of their members. Only a small percentage of these operated their own research institutions; most contracted with nonprofit institutes, profit-making research firms, or universities. The total amounts involved were quite small; $20 million is an outside estimate for spending in 1953.[24]

Imported Technology

One-fifth of all patents granted in the United States in 1953 went to foreigners, for inventions created abroad.[25] Because the difficulties of patenting are greater for foreigners, this probably understates the importance of foreign technology.[26] Examples of the U.S. debt to foreign technology are the ball-point pen (Hungary by way of Argentina), cellophane (France), crease resisting fabrics (England), DDT (Switzerland) and insulin (Canada). Studies of specific industries seeking to isolate the relative importance of imported technology also point to its major role.

Payments of patent royalties and license fees to foreign firms provide some measure of the industry direction of imported technology. The six most research-intensive industries (accounting for 92 percent of all industrial R&D in 1959) made two-thirds of all American payments. This

[24] Battelle Memorial Institute for National Science Foundation, *Research by Cooperative Organizations* (Washington: Government Printing Office, 1956).

[25] The latest year for which data are available is 1953. Source: Ministère de l'Industrie, Institut National de la Propriété Industrielle, *La Protection des Inventions en France et à l'Etranger* (Paris: 1960), Appendix Table. Although irrelevant to the discussion here, the United States exports considerably more technology than it imports. As measured by technological payments (royalties, license fees, etc.) the receipts from abroad were nine times the payments in 1961. See Organisation for Economic Co-operation and Development, *Science, Economic Growth and Government Policy* (Paris: The Organisation, 1964), p. 85.

[26] Obtaining a U.S. patent is a more complex and costly procedure for a foreigner than for a resident. Furthermore, since the foreigner is protected in his home country by his patent there and requires a U.S. patent only if the patent rights are to be exercised in the U.S. (either through licensing an American firm or by selling the patented product to a U.S. firm), foreigners only take out U.S. patents in situations where it is likely that they will be worked. On the other hand, patents are a poor measure of inventive output.

In contrast to the author's view, a much larger role is assigned to foreign technology by Edward F. Denison. He states: "To assume that half the advance in knowledge that affects United States growth originates in the United States would seem a very generous estimate." *The Sources of Economic Growth in the United States and the Alternative Before Us* (New York: Committee for Economic Development, 1962), p. 234. He based this conclusion in part upon the proportion of world patents received by Americans, noting that "From 1950 through 1957 the United

is largely because, as shown in Table III-9, the major industrial countries have the same pattern of R&D concentration as the United States.

Summary: *The Critical Concentrations*

While this chapter has explored various facets of the institutional structure of the invention industry, the most striking features are three types of concentration. First, industrial R&D is concentrated in about 400 large firms. Second, R&D is concentrated in a few industries and product lines. Third, apart from defense and space, industrial R&D is concentrated on short reach, applied work. Even though the existence of individual inventors, government laboratories, and universities partially offset these concentrations, they still raise important policy questions.

States received 474,759 patent applications from its own nationals, or 30 percent of the 1,580,089 applications received from their own nationals by twenty-three Free World countries (including the United States)." (*Ibid.*, p. 233). But the U.S. share of total worldwide patent applications, or patents granted, has two notable defects. First, a good many foreign patents relate to produce or processes applicable only to that country, as for example: various German patents on manual egg beaters which are almost valueless in America, or French patents for home shoe repair that in this country would not have been competitive with commercial shoe repair. The new technical knowledge embodied in such patents is largely irrelevant to the American economy. Second, the standards of patentability are markedly lower in some foreign countries. These two reasons, but particularly the first, explain why only about 10 percent of the inventions patented and granted abroad are also patented in the United States. This figure better represents the role of foreign technology than all the patents granted abroad.

4

Industrial R&D Concentration:
Causes and Significance

Some of the factors which lie behind the concentrations of R&D discussed in the last chapter will be examined here and their significance assessed. The observed concentrations are roughly what would be expected if, as suggested in Chapter 2, R&D allocation is strongly influenced by assessment of what is profitable. The question of significance for policy then turns on the issue: to what extent are true social costs and preferences accurately reflected in profit incentives, given the existing system of institutions and constraints.

R&D Concentration in Large Firms

John Kenneth Galbraith articulated the view of many people when he argued

> There is no more pleasant fiction than that technical change is the product of the matchless ingenuity of the small man forced by competition to employ his wits to better his neighbor. Unhappily, it is a fiction. Technical development has long since become the preserve of the scientist and the engineer. Most of the cheap and simple inventions have, to put it bluntly, been made . . . a benign Providence . . . has made the modern industry of a few large firms an almost perfect instrument for inducing technical change.[1]

[1] John Kenneth Galbraith, *American Capitalism* (Boston: Houghton Mifflin Co., 1952), p. 91.

The continuing presence and importance of private individuals and small firms in invention shows that Galbraith's statement is somewhat exaggerated. Nonetheless, Chapter 3 showed that industrial R&D spending is much more heavily concentrated in large firms than employment or sales. In 1961, firms with more than 5,000 employees accounted for about 86 percent of industrial R&D expenditures, as compared with 41 percent of manufacturing employment and 47 percent of sales.

Reasons for R&D Predominance in Large Firms

Chapter 3 indicated two principal reasons for the predominance of large firms. First, large firms are much more likely than small ones to have any R&D program at all. Second, of those firms which do have R&D programs, the larger firms spend more on R&D than do the smaller ones.

Larger firms also spend more on R&D as a fraction of sales. In 1961 the giants—those employing more than 5,000 persons—spent on R&D on the average of 5.2 percent of their sales; firms in the 1,000-5,000 range averaged 2.2 percent and firms with less than 1,000 employees, 2.0 percent. However, this largely results from certain industries, particularly aircraft, electronics and chemicals, being characterized by significantly higher than average R&D intensity for all firms in the industry regardless of size, and also by high average firm size. Within an industry the tendency for R&D spending to rise more than proportionately with sales is far less marked than in the aggregate. While in most (but not all) industries the R&D to sales ratios rise as one moves from the group of firms with less than 1,000 employees to the group in the 1,000-5,000 range, there is no clear tendency for these ratios to be larger for the giants in the above 5,000 range than for the firms in the 1,000-5,000 range.[2]

Assuming firms are interested in maximizing expected profits, this suggests three broad factors behind the distribution of R&D spending by firm size. First, in most industries there would appear to be a threshold on the size of an efficient program; if firms are not large enough to support a program of minimum efficient size, their efforts are ad hoc and informal or nonexistent. Second, large firms find it profitable to spend more on R&D than smaller firms. This in part reflects the role of market

[2] National Science Foundation, *Research and Development in Industry—1961* (Washington: Government Printing Office, 1964).

size in profitability, discussed in the preceding chapter. Because they already have a large market, the absolute gains from a given percentage reduction in cost or a given percentage increase in product attractiveness are larger for large firms, or at least come quicker. More projects then will be profitable for the large firm. In addition, large companies have more internal funds and find it easier to raise funds externally (their supply curve for external financing is more elastic). Third, in a few industries, like aircraft, large-scale projects are important sources of technical progress or there are other significant economies of scale in R&D. In these industries a firm must have a large R&D program, and be of sufficient size to carry it, or fail to survive.

Policy Implications

The data on R&D concentration suggest to some commentators that the way to create more (and hence more technical change) is to encourage the growth of large firms or at least not discourage their growth by antitrust or other actions. There is a corollary proposition: the low R&D intensity of industries such as textiles reflects the absence of large firms. Of course, the fact that large firms spend more on R&D than small firms is not sufficient to support the implied policy conclusions. The relevant question is: for a market of given size, will an industry comprised of a large number of small firms be less progressive technologically than an industry comprised of a few firms of large size, with the same aggregate sales?

The evidence suggests that if, by the wave of a magic wand, the small firms could be aggregated into units of about 1,000 employees, the result would be an increase in R&D spending.[3] However, it is unclear how much additional spending would be achieved by expansion of minimum firm size beyond the 1,000 employee level up to say, the 5,000 employee level. There would be some effect on the percentage of firms which engage in a formal R&D program. However, while in almost all industries the proportion of firms with R&D programs is greater in the 5,000 or more employee class than in the 1,000-5,000 employee class, differences here are far less within industries than in the aggregate. Beyond increasing somewhat the percentage of firms that have an R&D program, merging middle size firms in most industries would likely in-

---

[3] Needless to say, this is not a sufficient justification for arguing that such a policy would be desirable.

crease total R&D spending little if at all. As stated earlier, within any particular industry there is no systematic tendency for firms in the over 5,000 employee class to have higher R&D to sale ratios than firms in the 1,000-5,000 range.

Merging beyond the 5,000 employee level almost certainly would be pointless in most industries. The NSF data do not segregate firms by size above the 5,000 employee mark, but Scherer has examined R&D employment to sales ratios among 352 firms on *Fortune's* 1955 list of the 500 largest firms. Grouping these firms into industry categories and excluding major defense contractors, he found that the implication is that among firms big enough to appear on *Fortune's* 1955 list, the largest firms supported inventive and innovative activity less intensively relative to their size than did small firms.[4] It is at the high end of the size distribution that antitrust and other government actions have much of their influence, and it is with respect to such giant firms that the argument about bigness and progressivity is often made. Such arguments are not borne out by the kind of evidence just cited. A further point is, whatever the immediate effect on R&D effort, creating giants might well dilute competition and reduce the number of independent decision units. This could affect innovation by limiting the chances of a new idea getting a trial, and by reducing the competitive pressures to undertake R&D.

Further, the variable of concern is R&D output, not input. Scherer reports that in most industries patents per dollar of R&D spending among the super giants is less than for the mere giants.[5] Of course the "products" are not exactly comparable and patents per dollar of R&D input is a poor measure of productivity. In industries like aircraft and missiles, the size and complexity of the products call for massive R&D projects and require giant supporting firms. But the NSF and Scherer data, and the data on sources of inventions from Jewkes, Sawers, and Stillerman, suggest that in most industries major advances often can be achieved with modest sized programs.[6] Medium sized companies have the capability to support these programs, and many of them do.

Mansfield has examined the relative importance of the four largest firms in several industries in being the first to introduce inventions.

[4] Frederic M. Scherer, "Firm Size, Market Structure, Opportunity, and the Output of Patented Inventions," *American Economic Review*, Vol. 55 (December 1965).

[5] *Ibid.*

[6] Jewkes, Sawers, Stillerman, *op. cit.*

While not invention itself, it is closely related.[7] In petroleum and coal mining, where the costs of innovation tended to be large relative to the assets of all but the giants of the industry, the largest four firms accounted for a larger share of introductions than their share of the market. In steel where the required investment was much less relative to the assets of smaller firms, the largest four firms accounted for a smaller share of introductions than their share of the market. Thus the question of whether it is desirable social policy to encourage the growth of giants would appear to have different answers depending on the costs of making different kinds of inventions in different industries.

Mansfield has focused on average cost of innovation in different industries, but clearly a wide range of important R&D work exists within an industry, some projects requiring larger expenditures than others. Further, as will be seen in the following chapter, costs and uncertainties differ at various stages in the evolution of an invention. Many have low costs and high risks at the initial stages, and higher costs and lower risks at later stages. The low cost-high risk exploratory work is commonly initiated by a small company or independent inventor, with the subsequent lower risk, higher cost development work taken over by a large company. For example, Whittle was able to develop a working model of his jet engine with the financial and technical resources he could obtain on his own, but he had to turn to a larger English engine company to complete the development. Mueller reports that of the twenty-five important new products and processes introduced in America by Du Pont, fifteen were based on work initially done outside Du Pont, either by independent inventors or small companies.[8] While Du Pont's technical capabilities and financial and marketing resources played a major role in bringing the invention to market, the initial conception and early R&D work often came from smaller firms. Thus, even within an industry, there is no single answer to the question of optimum firm size for invention. Rather, optimum size appears to vary according to the kind of invention and the stage of work.

Even the notion of a distribution of firm sizes does not provide an ade-

---

[7] Edwin Mansfield, "Size of Firm, Market Structure, and Innovation," *Journal of Political Economy*, Vol. 71 (December 1963).

[8] See Willard F. Mueller, "The Origins of the Basic Inventions Underlying Du Pont's Major Product and Process Innovations, 1920 to 1950," *The Rate and Direction of Inventive Activity, op. cit.*

quate description of the optimum. The turnover of firms within any given size distribution is also important; in particular the relative ease with which new (and generally small) firms can enter the industry may be more important than the statical properties of the size distribution of firms. In many industries new entrants have been a prime source of invention; they were often founded by individuals for the specific purpose of carrying out inventions and innovations. Brown, in his study of new firms established in Connecticut after World War II, found a number started by inventors whose former employers were not interested in financing their inventions.[9] Thus, ease of entry serves as a check against the risk aversion tendencies of established firms.

Such new entrants may be particularly important when sharp discontinuities in technological evolution occur. At such times, the technical competence of established and new firms tends to be equalized. Old firms may be reluctant to abandon existing technology to gamble on radical inventions because of their success in an established field. The history of airframe propulsion illustrates this point. At the outset of World War II there were five major aircraft engine firms who had brought the art of gasoline propellor engines to a high state. The wartime jet engines, however, were pioneered by two outsiders, Westinghouse and General Electric, who remained major producers after the war. Likewise, rocket engines were pioneered by relative newcomers like Aerojet General, Grand Central Rocket, and Rocketdyne.[10]

These considerations and evidence suggest quite a different conclusion than the one equating large firms and technological advances. No single size firm is an optimum for conceiving and introducing all inventions of an industry. Rather, the optimum is a size distribution composed of small, medium, and large firms varying from industry to industry and from time to time. The optimum must further include a rate of turnover among firms sufficient to accommodate enough new firms to prevent excessive traditionalism.[11]

[9] Gilbert Brown, "Characteristics of New Enterprises," *New England Business Review* (June 1957 and July 1957).

[10] For a further discussion, see Merton J. Peck and Frederic M. Scherer, *The Weapons Acquisition Process: An Economic Analysis* (Boston: Harvard University Graduate School of Business Administration, Division of Research, 1962), chap. 7.

[11] Obviously this is only one dimension to the question of desirable industry structure.

Where cost-savings from large scale operation are not too great, or when turnover is not particularly important in stimulating or permitting desirable R&D, competition probably tends to produce a distribution of firms fairly well suited to exploiting R&D opportunities. If these opportunities shift toward high cost projects there are incentives and pressures to create more large firms through merger and expansion. The aerospace complex, the electronics and chemical industries have evolved large firms. A shift of technological opportunities towards the high risk, low cost inventions will stimulate the formation of new firms if established firms do not exploit the opportunities and if entry is not too costly.

However, major economies of scale in production or distribution or advertising may lead to an industry consisting of a few large firms, even though a more diversified size distribution and more turnover would be desirable for technological progress. In such a circumstance, even though there may be important unexploited opportunities for low cost R&D, entry into the industry may be costly and difficult. The ability to operate multiple plant units suggests that the opposite problem—economics of scale in R&D conflicting with efficiency of smaller production units—is unlikely to exist, at least in the long run. However, in industries where small firms are efficient in R&D and production and few large firms exist, sometimes opportunities for fruitful large-scale effort may be lost because of lack of sufficient resources. These problems—the blocking of progressive newcomers in industries with high entry costs, and an occasional important but expensive project which is too large and complex to be handled by the firms in an industry—call for public policy attention. It hardly appears that, as Galbraith suggests, the time is ripe to encourage giantism in all industries.

Industry and Product Field Concentration

Chapter 3 showed that a few industries and product fields dominate the industrial R&D picture—aircraft and missiles, electronics and electrical equipment, chemicals, and machinery. This concentration reflects the fact that about 55 percent of industrial R&D is financed through DOD and NASA contracts. But private funds also are highly concentrated—a large part in defense and space work, aiming for an eventual government contract; another large part in chemicals, and electrical and nonelectrical machinery and equipment, aiming for eventual sales to the civilian economy. While these industries are large, their share of R&D far exceeds their share of output or employment.

Reasons for Concentration

This concentration of R&D spending reflects the assessments of business firms (and outside supporters like the Department of Defense) as to how much R&D may be profitably undertaken in different fields. One would not expect the same ratio of R&D to sales to be optimal in all industries and product fields.

In the first place, returns on R&D aimed at product improvement or new products depend not only on the level of sales, but also on the value consumers place on improved product performance. This differs sharply from product line to product line. Improvements in aircraft performance have extremely high value to the DOD; thus the large volume of defense R&D contracts. Improvements in the quality of medicines have high value to consumers in the sense that they are willing to pay more for a more effective drug; thus the expected payoffs from R&D funds in this field are very high. People may value improved performance less highly in other areas.[12]

In the second place, as seen in Chapter 2, industries differ significantly in their capability for invention. The prominence of the science-based industries among those with high R&D to sales ratios partly reflects a greater ease of achieving advances. This accounts for the phenomenon described in the preceding chapter—failure of large R&D intensive firms to diversify their programs outside of a narrow range of product fields. Formal scientific and engineering competence of the sort established in a formal industrial research facility appears to have its greatest immediate payoff in fields where the technology is quite complex, but reasonably well understood in terms of scientific and engineering principles.[13]

---

[12] It is probable that higher horsepower automobile engines presently would not yield a company much competitive advantage.

[13] It is revealing that in 1957 corporations were credited with 97 percent of the patents on chemical inventions, 91 percent of the patents on electrical inventions, and only 12 percent of the patents on mechanical inventions. Corporations thus judged that their comparative advantage lay in the scientifically more complex fields.

Product field and industry differences in the profitability of R&D enter the budgetary decision process partly through rational calculation, partly through imitation. Mansfield's study of the decision making process in a large industrial laboratory showed a considerable effort dedicated to selecting a portfolio of projects that came close to maximizing expected profit. He further has shown that inter-firm differences in R&D to sales ratios can be explained by difference in the profitability of R&D. However, his studies also reveal that management's estimates are often inaccurate. Management presumably is aware of this.[14]

In such a situation rational calculation tends to be supplemented by rules of thumb, and particularly by imitation of the experience of successful competitors. For example, consider an industry or product field where R&D is productive and where a firm that does much of it has a strong advantage. Minasian has found that in the drug and pharmaceutical industry, where both conditions hold, the firms that did a significant amount of R&D in the late 1940's and early 1950's tended to be significantly more profitable in the late 1950's than those that slacked on R&D earlier.[15] Interviews for this study suggest that in such situations other firms are stimulated to increase their R&D spending. The success of laboratory management in arguing for a larger R&D to sales ratio seems to be enhanced when high profitability has been indicated by the success of R&D intensive competitors, particularly if the firm slacking in R&D is not doing well. In the absence of reliable objective criteria, a considerable part of the R&D decision making process appears to involve reaction to, and imitation of, the policies of competitors.

Implications of Inter-Industry Rates for Technical Advance

What are the implications of R&D concentration for the industry and product field distribution of technological advance? Chapter 3 suggested that the cost and performance of the products of one industry are influenced by the R&D done by other organizations, as well as by the industry directly involved. Some of the mechanisms will now be considered.

[14] Edwin Mansfield, *Econometric Studies of Industrial Research and Technological Innovation* (New York: W. W. Norton & Co., 1966).
[15] Jora Minasian, "The Economics of Research and Development," in *The Rate and Direction of Inventive Activity, op. cit.*

NEW COMPONENTS AND MATERIALS. As pointed out earlier, most firms do not do much R&D on their own processes. However, their processes are strongly influenced by the flow of new materials, components, and machinery which can stimulate major improvements in product performance and reductions in cost. Thus a firm experiencing rapid innovation by its suppliers may achieve relatively rapid improvement of its own products and processes with limited investment of its own. This is particularly so if it is assisted by the R&D staffs of its suppliers; often this assistance is willingly, sometimes eagerly, given.

The experience of the textile industries illustrates this strikingly. The textile mill products industry itself has done little R&D, yet has experienced gains in productivity faster than the average industry, with significant improvements in products. The principal reason is that supplying industries—particularly chemicals—have originated many new products for the textile mill products industries to use or process, and, in addition, have provided considerable technical assistance.

Almost all industries benefit from the new materials and components created by the R&D intensive producer goods industries. As pointed out in Chapter 1, most technologies have a large set of common elements. Many subprocesses (such as welding), many materials and components (such as steel and ball bearings), many kinds of equipment (such as electric motors and fork lift trucks), are widely used; technological advances in these fields benefit industry across the board.

This does not mean that all benefit equally. Most industries use at least a few specialized inputs, and the suppliers of some special inputs may be more progressive than others. Even if an industry is lucky enough to have R&D intensive suppliers, this does not mean that its own efforts do not matter. For many years, because of failure of the textile mills themselves, or their machinery producers, to redesign their equipment, nylon filament was used by cutting it up into short staples so that it could be spun like cotton. Only recently has equipment begun to be designed tailored to nylon. As this example illustrates, internal R&D is an important and sometimes necessary complement to that of suppliers; a considerable amount of redesigning of products or equipment may be needed to take full advantage of new inputs.

FLOW THROUGH KNOWLEDGE IN THE PUBLIC DOMAIN. The firms in one industry also benefit from the R&D done by other organizations through the enrichment of their stock of knowledge. As seen in Chapter 2, advances in scientific understanding have played a key role in facilitating invention and development. Most of the results of basic research are made public through publication. Universities are the major source of this flow of basic knowledge into the public domain. But the nonprofit, government agencies such as the National Bureau of Standards, the agricultural experimentation stations, the aviation laboratories of NASA, and the basic research laboratories of industry publish a vast amount of nonproprietary material. This body of knowledge entering the public domain ranges from new physical theories to the results of experiments on super conductivity, data on the strength of various materials under different loads, and reports on the most effective schedule for lubricating machine tools.

While the knowledge introduced through publication of research results has potentially widespread applicability, as with new material and components, those industries which do considerable research on their own probably benefit most. In the first place, the science-based industries directly or indirectly influence what kind of basic research is done. In their own laboratories, and through grants or contracts to the universities or other nonprofits, they tend to focus basic research on problems relevant to their technology. While the results often may be of use to other industries, analysis of the properties of high-speed gas flow, for example, is much more likely to be of use to the aerospace complex than to the textile industry. Further, as pointed out earlier, to understand and make use of the results tends to require a strong in-house capability working to that purpose.

Another important part of the knowledge introduced to the public domain consists of techniques and basic concepts behind various products and processes. Often these will have application far transcending the original purposes of the R&D, providing key techniques or insight into the solution of other problems.

The history of R&D on continuous casting of steel metals is illustrative. As early as 1890 there were experiments with continuous casting machines for steel, but the results were not promising. After World War I, interest developed in continuous casting of nonferrous metals. Progress was marked, and by 1940 the process was in general use. After World War II, development projects in the U.S., Austria, Germany, and Britain attempted to apply this experience to the ferrous metals. Certain aspects of nonferrous technology proved applicable, but only by the fifties, after extensive R&D, was steel successfully continuously cast. This history shows both a substantial share of the needed technical knowledge being created in other industries and an extensive development effort required in the receiving industry to adapt the progress elsewhere to its specific problems.[16]

There are at least nine similar cases which can be identified among the Jewkes, *et al.,* list of fifty major inventions. In each case a basic design concept developed for one purpose was, after considerable additional R&D, modified for use in another.

But again, like the other contributions to one firm's technology of R&D done by others, transfer of design concept tends to benefit most the industries that do a lot of R&D. This is not simply the result of the work generally required to make use of another's invention. While some techniques and designs have wide applicability, others are more limited, and transfer of a design concept from a product or process to a closely related one tends to be easier and more common than transfer to unrelated processes and products. Thus, while casting of steel is different from casting of nonferrous metals, metal casting processes have strong elements in common. Indeed, transfer appears to be most common within an industry. Thus, the design concepts proved successful in military aircraft later were applied to commercial aircraft. The result is that exploitation of the design concepts created by others is most prominent in industries where R&D is most intensive generally.

It is not clear how many of these transfers require the licensing of patents and to what extent the knowledge is in the public domain. But, if the Jewkes, Sawers, and Stillerman examples are a guide, it appears that while patent licensing may be involved, the unpatentable aspect of the design concept is often more important than a specific detailed patented product or process. This knowledge, like published nonproprietary data and basic research findings, usually enters the common domain outside the control of the firm that did the original work, although its use by others may require considerable additional R&D.

Importance of Internal R&D—A Summary Evaluation

Consideration of the mechanisms suggested above suggests that the product fields influenced by technological advance are far wider than the

---

[16] See Jewkes, Sawers, Stillerman, *op.cit.*

data on R&D concentration would indicate. Much of R&D has wide-spread impact leading to general purpose new components and materials, or to new data, relations, and theories that permit design problems to be solved more easily in advance, or to broadly applicable new design concepts. The studies cited below show that even industries with almost no R&D experience some productivity increase.

Still, the allocation of R&D resources among product fields and industries is an important determinant of the kinds of advances experienced. Minasian has shown that within an industry the R&D done by a particular firm is an important explanatory variable behind inter-firm differences in rates of productivity growth.[17] Looking across industries, Terleckyj has shown that R&D intensive industries tend to create new products at a faster rate, and to experience more rapid productivity growth.[18] In the six industries with the highest R&D intensity in 1958, products not in existence in 1956 averaged about 20 percent of 1960 sales and exceeded 10 percent in each case. (Table IV-1) No other industry had a new product percentage as large as 10 percent, and the average was about 5 percent. Similarly, there was a strong positive correlation between research intensity and the rate of growth of productivity. Mansfield's studies show similar results; he also has found that the rate of R&D spending helps to explain both inter-firm and inter-industry differences in productivity growth.[19] Griliches has found that R&D expenditures of agricultural experimentation stations in a particular state or region—presumably aimed at the problems and opportunities special to the area—are an important variable explaining different rates of productivity growth in agriculture.[20,21]

[17] Ibid.

[18] Nestor Terleckyj, "Sources of Productivity Change. A Pilot Study Based on the Experience of American Manufacturing Industries, 1899-1953" (unpublished doctoral dissertation, Columbia University, 1959).

[19] Edwin Mansfield, "Rates of Return from Industrial Research and Development," American Economic Review, Vol. 55, No. 2 (May 1965).

[20] Zvi Griliches, "Research Expenditures, Education, and the Aggregate Agricultural Production Function," American Economic Review, Vol. 54 (December 1964).

[21] Some of these studies treat the rate of R&D spending as the key variable; others the R&D to sales ratio. The analysis of this study would suggest the former to be more relevant; the fact that sales are twice as large should not cut the impact on productivity of a successful R&D project by a factor of two. Of course, to the extent firms or industries with a large volume of sales tend to produce a large number of different products, those with greater sales may need to undertake more

TABLE IV-1. *Rate of Growth of New Products Related to Intensity of Research and Development*

Industry	Total R&D spending as percent of industry net sales, 1958[a]	Sales of products not in existence in 1956 as percent of 1960 net sales
Aircraft, ships, and railroad equipment	*18.7*[b]	*35*
Electrical machinery	*12.9*[c]	*12*
Machinery	*4.4*	*14*
Chemicals	*4.3*	*16*
Motor vehicles and parts	*4.2*[d]	*10*
Fabricated metals and instruments	*3.5*	*17*
Rubber	*2.0*	*2*
Petroleum and coal products	*0.9*[e]	*2*
Nonferrous metals	*0.9*	*8*
Paper	*0.7*	*9*
Iron and steel	*0.6*	*5*
Food and beverages	*0.3*	*6*
Textiles	*0.2*	*9*
All manufacturing	*4.0*	*10*

Source: Nestor E. Terleckyj, assisted by Harriet J. Halper, *Research and Development: Its Growth and Composition* (New York: National Industrial Conference Board, 1963), p. 56.
[a] For companies performing R&D.
[b] Aircraft and missiles.
[c] Includes communication.
[d] Transportation equipment except aircraft.
[e] Petroleum refining and extraction.

While the quantitative results of these studies should be treated with great caution, the qualitative implications are clear. Even though there are strong common elements among technologies, the areas affected by a particular advance are likely to be numerous, and there are significant external economies, the allocation of R&D resources must be viewed as significantly affecting the kinds of advances an economy achieves.

Significance of Industry R&D Allocation

R&D concentration in the producer goods industries, and in defense and space, raise quite separate issues. The first concerns the efficiency of R&D

R&D in order to achieve the same increase in average productivity across the diversified product lines as a smaller firm or industry producing only one product and concentrating all its R&D. But this only indicates an accounting problem. If there is so little in common among the products of a diversified industry that there is little R&D spillover, the total R&D spending of the industry should be thought of as divided among the different product lines.

allocation in terms of achieving advances in a given set of final product fields. The second concerns the final product fields experiencing the most rapid technological advance.

CONCENTRATION ON PRODUCERS' GOODS. Prominent among the research intensive industries are those producing materials and components purchased by other industries. Sixty percent of the output of chemicals, 90 percent of the electrical industry's output, and almost all the output of the machinery industries go to other firms. In contrast, most of the industries which do little R&D sell most of their output to final consumers; thus the textile industry sells over 90 percent of its output to households and governments as contrasted with sales to other business firms. Many of the industries which do little R&D on their own, like textiles, purchase a considerable amount of their inputs from R&D intensive industries, like chemicals. The principal question posed by this situation is: Is this an efficient way to achieve better and lower cost final products?

As the case of textiles demonstrated earlier, it is important to remember that there are many different kinds of business firms producing many different products which play a direct or indirect role in the production of any final product or service. The amount of clothing output that a given amount of labor (direct and indirect) can produce, for example, can be increased in many different ways by many different kinds of R&D. The impact on the economy is the same whether the increase occurs as a result of R&D done by firms in the chemical industry on better synthetic fibers, dyes, and finishes; by firms in the machinery industry on more productive looms; by firms in the textile mill products industry on better techniques; by firms in the clothing industry on more productive ways to make shirts of cotton cloth; or by university research on the properties of fibers.

For any set of the final product fields where advances are desired, it is almost certainly true that considerable R&D concentration is efficient for society as a whole. Within the chain of industries from basic inputs to final products, some lend themselves more readily to improvement through R&D. They may have been fortuitously linked to science initially, and once the process of intensive R&D starts, the accumulation of a scientific base and the enrichment of the common stock of design concepts tends to build on the past. Where R&D resources and talent are limited and R&D in one industry can be substituted for that in another, the effort should probably be concentrated in a few industries rather than spread thinly over many.

R&D intensive industries can, and do, help their customers directly as well as indirectly. For example, the large chemical companies carry on R&D on the dye processes used by clothing manufacturers and indeed provide them with most of the technical information on this subject.[22] This kind of service is common whenever large firms sell to smaller ones. At the extreme, large companies have acted as if they and their customers were vertically integrated so far as R&D is concerned. When receptivity has been low, large companies have vertically integrated forward. Thus, prior to World War I the Aluminum Company of America (Alcoa) went into aluminum fabrication and even into a final product—aluminum pots and pans—because the existing metal fabricators and manufacturers were not familiar with aluminum and were reluctant to devise the new processes required.[23]

Although a considerable amount of R&D concentration probably represents an efficient division of labor, it can go too far. The extent to which a supplier needs to tailor its products to the processes and designs of the using industry, or to modify them through R&D, depends on the technical competence of the user firms. When the invention must be tailored to a relatively inflexible user, or R&D undertaken to facilitate adoption by the using industry, the supplier obviously incurs higher R&D costs. This cost would be paid in part by the firms in the using industry if the work was not done by the material supplier, but placing the total cost and risk on one firm may weaken incentive or strain financial capability.

Further, the single firm is likely to reach a point where the division of labor becomes uneconomic, resulting in higher R&D expense or less effective technological advance than had the research been performed in part in the consuming industry. No matter how strong its supply of scientific and technical talent, the supplying firm may lack knowledge of the processes and other inputs used by its customers and hence miss problems

[22] The same process can occur in the other direction: large R&D intensive firms can do R&D and provide technical assistance for their suppliers. Thus, petroleum companies do R&D on the equipment provided to them by smaller firms.
[23] Merton J. Peck, *Competition in the Aluminum Industry, 1945-1958* (Cambridge: Harvard University Press, 1961).

and opportunities that might be evident to an R&D staff in the receiving industry. The good-supplying firm, one step removed from the customers of its customer, may not recognize what new products or changes in product performances have high value. In addition, there are some problems and opportunities which the supplying industries have little incentive to work on, such as more economical production methods or ways to improve a product (except as these embody materials or equipment that they can supply).

In short, a firm often has a strong comparative advantage with respect to R&D on certain aspects of its products and processes. In other cases incentives do not extend back to suppliers, and if the firm does not do the R&D it will be done less efficiently by others, or not at all.

It is not known whether concentration of R&D in the producer goods industries generally has gone too far. However, there might be high payoffs from increasing the technological capabilities of some of the industries which do little R&D. There are a few clearcut cases, characterized by extreme industry fragmentation and firms with profit interest in the status quo, that frustrate the efforts of large supplying firms to offset the low level of R&D by their customers. This is illustrated by McDonald's description of the efforts to popularize plastics as a building material. McDonald comments: "Like other sellers who are basic material producers, it (Monsanto) has had difficulties with distribution and is still looking for ways to get its products from the factory to the customer. Ordinary builders tend not to be interested in selling houses that may pose a competitive threat, and lumber yard dealers, the main wholesalers of the industry, are not apt to welcome a house that can bypass most of their own line of materials."[24]

These kinds of situations cannot be identified by data showing low R&D efforts; they require a detailed industry study. The problems and policy guidelines for these situations are considered later.

CONCENTRATION ON DEFENSE AND SPACE. The concentration of R&D resources in defense and space raises quite different issues than concentration in the producer goods industries. In defense and space it is aimed at creating final products, not inputs to be used in producing other products. The principal benefit from this kind of R&D is im-

---

[24] John McDonald, "Where's the Ceiling on New Houses?" *Fortune* (June 1963), p. 216.

proved, or less costly, defense. The principal question posed by this concentration is: is this a sensible allocation of scarce R&D resources, given the multiple final wants of society?

The issue is somewhat blurred because certain military products, materials, or components find their way into other uses with widespread application. This unintended spread of benefits has been termed "spillover." A study by the Operations Research Office at Johns Hopkins cites many examples of defense R&D during World War II with broader applications, from the development of cloth suitable for the tropics to the design of trucks that could operate where no roads exist.[25] The expense of developing a way to produce penicillin was largely supported by defense R&D funds, as was much of the early work in computers. The jet engines used in commercial flights are almost identical with those developed for the military, and a considerable amount of knowledge going into civil jet passenger airframe design is the result of military R&D. For defense R&D spending of this sort, it could well be argued that alternative costs in terms of foregone improvements on civilian final products were relatively low.

However, this would not appear to be the case today. Direct spillover is less likely to occur. The Army still supports some R&D on such items as personnel vehicles, the Air Force supports it for cargo aircraft, and there still is a substantial medical R&D program. But the bulk of defense and space R&D is on strategic weapons systems and specialized products that do not have close civilian analogues or obvious spillover applications.

However, because today military and space R&D reaches so far, special new subcomponents, materials, and processes must often be created. For example, tubes and circuits manufactured by existing processes were inadequate to meet the requirements of supersonic aircraft and Intercontinental Ballistics Missiles (ICBM's). Hence, the Air Force found it necessary to sponsor considerable R&D to develop new items and production processes that could meet its requirements. These efforts would appear to yield spillover, though not of the more direct kind typical of World War II.

The list of civilian applications of NASA research and development (collected by the Denver Research Institute) makes an interesting con-

[25] Operations Research Office, Johns Hopkins University, *"Defense Spending and the U.S. Economy"* (Baltimore: Johns Hopkins University Press, 1959), p. 107.

trast with the old ORO list of applications of Army R&D.[26] It includes a few interesting final products with high performance properties—a rapid-sequence camera and a better life raft, for example. The bulk of the list, however, comprises small scale industrial components—a rapid actuating valve—and new materials, like ceramics. There also are many potentially interesting new ideas in the form of techniques—a process of thin wall casting, printed electrical cables, coatings, sealings and soldering techniques.

There is little question that many of these have great potential importance. But patent statistics suggest that, to date at least, only a small percentage of the R&D financed by DOD and NASA has resulted in elements with sufficient commercial application to patent, and even these have not generally been used commercially in the form in which they were created for the DOD and NASA. From 1954 to 1956 about 4 percent of all corporate applications originated from work funded by DOD contracts, and yet during this same period DOD financed about half the R&D expenditures of private firms.[27] Furthermore, patents granted for defense-funded R&D were put to commercial use far less frequently than nondefense patents. Holman, examining a sample of patents, found that the rate of commercial utilization of privately owned patented inventions originating under federally financed R&D contracts is between 10 and 15 percent. In contrast, privately developed patented inventions are utilized at a rate of between 55 and 65 percent.[28]

The NASA experience confirms the limited direct commercial utility of space research. Unlike DOD, NASA takes title to patents which arise

[26] Denver Research Institute, *The Commercial Application of Missile/Space Technology* (Denver: University of Denver, 1963).

[27] This across-the-board data is confirmed by the patent history of one large defense contractor. Aerojet General has been a producer of rocket engines with a substantial government funded R&D program since 1944. By 1959 Aerojet had accumulated 400 patent applications, covering a wide range of advanced technology. According to Emerson S. Reichard, the company's Director of Contracts, "We have found that out of all our patent applications only three currently have commercial application. We are hopeful that other of our patent applications will some day find commercial values, but because of the very nature of our business, being as specialized as it is, we really have only one customer, and that is the government and we do not foresee in any particular instance an immediate use of these 400-odd inventions that we have made since our company started."

[28] Mary A. Holman, "The Utilization of Government-Owned Patented Inventions," *The Patent, Trademark and Copyright Journal of Research and Education* (Summer 1963 and Fall 1963).

from the R&D it sponsors. NASA, however, offers to waive title or grant exclusive licenses to contractors and has done so generously in those cases where a request was made. While NASA now has title to between 600 and 700 patents, in only seventy-five to eighty-five instances has the contractor applied for a waiver, suggesting that only about a sixth of these inventions are considered to be of possible commercial value.

These patent statistics, interpreted literally, underestimate the spillover from defense and space R&D. The Denver Research Institute list is rich with processes and design concepts which transcend the scope of any patent. Many of the components and materials developed for defense and space will likely find civilian use, after they have been suitably modified. But this will require a significant amount of imaginative follow-up R&D.

Defense R&D need not and should not be justified on the basis of spillover; its principal purpose is enhancing national security. Judgments as to whether too much or too little is spent on defense R&D should consider the importance of national security and other national objectives, and the importance of R&D to the achievement of these objectives. However, it should be recognized that spillover is limited and the price of security may come high in terms of foregone technological advances in other fields.

Concentration on Modest Design Improvement

Chapter 3 suggested that, outside of defense and space work, the bulk of the nation's R&D resources are allocated to projects seeking relatively minor improvements or modifications in products and processes. Basic research comprises only 9 percent of the national total; industrial basic research only 4 percent of corporate R&D activity. For applied R&D, the decision rules of business firms tend to screen out most far reaching projects.

Factors Leading to R&D Conservatism

Expected R&D costs and risks are largely dependent on the magnitude of the advance sought. In many cases a relatively secure competitive position can be held with a product possessing only a relatively small performance or cost advantage over that of a competitor. Clearly there are strong incentives for doing enough R&D to maintain technical parity or a slight advantage over the competition: it may spell the difference between long-run survival and going out of business. However, the additional returns from a far reaching R&D project may not be viewed by a cautious businessman as being worth the added uncertainties and costs, even though its success might place the firm far ahead of its competition. When a strong science base has been laid and a lower cost or better product gives a major competitive advantage, R&D competition may easily escalate and a company may have to seek relatively major advances just to stay on a parity with competitors—this seems to be the case in the drug industry, and clearly is the principal driving force behind the heavy expenditures on long-range military R&D. In view of the high costs involved, however, there are good reasons not to reach for more major advances than are needed to stay up with or just ahead of the competition.

As pointed out in Chapter 2, the total costs and risks of development efforts aimed directly at creating new products can be considerably reduced by undertaking basic research and experimental development to probe and open up interesting possibilities before commitment to full-scale design and development. Carothers' nylon project initially involved a very small group. Langley and Wright worked with only a few people in their experimental aircraft development efforts; Watson Watt worked with six assistants in the project that led to workable radar; the pre-1935 work on television at R.C.A. and Philco did not involve large projects.[29] But, while it reduces subsequent development risk, such work is very risky itself: it may extend over rather long periods of time, and the chances of a profitable outcome may be far from clear in advance. Furthermore, this work often may not produce a finished design, but simply demonstrate the feasibility and key attributes of a broad design concept or general approach—knowledge which may be hard to protect by a specific patent, or which may require much further development. For these reasons this work generally is considered to be similar to basic research, and is conducted in that spirit by scientists, engineers, and technological enthusiasts.

The data presented in Chapter 3 show that only a few firms in a few industries have found it worthwhile to support this kind of R&D. Firms have an incentive to watch for developments, but most of them are content to let others do such work.

[29] For case studies of some of these see Jewkes, Sawers, and Stillerman, *op. cit.*

Implications of the Conservative Bias

The emphasis on short-reach work within the applied part of the R&D budget may be rational from the point of view of the individual business firm, but it may be less desirable for the economy as a whole. The modesty of private incentives may sometimes indicate that there is little extra social utility in the major advance. More often, however, it reflects the firm's high premium on its own long-term survival and its aversion to large risks which are not necessary to assure survival—a valuation not necessarily shared by society. Furthermore, risk aversion aside, it is probably true that firms reap a smaller share of profits from the social benefits of major advances than from minor ones. New products or processes with significantly different attributes may have higher advantages for some users than for others; yet the supplier of a new product is generally limited in the extent to which he can charge different prices to different purchasers and users. Thus, for major advances, the price charged to many users may be only a small fraction of its value to them.[30] Within applied R&D the concentration on modest design improvement therefore probably represents a failure of market incentives to reflect the public interest in major technological advances.

The problem is compounded by widespread neglect of the indirect route to major advances—basic research and experimental development. Just as there is a trade-off between R&D done in producer goods industries, and that done by their customers, there is a trade-off between effort in basic research and experimental development, and in applied design and development efforts. The stronger the prior basic and experimental work, the fewer resources are needed in applied development to achieve a given advance. In many fields, a reallocation to increase the share of basic research and exploratory developments would, very likely, lead to more rapid technological progress than the same quantity of resources could achieve with the existing allocation. The fact that much of the knowledge created through basic research and experimental development goes into the public domain means that private decision mak-

[30] Dan Usher in his "The Welfare Economics of Invention," *Economica*, Vol. 31 (August 1964), presents an analysis in which the above discussion is implicit. Hla Myint, in his *Theories of Welfare Economics* (London: Longmans, Green & Co., 1948), discusses at some length the "surplus" problem that arises when changes are discrete. A new invention is, by its nature, a discrete change.

ing, guided by the profit incentive, will fail to seize many opportunities which have a high rate of return for the economy as a whole. This is a distortion distinct from, but additive with, the failure of market prices to reflect more fully the social returns to patented major advances.[31]

In a few fields, the interests of a scientific discipline happen to lead to research which improves scientific understanding of a technology or technique—as the interest in genetics aided agricultural technology—and basic research is undertaken without technology motivated financing. But few fields are so lucky. In some, as in agriculture, health, and aviation, the government has provided funds to universities as well as to business firms. But such public investments to offset the lack of corporate financed basic and experimental work hardly exist in most technological fields.

The concentration on short-reach applied R&D probably distorts the process of technological advance far more severely than concentration in large firms and in a few industries and product fields. This problem will be a principal concern of Part III.

[31] For a discussion of the external economies generated by basic research see Richard R. Nelson, "The Simple Economics of Basic Scientific Research—A Theoretical Analysis," *Journal of Political Economy*, Vol. 67 (June 1959).

5

Screening and Adoption of New Technological Knowledge

Previous chapters have focused upon inputs and outputs, the factors that determine them, the institutions involved, and the characteristics of present allocation. This chapter views the technological change process as it proceeds over time, following a new idea from its inception to its economic acceptance.

There are always a vast number of efforts underway to create new or improved products and processes, although only a small percentage of these result in anything significant. It is useful to visualize the process by which new ideas are rejected, or accepted, in terms of two successive screenings. First, assessments of technical promise and potential market become more realistic and tough minded as the project proceeds along the R&D path from embryonic design concept through development to the decision to introduce it to the market. Second, if it is brought to the market, there is the period of trial use by both producers and potential consumers, during which the fate of the new product or process is very much in doubt.

If it passes the early use test, the new product or process finds those sectors and uses where it is applicable and worthwhile. Neither demand nor supply adjusts instantaneously; only with time does the economy learn the nature of new opportunities and acquire the capability to take maximum advantage of them.

Screening

The stock of embryonic ideas for new or improved products and processes is very large. At any time many ideas are being worked on in a limited way with the objective of making their concepts more explicit, testing their technical feasibility, and assessing their value and cost. This kind of exploratory work often can proceed with a moderate investment. Relatively routine ideas for product or process modification may require no more than a few paper and pencil calculations, the drawing of a rough blueprint, and the building of a simple test and demonstration model. For more complex products, like a new automobile model, more people may be involved and the work may take longer but even here it is unlikely that substantial resources will be required. For a radically new product, a workable design concept may require considerable time, and there is no guarantee of success, but even for these efforts the staffing and rate of expenditure in the exploratory stage often can be quite small and there need not be a large-scale commitment of funds.[1]

Weeding Out of R&D Projects

Once a workable design concept is achieved, the outlays required to take the next steps toward a production version tend to be higher than the costs of the very early stages reflecting generally higher labor requirements for working out and testing the details of a design. Typically, moving from the design study to the early development work involves a significant increase in staff. As the development task approaches its final stages where the smallest details must be decided and the full system tested, costs of proceeding further may be still greater and may involve considerable production expense. It is important to find out how durable a product is, and this may involve multiple tests. Often it is useful to gain information about a product under a wide range of conditions. To do so in a reasonable period of time may require a number of items of the product for testing and to produce enough test items may involve considerable expense, if special processes or equipment are needed.[2]

As a result, the rate of expenditure curve for an R&D project tends to

---

[1] Often military and occasionally civilian R&D do not follow this low-cost uncertainty resolving pattern. This point is discussed subsequently.

[2] A dramatic, but highly specialized, example is missile systems where the test vehicles can be used for only one test.

Chart V-1

Du Pont's Annual Investment in Nylon, 1928-40

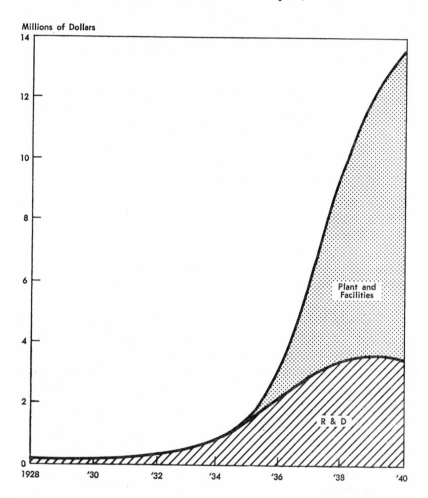

Millions of Dollars

Plant and
Facilities

R & D

1928   '30   '32   '34   '36   '38   '40

Source: F. M. Scherer, et al., *Patents and the Corporation* (Boston: J. J. Galvin, 1958), p. 30.

91

look like a logistic, or cumulative normal, function, as illustrated by Chart V-1, which depicts the time pattern of Du Pont's expenditures on nylon.[3] The first polymers were produced and shown to be useful for textile fibers in 1934. Up to that point, Du Pont had invested only about $1 million in R&D. The large expenses occurred later. Ways had to be found to process the polymer into filaments and to spin them into useful fibers. Some of this work could be done relatively inexpensively in the laboratory, but difficulties in extrapolating the results of some small-scale reactions made it necessary to build and experiment with large scale equipment. Between 1934 and 1939, the year that large-scale production of nylon stockings was begun, Du Pont invested $26 million; $5 million more in R&D, and $21 million in plant.[4] (See Chart V-1.)

Rising costs of continuing an R&D effort require a more hard-headed appraisal of costs and benefits. While the early work often can be carried on by an enthusiast despite the scepticism of the majority of experts— thus Whittle and his jet engine—the middle and later stages require someone or some organization to commit large quantities of resources. This often means that new sources of funds or sponsorship must be obtained.

As rising costs force a more calculating appraisal, this is often made possible by the knowledge created by earlier work. For more modest design improvements the initial uncertainties may be relatively small. Even here, however, articulating the objective and making the design concept or alternative concepts explicit may significantly improve the ability to estimate R&D costs, production costs, and the potential market. In most far-reaching efforts the initial uncertainties may be extremely great, and the probing for a workable design concept may be the only practicable key to their resolution.[5] In some cases an explicit design concept that proves technically workable may prove impossible to achieve. Sometimes a technically workable concept is achieved, but calculations of

[3] This discussion rests heavily on Willard Mueller, "A Case Study of Product Discovery and Innovation Costs," *Southern Economic Journal*, Vol. 24 (July 1957), and on Frederic M. Scherer and others, *Patents and the Corporation* (Boston: J. J. Galvin, 1959).

[4] The $21 million probably overstates the R&D requirements. Mueller points out that Du Pont intended the pilot plants to be used for production, and hence built more capacity than was needed for development alone.

[5] For an analysis and some data relating to the gradual resolution of uncertainty in the course of a development project, see A. W. Marshall and W. H. Meckling, "Predictability of the Costs, Time, and Success of Development," *The Rate and Direction of Inventive Activity, op. cit.*

benefits and costs indicate that it is unlikely to pay economically, and the work is abandoned. Sometimes the results are not sufficient to justify a major development project, but provide another piece to the jigsaw puzzle, and the work may continue.[6]

Marshalling major resources to a project usually awaits the articulation of a design concept which appears technically workable, and its careful economic evaluation.[7] With a concrete design concept to work with, rough tests completed, and more reliable estimates of development and production costs and potential market, projects which pass these tests and attract the needed resources are put into subsequent stages of development. Sometimes there is no real break between the stages. In other cases there may be a significant time lag as organizational changes are made reflecting the increased input requirements. There was a ten-year interval between the time Fleming discovered penicillin and its properties, and the time significant resources were marshalled for development.[8]

While major efforts to develop the details of a design generally are not started until there is high confidence that the concept is technically feasible and economically attractive, often major developments in military and, occasionally, in civilian R&D are initiated, while considerable uncertainties still remain. In military developments the inaccuracies of early estimates of cost and value are notorious. For example, one missile program achieved half the forecasted accuracy in the course of a development lasting three times longer and costing many times more than originally estimated. One guidance system after long and costly development, achieved only one-half the expected performance, and this required a package weighing four times the original specifications.[9] In civilian developments there are fewer such examples, because decisions to go ahead with development are made more conservatively; still Edison[10]

---

[6] Sometimes someone else will take up the hunt. As clues accumulate that a good design concept is achievable, there may be a competitive race. Thus half a dozen inventors worked on the steamboat, perhaps an equal number on the electric light, and several individuals and large companies were working on television in the stages just before the final breakthroughs.

[7] In some cases it is meaningful to think of the successful achievement of a workable design concept as the "invention," and the subsequent stage as "development." However, in many cases there is no sharp break between these stages.

[8] Jewkes, Sawers, and Stillerman, *op. cit.*

[9] Burton H. Klein, "The Decision Making Problem in Development," *The Rate and Direction of Inventive Activity, op. cit.*

[10] The examples above are of overoptimism. There are many examples where

vastly underestimated the difficulties of developing his concept for refining low-grade iron ore.[11]

As development proceeds, assessments become sharper. Sometimes the early uncertainties are resolved easily and development proceeds on the "best bet" course. In other cases, problems prove much harder to solve than had been hoped and expected. In some of these cases developments are pushed through the middle and late stages despite adversely changing evaluations of cost and merit. Many projects, however, which appeared promising as they entered middle development are dropped as more is learned, easy solutions to the design problems fail, and assessments of cost and merit become more pessimistic. Thus, in the early 1950's the Air Force had high hopes for the air breathing Navaho missile. By the end of the decade the project was cancelled, partly because estimated costs had soared, partly because assessments of its utility had changed sharply, and partly because ballistic missiles had progressed much faster than expected. Edison abandoned his venture on low-yield iron ore processing as the working out of the basic idea appeared increasingly expensive, and when the Mesabi range discovery drastically reduced the value of techniques for tapping low-yield ores.[12]

As with the projects that are dropped at earlier stages, those which are pushed far before they are abandoned often leave heirs. Sometimes certain components or ideas created for them prove valuable in other uses; the booster created for the Navaho missile powered the early ballistic missiles. Some of the design solutions achieved may provide a base for further work, and the problems which proved insurmountable are solved at some later time; the history of R&D on continuous casting of steel, mentioned in the last chapter, is a good example.

Thus, as work on a project proceeds the cost of continuing increases, perception of cost and value becomes sharper, and projects are screened out. Some never reach a technically satisfactory design concept. Others do, but do not appear promising enough economically for investment of major development resources. Some that go into the middle and later

experts overestimated the difficulty of achieving a satisfactory design or underestimated its value. Developing a ballistic missile re-entry vehicle proved much easier than many experts expected. The difficulties in achieving a jet engine were overestimated and its value underestimated during the mid-1930's by experts in the United Kingdom, the United States, and Germany.

[11] Matthew Josephson, *Edison* (New York: McGraw-Hill Book Co., 1959).
[12] *Ibid.*

stages of development are ultimately abandoned when unforeseen difficulties occur or circumstances change. It is hard to determine what percentage of initial ideas reach the market. Some indication is provided by a Booz, Allen, and Hamilton study in which only a few of the companies interviewed reported that more than half of their R&D projects ever resulted in something that was used commercially; in most of the companies this figure was much smaller than 50 percent.[13,14]

Early Use Incubator

In much of the literature on the process of technological advance a sharp distinction is made between invention and innovation: the former is defined as the creation of a satisfactory design; the latter as its introduction to the market.[15] As has been seen, with respect to the decisions involved and the committal of money and resources, the distinction often is far less sharp than many people believe. If invention is considered the achievement of workable design concept, there often remains a substantial amount of technological uncertainty and a requirement for considerable ingenuity in development, as well as the risks and costs involved in getting into the market. Watts's first crude working steam engine was achieved in 1765. It took ten more years before he achieved a detailed design he felt ready to introduce to the market.[16] If invention is defined as including full development, the last stages generally involve commitment to market, and the capacity to do so, at least on a small scale. In

[13] See "Is R&D Management Effective?" *Chemical and Engineering News,* Vol. 35 (June 10, 1957), p. 38.

[14] Studies of patent utilization yield roughly the same result. About half the patents issued in the United States are used; about half are not. In one way, these figures drastically understate the percentage of ideas for new products and processes which are worked on but never actually tested out in practice. Many ideas never progress far enough to be classified as a "project" by an industrial laboratory, or to warrant a patent. However, these figures also probably exaggerate the percentage of research and development effort and resources devoted to projects which are abandoned before they are tried out in practice. The bulk of development expenditures are spent on the last stages of a design effort, and as pointed out earlier, while many companies (and private inventors) have relatively loose controls over small-scale expenditures, the decision to engage in an intensive expensive development effort is much more carefully considered.

[15] For a good review see Vernon W. Ruttan, "Usher and Schumpeter on Invention, Innovation, and Technological Change," *Quarterly Journal of Economics,* Vol. 73 (November 1959).

[16] For an analysis see Frederic M. Scherer, "The Watt-Boulton Steam Engine: A Case Study in the Economics of Technological Change," unpublished manuscript.

the nylon case, the pilot plants were adapted to production for the market. In military R&D the plant and equipment used to produce aircraft and missile test items also are used for production items.

The productive capacity and labor force required for the last stages of development often will not be considered adequate for the scale of output deemed desirable for effective introduction to the market and practical use. Thus, there may be high extra costs involved in moving from development into a market test. In cases where these costs are high and the costs and risks of development low, the classical break between invention and innovation may be quite meaningful. Where middle and late stage development costs and risks are high and where some productive capacity is built in the course of development, the break between achievement of a roughly worked out concept and the decision to initiate major development may be more important.

In either case, what happens in actual use is crucial. Research and development, and pilot plant operation, can demonstrate technical feasibility and many of the qualities of the product or process, and often provide reasonably good estimates of average production costs. However, the residual element of uncertainty may still be high. If special production techniques are required for mass production, cost estimates may not be accurate. Further, the demand for the product, and even the uses to which customers will put it, are often extremely difficult to predict. The only way to resolve these uncertainties is the practical production and market test. This period of early use provides an important feedback to management and engineers, and is often viewed by both as an exploratory learning experience, rather than as a long-term committal.

The early use period also tends to be viewed as a period of experimentation by potential users. It is relatively easy to induce consumers to try out a product when there is little risk for them. Early wearers of nylons, for example, simply risked the two dollars for a pair of stockings. With more expensive goods and those involving life and limb, consumers take a considerable risk. Quite generally with producer goods, users have to redesign their product and alter their operations before the value of the invention is fully proved.

In many cases a new product or process, once introduced to the market, is an immediate success; in many other cases it is not. Often commercial application shows that additional R&D is required. Various models of automatic cotton pickers were produced for sale long before the successful models of the 1940's, but none proved adequate for a large market. Continuous hot strip rolling of steel was tried out as early as 1902, but the design was not good enough to be used widely until 1923. Diesel electric locomotives were in wide use in Europe by the 1920's, and several were produced in the United States, but not until 1934 was a diesel developed suited to the long haul nature of most American railroad traffic.[17]

In addition to modifications in design, there may be significant changes in the perception of appropriate uses. Whittle believed his jet engine would find its principal use in long-range mail planes. Edison believed his electric trolley would replace long-haul steam engines.

While additional R&D and better perception of appropriate applications enable many new products and processes to achieve a market niche, many never make it. The autogyro never replaced the private automobile, nor has it found any other significant application. Schmookler reports that about half of the new products and processes that pass through the sequential R&D screen are never used widely enough to yield a profit.[18]

So the attrition rate is high, both in the R&D and early use stages. Many of the ideas that fail, however, are far from valueless. They comprise a large share of the stock of ideas in various stages of articulation and development among which inventors, developers, and innovators with richer knowledge, an expanded stock of components and materials, and facing different economic circumstances will scan and select.

The Adoption of New Technology

This section considers the innovations which pass the early use test and find a use or set of uses for which they are profitable and worthwhile.

The New Equilibrium and the Diffusion and Learning Process

The diffusion process may be viewed as a movement from the old to the new economic equilibrium. Prior to the time when the new product or process proved itself in trial use, there was one equilibrium set of levels of use of various processes and sales of various products. The intro-

---

[17] Jewkes, Sawers, and Stillerman, *op. cit.*

[18] Jacob Schmookler, *Invention and Economic Growth* (Cambridge: Harvard University Press, 1966).

duction of a new product or processes broadens the range of choice of producers and consumers and the equilibrium is altered. For a producer's good, such as a new machine used in the manufacture of an established good or service, the equilibrium level of use depends on its economic advantages relative to the inputs it replaces. The new equilibrium also depends on demand characteristics of the product in which the input is used; that is, the quantity changes in response to price declines or quality increases. For a new final good, the equilibrium level of use is a function of the quantity sold at a profitable price.

Many innovations, both producer and consumer goods, can be used in a wide variety of ways and whether, and to what extent, it will have an advantage over existing goods will differ from case to case. Nylon, for example, performs some functions cheaper or better than cotton, but not others. In some uses the new product or process may perform a function that others cannot. Television is partly a substitute for radio and the movies, and it also does things that radio and the movies cannot do. The demand for a new product or process depends on how effectively it competes with existing products, and also on the demand for the new functions it performs.

While many producer good or process innovations require less of every kind of input than the equipment or process they replace, many others do not. When it was introduced, the tank and tube process for cracking petroleum economized on labor, fuel, and raw materials cost per gallon of gasoline produced; in addition, its equipment was less costly than that required by the older process. The modern fluid catalyst cracking process seems to require more expensive capital equipment, but more than makes up for this in lower labor costs, given the high wage rates in the United States. If labor were less expensive, the advantages of the process would be less.[19] Thus, the attractiveness of a new machine depends partly on its cost or price relative to the machine it directly replaces and partly on the cost of other inputs it releases and uses.

For innovations which create a new consumer good, the tastes and preferences of consumers play a key role. Unlike a new producer's good where merit can be judged by its effect on the cost of producing a given end product, the merit of a new consumers' good can only be judged in terms of how well it meets wants. Thus, hybrid corn was re-

[19] See John Enos, *Petroleum Progress and Profits* (Cambridge: The M.I.T. Press, 1962).

jected after a trial by a Spanish American community in New Mexico despite the fact that it clearly had a higher yield than conventional corn seed, because the tortillas it produced had a taste which the community did not like.[20]

The movement to the new equilibrium does not proceed all at once. For the twelve industrial innovations studied by Mansfield, the average time between first use and use by 50 percent of the ultimate users was twelve years.[21] Ten more years elapsed before 90 percent of the ultimate acceptance was reached. The speed of diffusion varies from case to case. For Mansfield's innovations, the time between first use and use by 50 percent of those who ultimately accepted the innovation varied from nine to fifteen years. Many other studies confirm both the median long duration and its wide dispersion.

What accounts for this long time lag and the difference among innovations in their rate of diffusion? There are factors at work on both the demand and supply sides.

The Dynamics of Demand Adjustment

Typically, the number of users of an innovation grows slowly at the start, then accelerates, and then decreases its rate of growth as full equilibrium demand is reached. Mansfield has found such an acceptance curve for twelve industrial innovations; Dernberg for television, Ryan for hybrid corn, Jerome for machine tools.[22] Perhaps the principal factor explaining the slow start and later step up of the diffusion process is that a principal stimulus to try out a new product is the knowledge that others have used it successfully. This phenomenon will be examined in detail later in this chapter.[23]

[20] Reported in Everett M. Rogers, *The Diffusion of Innovations* (New York: The Free Press of Glencoe, 1962).

[21] Edwin Mansfield, "Technical Change and the Rate of Imitation," *Econometrica*, Vol. 29 (October 1961).

[22] Mansfield, *ibid.;* Thomas Dernburg, "Consumer Response to Innovation: Television," in *Studies in Household Economic Behavior* (New Haven: Yale University Press, 1958); Bryce Ryan, "A Study of Technological Diffusion," *Rural Sociology* (September 1948); Harry Jerome, *Mechanization in Industry* (New York: National Bureau of Economic Research, 1934).

[23] The S-shaped curve also could be the result of factors that would lead the number of new adapters to be normally distributed against time. However, such variables as age of capital stock would not appear to be distributed in such a manner as to lead to this result. For a discussion see A. D. Bain, "The Growth of Demand for New Commodities," *Journal of the Royal Statistical Association*, Vol. 126, Series A (1963).

Three factors determine the speed at which diffusion proceeds, compressing or stretching out the S-shape curve: (1) the long run advantage of the new product or process over older ones; (2) the transition costs and frictions, on the one hand, and the costs and dangers of maintaining the status quo, on the other; and (3) the uncertainty about the superiority of the new product and the ease or difficulty of overcoming these uncertainties.

LONG RUN PROFITABILITY OR UTILITY. If a new product is better or cheaper than an old one, or meets a want that could not be met before at a reasonable price, it eventually will be used in all or most situations where it has positive net value. If it is very desirable and profitable, it will be adopted faster than if it is only marginally profitable. The rapid spread of use of penicillin was due to its effectiveness. Griliches' study of the diffusion of hybrid corn shows that in Iowa, where the innovation was extremely profitable, it took five years before 50 percent of the farmers switched over; in Alabama, where hybrids had smaller advantage over conventional seed, ten years.[24] Mansfield's study of twelve industrial innovations shows similar results—the more profitable inventions diffused more rapidly.[25]

TRANSITION FRICTIONS AND PRESSURES. Relative profits are not perceived and calculated as though the world were continuously beginning from scratch. Capital stock, education, and organizational form all reflect existing technology, and generally must be altered to suit new developments.

The necessity of acquiring new physical capital frequently makes rapid transition uneconomic. Where the innovation is a new consumer good performing a radically new function, or is in a product field for which demand is growing rapidly, or is equipment used in an expanding field, there is no major competition with existing capital. If a new consumer or producer durable competes strongly with existing durable goods—and must win its way largely by replacing them—there is an element of friction. However great the long run profitability of the invention, its shorter run profitability is considerably less when the new product must win its place in competition with an accumulated stock of older

[24] Zvi Griliches, "Hybrid Corn: An Exploration in the Economics of Technological Change," *Econometrica*, Vol. 25 (October 1957).
[25] Mansfield, *loc. cit.*

goods whose purchase price already has been incurred. The user's comparison is the purchase price of the invention plus its operating cost against the operating cost of the old goods plus resale value. The higher the purchase price, the greater must be the operating cost advantage to make replacement economical. As an existing stock of capital ages and deteriorates replacement becomes progressively economical but again, the higher the purchase price, the slower the initial replacement will proceed, at the outset.[26]

Likewise, adoption will be delayed if the new technique requires new kinds of knowledge or patterns of behavior which are costly in terms of resources, effort, or time. For instance, some farmers were reticent about purchasing automatic cotton pickers because they required significant changes in the way fields were planted and spaced. The switchover from horse-drawn plows to tractors also was undoubtedly retarded because many farmers were unfamiliar with tractor operation and maintenance.[27] In manufacturing, the requirement for labor retraining or for new skills may retard acceptance. As with innovations requiring new capital, those requiring significant special education or training must win their way against older technologies for which such costs already have been incurred.

Requirements for interorganizational coordination also may slow adoption. In some cases no real problem exists; thus the success of the catalytic cracking process depended almost entirely on changes internal to the adapting company. Sometimes, however, there may be fragmentation of authority. The effective introduction of prefabrication in the building industry thus may require a revision of building codes by local governments and modification of behavior by architects, structural engineers, contractors, and labor unions, with the incentives for any one group to change being relatively small until the other groups change their practices.

Finally, the speed of diffusion may be slowed by simple lethargy, which has a cost. A firm may dawdle if the result is merely slower growth of profits, but it is likely to be activated when the result is a serious erosion of a previous profit or market share position. The pressures

[26] Mansfield, *loc. cit.*, has shown that the capital cost of an innovation is an important variable influencing the adaption rate.

[27] These examples can be contrasted with switching over to a new machine that simply is more durable and less prone to break down than the old, and which is operated the same way.

to adopt producers goods innovations rapidly will be greater in reasonably competitive than in more sheltered industries. Once some firms switch over, the pressure on the other firms depends on whether early users push their advantage aggressively by cutting prices or otherwise pressing for a bigger market share, or whether they sit back and only reap those benefits of lower cost which can be attained without expanding output.[28]

UNCERTAINTY AND ITS RESOLUTION. Some innovations, representing only marginal modifications from existing equipment, may be relatively easy to demonstrate and evaluate. For major innovations it may be considerably more difficult for sellers to demonstrate that a potential user could effectively and beneficially adopt the new technique or product, or for potential users confidently to make their own evaluation.

Problems of uncertainty and its resolution are, like the factors discussed above, elements of friction in the diffusion process. However, they warrant separate treatment. Three factors influencing uncertainty resolution appear to play a major role in determining the pace of adaptation: (1) the extent to which an innovation may be tried out on a small scale; (2) the extent to which potential users include a group with education and training which permits information about the new product to be decoded and understood and experiments to be performed effectively and confidently; and (3) the strength of the information dissemination system.

Various studies show that, where possible, early users of a new product proceeded experimentally. Early adopters of hybrid corn tended to plant initially less than 15 percent of their land in hybrids; when performance was proved they increased their commitment.[29] Physicians generally engage in small-scale testing of new drugs before adopting.[30] Early

[28] In a number of cases, sheltered companies failed to adopt an innovation until new firms showed the way. However, there is little statistical evidence to demonstrate that competition spurs the diffusion process, in part because the effect of competition cannot generally be separated from other factors. Mansfield reports on his study: "These (intra-industry) differences seem to be broadly consistent with the hypothesis often advanced that the rate of imitation (diffusion) is higher in the more competitive industries, but there are too few data to warrant any real conclusions of this score."

[29] Ryan, *loc. cit.*

[30] James Coleman, Elihu Katz, and Herbert Menzel, "The Diffusion of an Innovation Among Physicians," *Sociometry* (December 1957).

users of machine tools and diesel locomotives purchased just a few.[31] Innovations differ significantly in the extent to which small-scale experimentation is possible. For example, the decision to adopt catalytic cracking had to be largely an all-or-none decision to convert the entire refinery.

Several studies also indicate the importance of a group of technically sophisticated people who are capable of evaluating the new possibility.[32] Not everyone in the industry must be competent and self-confident enough to evaluate claims and check them out, but some people must be, and they must be in a position to influence the decision to start the process. Carter and Williams found that the early adopters of a new process tend to be firms which include a number of technically trained people.[33] The early adopters of hybrid corn tended to be farmers with higher than average education who read technical journals and bulletins. Often they had contacts at the universities.[34] Similarly, the early adopters of new drugs generally were doctors who were current with the medical literature and who had worked on the staffs of university hospitals.[35]

After the early users have set an example, their less venturesome and knowledgeable colleagues follow. The late adopters of hybrid corn mention the influence of direct contact with the early users, or with salesmen and extension agents who pointed out the experience of the early users. There is little evidence that the later adopters heard of the new product much after the earlier adopters. Indeed, in the hybrid corn case, the data suggest no significant differences in this respect.[36] However, later users are less able to evaluate the claims of salesmen, newspapers, advertisements, and other communication agents. Apparently, these sources often are not considered reliable unless their message is backed by one or

[31] Edwin Mansfield, "Intrafirm Rates of Diffusion of an Innovation," *Review of Economics and Statistics,* Vol. 45 (November 1963).

[32] A more formal presentation of this model is in R. R. Nelson and E. S. Phelps, "Investment in Humans, Technological Diffusion, and Economic Growth," *American Economic Review,* Vol. 56 (May 1966).

[33] Charles Carter and Bruce Williams, *Industry and Technical Progress: Factors Governing the Speed and Application of Science* (London: Oxford University Press, 1957).

[34] Bryce Ryan and Neal C. Gross, "The Diffusion of Hybrid Seed Corn in Two Iowa Communities," *Rural Sociology* (March 1943).

[35] Coleman, Katz, and Menzel, *loc. cit.*

[36] Ryan and Gross, and Ryan, *loc. cit.*

more members of a peer group, particularly by a member considered to be an expert.[37] Katz describes this phenomenon as the "two-step flow of communications" in diffusion.[38]

There is little reliable information on the importance of the various communications media in determining the rate of acceptance of a new product or process. They certainly can be effective in determining how fast the news of successful early adoption spreads. They can also influence the ability of potential adopters to learn what is needed to make a successful switchover. Some tentative evidence suggests that the amount of effort put forth by agricultural extension agents makes a difference once they can point to the success of some early users.[39] The intensive and extensive use of salesmen and advertising certainly suggests that firms believe that communication matters.

Thus, one variable that might significantly influence the pace of diffusion in its middle and later stages is the existence and effectiveness of organizations with direct interest in rapid acceptance. For marketed products the producing firm certainly has strong incentives to proselytize, but firms differ greatly in the strength of their sales force and advertising reach. It is likely that the new products of large firms tend to diffuse more rapidly than those of smaller firms aiming at a comparable market. For techniques and practices that do not involve a marketable product, or are not strongly associated with the use of one, there is an institutional gap. The technical professional associations, trade associations, and industry publications reporting on new developments partially fill this gap, as do the services of private consultants. In agriculture the Federal-State extension service proselytizes new techniques generally—not just those embodied in products.[40] But outside of agriculture, and those industries with strong associated technological professions, the

[37] Katz reports evidence that there may be three steps in instances when the bulk of the group do not consider the early users as peers. This can occur either when the innovators are believed to have special competence or conditions, or when they are not respected in the community. In these cases an intermediary group of adapters is necessary before the diffusion process starts.

[38] Elihu Katz, "The Two-Step Flow of Communication: An Up-To-Date Report on An Hypothesis," *Public Opinion Quarterly*, Vol. 21 (Spring 1957).

[39] See Ryan, and Ryan and Gross, *loc. cit.*

[40] For a history and discussion of the Agricultural Extension Service see A. C. True, *A History of Agricultural Extension Work in the United States, 1785-1923*, U.S. Department of Agriculture, Misc. Publication No. 15 (Washington: Government Printing Office, 1928).

pace of diffusion of new techniques not embodied in marketable products may be far slower than economically desirable because effective organizations are lacking to promote the new development and provide assistance in adoption.

Supply Adjustment and Producer Learning

So far, the process has been assumed to be limited by demand. Yet on the supply side, financing must be arranged, productive capacity built, intermediate materials and components obtained, and labor trained and employed.

There may be bottlenecks. In the early years of penicillin, for example, after the technological problems of quantity production had been solved there were large unmet demands by the armed services because productive capacity took time to build. All the early orders for the Boeing 707 were not filled for years after the first new jet transport was built. However, in both examples, the potential buyers (the government in the one case and the airlines in the other) had made up their minds to buy before the product reached the market. Where buyers stand willing and ready, the pace of diffusion clearly is limited by supply factors. But when the growth of demand takes time, as in most cases that have been studied, there is little evidence that bottlenecks on the supply side have been important.[41]

In most cases there is a more or less steady adjustment in supply conditions—keyed to the growth of demand and of output—which is important because it results in lower unit costs or an improved product. As indicated earlier, the initial versions of a new product or process often have serious technical defects. Consumers often have reason to be reluctant to buy early versions of a new automobile or appliance. The early versions also tend to be more costly. As experience accumulates the defects are identified and eliminated, performance is improved, and cost is reduced.

This phenomenon is well known and striking. Asher has documented cost declines for military aircraft.[42] Enos has found that for each of four

[41] This statement applies to recent experience in the United States. In a less highly industrialized and flexible economy there may be some serious bottlenecks to the creation of a labor force with the requisite skills, the obtaining of sufficient capital, and the obtaining of other inputs.

[42] Harold Asher, *Cost Quantity Relationships in the Airframe Industry* (Santa Monica: The RAND Corporation, R-291, July 1956).

major petroleum process innovations, capital costs per unit of capacity were halved after five years.[43] Hirsch has observed that unit costs for new machine tools are typically reduced by 20 percent for each doubling of cumulated output.[44] In all of these cases improvements over the first few years were significant, but far less important in later years. Part of the cost reduction reflects the redesign of product stressed by Gilfillan. Part is the result of better understanding of the production process which enables various economies to be made.

One important kind of economy created as understanding of the production process increases is enhanced ability to substitute machinery and relatively unskilled workers for highly educated workers. The observers of the early production of transistors remarked on the high percentage of physicists and engineers required to control the processes. As experience accumulated, however, it became possible to design machines to do some of the jobs formerly requiring highly educated talent, and to develop training programs to teach less educated workers the special things that they needed to know to be effective workers. It is difficult to prove that this phenomenon is general. However, one demonstration of this tendency would be for R&D intensive industries, which would have a larger percentage of new products and processes, to use a larger number of scientists and engineers outside R&D activities. Donald Keesing has found a strong positive correlation between R&D scientists and engineers and other scientists and engineers as a fraction of the work force.[45] More detailed observation would probably reveal that these other scientists and engineers are predominately involved with products and processes that have only recently emerged from the R&D laboratories.

This ability to redesign the production process and to design training programs to reduce education requirements is one important aspect of the "learning process." In addition, as the work force gains in experience, its efficiency improves. Management becomes experienced, problems are anticipated, and procedures developed to deal with them are put on a routine basis; the master coordinating programs and the command and control system are improved.

[43] John L. Enos, "A Measure of the Rate of Technological Progress in the Petroleum Refining Industry," *Journal of Industrial Economics,* Vol. 6 (June 1958).

[44] Werner Z. Hirsch, "Manufacturing Progress Functions," *Review of Economics and Statistics,* Vol. 34 (May 1952).

[45] Donald B. Keesing, "The Impact of Research and Development in United States Trade," Columbia University, mimeo., April 1, 1966.

The improvement process spreads out from innovating firm to its sources of supply. As the size of the market for material inputs grows, opportunities for economies of scale and more competitive markets are opened. A new industry of specialized material suppliers may come into existence. As the nature of the labor skill requirements becomes better known, the availability of these skills increases. Bankers and other sources become less reticent about providing funds for investment. As engineers and technicians become more experienced with the new technology, the exchange of ideas and experience tends to develop and become formalized in a technical literature. If the new technology is intellectually significant or occupationally important, some of its elements are introduced into general education and professional training.

Interactions in the Growth Process—Generalized Embodiment

In short, the shifting outward of the production possibility frontier which results from the creation of new technology does not occur all at once, but gradually. This is partly because of the importance of learning by trying and doing, on both the demand and supply side. It is also a natural consequence of the strong interaction among different forms of investment discussed in Chapter 1.

Adoption of new technology generally must await the acquisition of new capital in the industries using the new process, and sometimes in those industries producing the new product, be it a producer or consumer good. The pace at which this occurs is not only dependent on the profitability of the invention, but also on savings propensities and the working of financial markets—factors which influence the rate of investment in physical capital generally. Effective adoption requires understanding of the value of the new item and how to use it; the ease or cost of such understanding is strongly dependent upon the supply of people who have the knowledge to understand the new technology, and the existing education and training of the work force which determines how much additional or different knowledge they must receive concerning the new technology. Organization often must change and the speed with which this occurs depends on the basic flexibility and rationality of the economic structure generally.

Solow[46] has introduced to economic theory the concept of "embodiment" to denote the new physical capital necessary for the production of

[46] Robert M. Solow, "Investment and Technical Progress," in *Mathematical Methods in the Social Sciences, 1959* (Stanford: Stanford University Press, 1960).

a new good or the use of a new process. What is suggested here is that the needs for "embodiment" of a new technology transcend the creation of new physical capital. New investment in human capital in formal training and experience, and the investment of time and effort into remolding old or creating new institutions, are required as well.

An examination of all of the implications of the model sketched above for problems of development in the less developed economies, and upon patterns of world trade, is outside the scope of this volume. One of the implications worth noting is that a country like the United States, which engages in considerable research and development, which has invested heavily in creating a stock of well educated workers, thus reducing the training costs in shifting to new technology created by R&D, and which has relatively flexible economic institutions, should have a comparative advantage in producing new products. Keesing has found that the most important factors explaining why the U.S. exports considerable amounts of certain products, and smaller amounts of others, are the R&D intensity of the industry and the educational composition of the work force. In manufacturing industries where little R&D is undertaken and educational requirements of the work force are low, the U.S. exports little and tends to be a net importer from other countries.[47] The comparative advantage of the United States in relation to new products and processes certainly is partly the result of the fact that it is American R&D that creates a large number of them. It also is a result of the fact that the economy, through major investments in general and professional education, and because of a basic flexibility of economic institutions, has unusually great capability to exploit new technology efficiently and rapidly.

Sequential Screening as a Rational Response to Uncertainty

Many writers have commented on the apparent waste in the technological change process: a large number of projects never result in anything useful, duplication of effort is involved in competitive and parallel approaches when only one solution is needed, many people and organizations resist new technology.

Yet sequential decision making in situations of great uncertainty which can be reduced, either by small-scale efforts or by waiting, is ra-

[47] Donald B. Keesing, see also his "Labor Skills and Comparative Advantage," *American Economic Review*, Vol. 56 (May 1966).

tional both from the point of view of individuals and the economy as a whole. If waste is involved in duplicate efforts, it is also involved in commitment too early to an inferior approach. If there are economic costs of delay in accepting superior technology, there also are costs in accepting new technology that turns out to be uneconomic.

Yet there is doubt as to whether the sequential screens are exactly of the right size mesh, or that the pace of diffusion is close to optimal. The preceding chapter has pointed out that externalities and uncertainties probably produce a less than optimal allocation of R&D resources to technology-motivated basic research and experimental development. The same factors probably tend to result in a less than optimal flow of radical new inventions into the early use stage. On the supply side, development cost uncertainties, inability to spread the risk over multiple projects, and lack of ability to appropriate many of the benefits, compounded by great uncertainties with respect to consumer response, tend to deter companies from pushing far-reach projects through to the market. On the demand side, potential users of new products have an incentive to let others try them first and identify the defects. Since for society as a whole these risks and externalities are spread widely, the tendency of individual decision makers to wait is a source of economic inefficiency—an Alphonse-Gaston attitude toward major innovations.

There also may be major inefficiencies in the diffusion process itself, particularly for innovations not embodied in new products. The long duration of diffusion is reflected in striking differences between best and average practice among business firms. Salter,[48] for example, has noted that in the blast furnace industry, output per worker in the most productive plant was roughly double that in the average plant. Much of the difference was accounted for by the modernity of the processes in use, which is largely a reflection of the location of firms along the diffusion curve.

These gaps between best and average practice are to be expected, for it would not pay either the firm or the economy to scrap the old and buy the new overnight. Still the gap seems to reflect too many laggards lagging too long. There is a group of firms that seem too far removed from the forces of the diffusion process, and the social costs of their isolation are the higher cost and lower quality of their output.

[48] W. E. G. Salter, *Productivity and Technical Change* (Cambridge: Cambridge University Department of Applied Economics, 1960).

PART II

Adjustment to Growth and Technological Change

6

Technological Change and Employment

As new technological knowledge is created, the production possibilities open to society are expanded. As physical capital is formed and labor trained, and as intra and inter-firm organization is modified, society becomes more capable of exploiting the possibilities of the new technology.

The ability of society to reap the benefits of technological change, however, depends on a variety of adjustment mechanisms that transcend those directly connected with the process of technological change itself. These mechanisms, as well as those directly related to the creation and utilization of new technology, determine the extent to which the range of economic choice is expanded. If the mechanisms do not work well, the expansion of choice will be limited; in addition there may be serious social costs.

Among the most prominent of the adjustments required by technological advance are those involved in reallocating labor and other resources to correspond to the changes in the general equilibrium and those involved in assuring that growth in aggregate demand matches the expansion of economic potential. If these mechanisms do not work well, much of the potential gain of technological progress will be dissipated in unemployment, and a policy of encouraging even more rapid technological advance scarcely would be rational. A current body of thought maintains that automation is rapidly overwhelming these adjustment mechanisms and bringing on an era of high unemployment. To quote one commentator, W. H. Ferry:

113

Our growing inability to absorb available workers into the economy will give this question of 'just' distribution a point it has never before had. These technologically displaced people will comprise a new class, which I shall hereafter refer to as the 'liberated margin' . . . permanently liberated —from traditional toil, not because they want it so, but because the imperatives of efficiency have sent them to the sidelines. . . . Many questions arise. How will they live? Who will provide for them? What should be the community's attitude?[1]

The analysis in this chapter uncovers no trail pointing to such a dismal future. Rather, in examining the adjustment mechanisms which defend against high unemployment and wasteful allocation, it reveals a picture both more balanced and rapidly improving.

Supply Adjustment and Reallocation of Resources

The shifting of human and material resources is an essential part of the mechanism by which society exploits the possibilities opened by technological progress. If diesel engines are to be produced, capital, labor, and materials must be marshalled; the flow of resources into new activities is the supply aspect of the diffusion process discussed in the last chapter. However, the allocation of resources to apply the new technology is only one part of the reallocation necessary. Full exploitation of the benefits of technological advance requires also that those released from superseded activities find productive work. If the men previously involved in producing steam engines stand idle for long and the resources newly employed in the production of diesels are drawn from high value alternative uses, the net value of the output increase generated by technological advance may even be negative.

New General Equilibrium—Reflection of Choice

Even without technological advance, the allocation of resources would not be static, but would change in response to changing tastes and factor supplies. Yet technological progress is clearly the principal source of changes in the general equilibrium. The uneven pace of technological progress permits certain industries to become relatively more efficient than others in meeting wants. As pointed out in Chapter 4, the R&D intensive industries tend to introduce new products and product im-

[1] W. H. Ferry, *Caught on the Horn of Plenty* (Santa Barbara: Center for the Study of Democratic Institutions, January 1962).

provements at a faster rate and to experience more rapid productivity growth. Businesses and labor unions have not been able to appropriate all of the productivity differentials in profits and wages. While these industries have generally been profit and wage leaders, their leadership has been a limited one. High profits have led to expansion. Stigler has shown that where the returns to capital were high, capital growth rates often have exceeded 10 percent a year; where returns were low, growth has been slow or negative.[2] As a result, while an industry with a high rate of return in one year also tends to show a high rate in the next, capital expansion is likely to have driven returns back close to the average by the end of six years. Similarly, even when unions in the industry are strong, they have shown only limited ability to capture the benefits of higher productivity advances in the form of higher wages. While rapid progress plus strong unions make higher than average wages possible, over the long run labor competition has limited the extent of wage dispersion.[3] Thus, differential rates of technical advance have been largely translated into differential rates of consumer gains in terms of better or more products per dollar.[4]

Demand has been responsive to quality improvements and to price reductions, and technically progressive industries have shown above average expansion in output.[5] The relative size of the output expansion and labor-saving effects determines what happens to employment in industries which experience rapid technological progress. If demand is sufficiently sensitive to price reduction or product improvement, employment will increase. In automobiles during the 1920's and more recently in airlines, office machinery, and electronic and communications equipment, the technologically induced lowering of prices and raising of qual-

[2] George Stigler, *Capital and Rates of Return in Manufacturing Industries,* National Bureau of Economic Research (Princeton: Princeton University Press, 1963).

[3] W. E. G. Salter has shown that the correlation is low between the rate of productivity growth in an industry and the rate of growth of the wage rate in that industry if long periods of time are considered. See his *Productivity and Technical Change* (Cambridge: Cambridge University Department of Applied Economics, 1960).

[4] Both Salter, *ibid.,* and John W. Kendrick, *Productivity Trends in the United States,* National Bureau of Economic Research (Princeton: Princeton University Press, 1961), show a high correlation between the rate of technical progress and change in relative price.

[5] Salter and Kendrick, *ibid.*

ity led to enough expansion of demand to increase employment considerably. On the other hand, if demand is not sufficiently sensitive to declines in price (as often is the case in mature industries), productivity increases will result in less than proportional output increases and bring about a release of labor and other inputs. Coal and agriculture are cases where high productivity growth led to employment cutbacks because demand did not respond sufficiently to falling relative prices.[6] In these cases, the benefits of technical change were reaped largely by freeing resources for use in other industries.

Technical change has implications for employment composition far beyond the industry where the change is occurring. These implications cannot be fully examined except in terms of the general equilibrium analysis.[7] Employment in any industry is affected not only by its own technical change and productivity advance, but also by progress elsewhere. Reductions in price or improvements in quality will have an affirmative effect if they occur in industries producing inputs or complementary goods, and a negative effect if they occur in industries producing substitutes. For instance, advances in airline technology have increased employment in resort areas and in aluminum production, but reduced employment in railroads.

Thus, in order to obtain full benefit from an increase in productivity in a specific product line, purchases of a wide variety of other goods must be altered. This almost always requires changes in the location of job opportunities and the allocation of physical capital extending far beyond the industry where technical change is occurring. The efficiency and smoothness with which this reallocation proceeds is a major factor determining both the benefits of technical change and its human costs.

Adjustment Mechanisms and Burdens

Chapter 5 focused on that part of the adjustment process which involved the expansion of capital and the employment of workers with appropriate

---

[6] In the case of agriculture the problem was compounded by government policies which kept a floor under many prices.

[7] The complexity of this relationship may explain why the association between employment and productivity changes in specific industries is not at all close. For eighty manufacturing industries, Kendrick (loc.cit.) has computed the following coefficients of rank correlation between relative changes in output per man hour and in persons engaged: for 1899-1909, —0.01; for 1909-19, —0.28; for 1919-29, —0.5; for 1929-37, 0.09; for 1937-47, —0.19; for 1948-54, —0.02; and for the entire period, 0.33. Only the 1909-19 and 1899-1954 observations are significant at the 0.05 percent level or below.

skills to produce or use a new product or process. The human costs of adjustment are concentrated on those aspects of the reallocation which involve retrenchment of other activity.[8] As certain kinds of employment contract, and others expand, young people are unable to take the existing pattern of demand as a good indicator of what opportunities will exist when they enter the labor force. This uncertainty requires them to be more flexible regarding their job expectations. More important, job tenure of employed workers also becomes less certain. As particular jobs become obsolete, workers must be prepared to shift jobs.

The broad education acquired by most young Americans gives them the ability to learn to perform a wide variety of jobs. Further, they show considerable willingness to move in order to find an attractive job. Therefore, the human costs of foreclosing certain job opportunities which employed a significant fraction of the older generation would not appear to be particularly serious for youth. To be sure, society may develop a certain footloose quality, and the gap between generations may be widened, but compared with the problem of job insecurity, these costs appear minor.

The major human costs stem from the erosion of jobs of established workers. And yet the turnover and mobility characteristics of the American labor force permit considerable labor reallocation without extensive lay-offs of established workers. Each year between one and two percent of the labor force leave the labor market because of death, retirement, or for other reasons; and new entrants amount to 2 or 3 percent, so a considerable reallocation can be effected without anyone changing a job. In addition, voluntary job shifting is an important characteristic of the American labor market. During 1961 4.5 million persons, or 5 percent of all who worked, changed jobs voluntarily.[9] A significant fraction were young men, women with limited interest in the labor market, and workers in low wage industries—generally people who were seeking to improve their jobs or change their scenery. To the extent that attrition (retirements and voluntary departures) is the primary mechanism of employment reduction in declining industries, occupations, and regions, the human costs of reallocation can be kept relatively modest.

---

[8] It is assumed for the moment that the total number of employment opportunities is not adversely affected by the concurrent expansion and contraction. Later, this chapter will examine the effect of technological progress on employment opportunities in the aggregate.

[9] Gertrude Bancroft and Stuart Garfinkle, "Job Mobility in 1961," *Monthly Labor Review*, Vol. 86 (August 1963).

Not only do labor force turnover and mobility characteristics permit considerable reliance on the attrition mechanism; business firms, faced with pressures to cut back, have incentives to use attrition where possible because of concern for morale among the remaining work force and possible adverse effects of firings on future recruiting. This preference tends to prevail when work-force reductions proceed at moderate rates and for a moderate period of time.[10] Reliance upon retirements and voluntary quitting is further facilitated when reduction can be anticipated, as, for example, in the introduction of a process with a long planning period. For highly mechanized processes, the gestation period between initiation of the investment decision and actual operation of the new facility is frequently as long as one to three years,[11] allowing the employer considerable flexibility for planning, and for cutting the work force through quits and retirements, while meeting interim labor needs by use of overtime or provisional employees. Finally, when one kind of job is cut back and another is expanded within the same firm, attrition is facilitated when the job shifts do not require significantly different general educational

[10] Reliance on attrition is stated company policy in many large firms like General Electric and American Telephone and Telegraph. See the statements of Ralph J. Cordiner of the General Electric Company, Don G. Mitchell of the Sylvania Electric Products Corp., and C. W. Phalen of the American Telephone and Telegraph Co. in Howard B. Jacobson and Joseph S. Roucek (eds.), *Automation and Society* (New York: Philosophical Library, 1959). Also, a small number of studies by the Bureau of Labor Statistics on the installation of automatic technology—in a bakery, petroleum refinery, insurance company, electronics plant, and in general company offices—disclosed considerable advance planning aimed at avoiding layoffs, and resulting in surprisingly few layoffs. See U.S. Department of Labor, Bureau of Labor Statistics, *Adjustments to the Introduction of Office Automation,* Bulletin No. 1276 (Washington: Government Printing Office, May, 1960); and *Impact of Automation,* Bulletin No. 1287 (Washington: Government Printing Office, 1960).

The impact of a specific technical advance on plant labor requirements is frequently exaggerated, because attention is focused on specific production processes, rather than on the product line or employing unit. Innovations can have major impacts on particular departments or processes, without perceptibly affecting establishment employment levels. For instance, James Bright cites an automated facility which increased labor productivity in foam rubber production by 425 percent. At constant output levels, the introduction of this facility would have reduced the molding work force by 45 percent, the total foam rubber mattress line force by only 16 percent, and the total plant force by only 1.4 percent. James R. Bright, *Automation and Management* (Boston: Harvard Business School, Division of Research, 1958), Chap. 12.

[11] The Department of Labor case studies, reported in Bulletin Nos. 1276 and 1287, were all characterized by quite lengthy gestation periods.

background; retraining time then is generally minimal, thus lessening the costs of retaining existing workers.[12]

If labor requirements are declining at too rapid a rate, reliance on attrition alone becomes economically disadvantageous for the firm, and layoffs result. Even if new jobs are opening within the firm as old ones are closing down, if the jobs require considerably more educational background, firms will generally prefer to dismiss current employees and hire workers with more appropriate skills. Length of training time and difficulties of making sure employees stay with the firm until the training investment is recaptured deter most firms from significant investments in education.

If a small proportion of the plant work force is displaced the workers laid off are likely to be young, and with relatively short job tenure. In a full employment economy, reasonably well educated young layoffs have a high probability of finding a new job rather quickly. It is well known that young workers account for most labor force mobility.[13] Their ability to find employment in expanding sectors is suggested by high overall rates of industrial, occupational and geographical mobility. Of the eleven million job shifts which occurred in 1961, over half involved movements of workers from one of fourteen major industry groups to another. Slightly less than half involved a shift between one to another of the twenty-two major occupational groups.[14] The Survey Research Center of the University of Michigan reported that 30 percent of all heads of families moved to a new labor market area between 1950 and 1964, and that 65 percent of all family heads were living in a different labor market area than the one in which they were born.[15]

[12] For instance, a General Electric spokesman states: "Naturally, the Company provides any training required to enable employees to handle new assignments. Most of this training is informal in nature and is done by individual supervisors on the job or through vestibule training schools that run from one to two weeks, in preparation for a specific kind of work." Ralph J. Cordiner, "Automation in the Manufacturing Industries," in Howard B. Jacobson and Joseph S. Roucek, *op.cit.*

[13] In 1961, for instance, workers between the ages of eighteen and thirty-four accounted for 34 percent of total employment and 56 percent of all job changers. See Gertrude Bancroft and Stuart Garfinkle, "Job Mobility in 1961," *op.cit.*

[14] *Ibid.*, pp. A-9 - A-11. The data contained in this article also suggests that the matching of jobs and workers is frequently accomplished in an expeditious manner. In the recession year of 1961, 40 percent of all job changers found new employment without an intervening experience of joblessness, and another 25 percent found jobs within four weeks.

[15] U.S. Department of Commerce, Area Redevelopment Administration, *Eco-*

The serious problems of adjustment occur when layoffs cut deeper into the seniority list. Age is correlated with job tenure; as a worker's job tenure lengthens, the ratio of specific to more general skills rises and these skills become more valuable to the current employer (or to a small group of closely related employers) than in the general labor market. In addition, employers—particularly the government and private unionized firms—tend to offer significant rewards for employment longevity. In a large number of establishments, where steps in the job hierarchy below supervisory level represent only minor and easily learned gradations in skill, employment tenure is the major differentiator between those in the common labor pool and those with preferred semiskilled jobs. Thus, when older workers are laid off, their next job is likely to pay less. The financial costs may, of course, be compounded by the psychological costs of losing status or leaving the community in which deep roots have been sunk over the years. Further, employers are reluctant to invest in hiring and training employees who are approaching retirement age. Once unemployed, older workers may have considerable difficulty finding any job at all.[16]

The trauma felt by mature workers when they are tossed into the job market again, and the frequent necessity to lower standards of living which they reasonably expected to be perpetuated, rank among the major inequities of technical change.[17]

---

nomic Redevelopment Research: The Geographic Mobility of Labor, Summary Report (Washington: Government Printing Office, 1964).

[16] During the first half of 1965, 37 percent of all unemployed men, ages forty-five and over, had been jobless for fifteen weeks or longer. This compares with 17 percent for men ages 20-24 and 26 percent for men ages 25-44. See Susan S. Holland, U.S. Department of Labor, Bureau of Labor Statistics, "Long-Term Unemployment in the 1960's, *Monthly Labor Review,* Vol. 88 (September 1965). Special Labor Force Report no. 58.

Note that the labor market is structured differently for many white collar and skilled blue collar occupations, where lateral transfer is quite possible. Indeed, considering the wage dispersion that results from the cost of job search and the "satisficing" behavior of many workers, displacement often results in the finding of a higher paying job. ("Satisficing" denotes the willingness to settle for a traditionally satisfactory outcome rather than search for the best.) Nonetheless, after a certain point, the ratio of a man's current income to his opportunities in alternative employment probably rises with length of service; so inevitably does the capital loss associated with involuntary job transfer.

[17] There are no comprehensive statistics on the income experience of involuntary job changers, but a number of special studies indicate that significant capital losses

Performance of the Adjustment Mechanism

The ability of the American economy to reallocate labor to better meet needs and exploit new opportunities is quite impressive. Rapid technological progress in agriculture and mining, where demand remains relatively static, has driven resources out of those sectors into others where the marginal value of output was higher. Over the past twenty-five years employment in agriculture and mining has been cut in half. Even in the short-run, the economy has shown great ability to reallocate resources to meet changing relative needs. Three years after World War II, defense expenditures had fallen from 40 percent of GNP to 5 percent. Despite vast declines in the demand for many final goods and services, however, unemployment stayed under 4 percent of the labor force throughout the period, due to the rise in private consumption and investment demand. This was an extreme example of a reallocation burden imposed upon the labor market, and still it performed well.

Table VI-1 illustrates why reallocation is frequently a rapid and relatively painless process. Where labor requirements are being reduced, a significant portion of the decline can be accommodated simply by terminating new hires. Where employment is expanding, a significant portion of each year's crop of new workers is attracted. Between 1950 and 1960, the number of younger workers (ages 20-29) dropped by one-third in the twenty-seven major nonfarm industries and fifty-four major nonfarm occupations in which employment declined. It rose by 800,000 or 20 percent in expanding activities. In industries and occupations

---

are frequent. For 141 International Harvester workers displaced in 1950, Adams and Aronson found that the average starting wage at their new job was 45 to 50 cents an hour less than previous average earnings. Leonard P. Adams and Robert L. Aronson, *Workers and Industrial Change; A Case Study of Labor Mobility* (Ithaca: Cornell University Press, 1957). In a study of a textile plant closing, Miernyk reported that 64 percent of the displaced workers who found new employment received lower weekly earnings. William H. Miernyk, *Inter-Industry Labor Mobility; The Case of the Displaced Textile Worker* (Boston: Northeastern University Press, 1955). In a depth survey conducted in 1962, with a heavy representation of older workers, Sobel and Folk found that one-third of 1,100 short-term unemployed workers earned an hourly wage of 25 cents or more lower on their last job than on their longest job. Irvin Sobel and Hugh Folk, "Labor Market Adjustments by Unemployed Older Workers," in Arthur M. Ross (ed.), *Employment Policy and the Labor Market* (Berkeley: University of California Press, 1965).

TABLE VI-1. *Changes in Male Employment in Nonfarm Activities, 1950–1960*

By Industry				
Percentage Change in Total Employment	Absolute Change (thousands)		Changes Age 20-29 As a Percent of Total Changes	Number of Industries
	Total	Ages 20-29		
−25 to −49	−1,028	−378	35	6
−11 to −24	− 461	−261	57	10
0 to −10	− 331	−208	63	11
0 to 20	846	−142	*	11
21 to 30	1,381	37	3	9
31 to 40	1,200	136	11	8
41 to 60	1,378	244	18	8
Over 60	1,506	342	23	5

By Occupation				
Percentage Change in Total Employment	Absolute Change (thousands)		Changes Age 20-29 As a Percent of Total Changes	Number of Occupations
	Total	Ages 20-29		
−50 to −80	− 200	− 58	29	4
−25 to −49	− 688	−196	28	12
−11 to −24	−1,873	−630	34	27
0 to −10	− 152	−124	81	11
0 to 20	1,223	− 65	*	28
21 to 30	1,240	311	3	17
31 to 40	367	110	30	6
41 to 60	1,419	118	8	10
Over 60	2,510	736	29	13

Sources: U. S. Department of Commerce, Bureau of the Census, *U. S. Census of Population: 1950*, Vol. II, *Characteristics of the Population*, Part I, *United States Summary*, Tables 127 and 132, and *U. S. Census of Population: 1960*, Vol. I, *Characteristics of the Population*, Part I, *United States Summary*, Tables 204 and 212.
* Percentage cannot be computed.

where decreases in employment were moderate, the bulk of the change was accounted for simply by nonreplacement of retiring workers.[18] In instances where employment fell by less than 10 percent, non-replacement accounted for 60 to 80 percent of the decline.

It is reasonable to conclude that voluntary mobility, and the normal turnover cycle, are important contributors to the reallocation process,

[18] Table VI-1 would be a measure of the relative importance of attrition in declining activities only if maintaining a constant sized work force ages twenty to twenty-nine were necessary and sufficient for maintaining a constant sized total work force, and only if the data pertained to establishments, and were segregated by periods of employment increase and decrease. Since these conditions are not met, the data are merely suggestive.

and that much of the burden of involuntary mobility falls on younger workers with only a limited attachment to their current work endeavors. At the same time, the process of matching jobs and workers is still marred by unnecessary market imperfections. Plant closings and mass layoffs are the exceptional response to technical advance, rather than the rule, but when they occur, they impose high costs on the older workers affected.

Labor Market Policies

The general recognition of defects and inequities in operation of labor markets has led recently to a major expansion in government labor market programs.[19] The new programs are largely oriented to general labor market inefficiencies, and to the problems of groups disadvantaged for reasons only tangential to technical change. However, as has been seen, technical change is not a foreign intrusion, but an integral part of the economic system. Its impact on layoffs is not centered in establishments adopting new technology, but frequently may occur in backward establishments, and in industries producing substitutes and inputs to substitutes. Since its effect is so pervasive, measures increasing the flexibility of the work force or the efficiency of labor markets naturally facilitate adjustment to technical change. Still, such programs do not fully come to grips with the capital losses and long-term unemployment frequently experienced by displaced senior workers.

Private Policies

Traditionally, public policy has been concerned with maintaining an adequate number of job opportunities, providing an appropriate educational background for workers, compensating for periods of unemployment, and undertaking various functions to match job hunters and jobs.

---

[19] These programs include the National Defense Education Act, the Vocational Education Act of 1963, the Manpower Development and Training Act, the Area Redevelopment Act, efforts to modernize the United States Employment Service, and many aspects of the Economic Opportunity Act, particularly the Adult Literacy Program, the Job Corps and the Neighborhood Youth Corps. They are designed to raise the educational level and adaptability of future labor force members, to retrain some of the currently unemployed, to reorient and acquaint with work disciplines those who for psychological or social reasons have not realistically interacted with the world of urban work values, and to improve the flow of labor market information.

In contrast, private policies evolved in personnel departments or through collective bargaining have been concerned with the relationship between individual workers and specific jobs. They have concentrated on determining who is displaced, and providing them with some compensation based on length of service. Attrition policies and the determination of layoffs on the basis of seniority have created protected enclaves for already employed workers, particularly for those with lengthy job tenure.[20]

This division of labor between private and public policies is felicitous. Public policy is highly deficient in assisting displaced experienced workers to new jobs on a par with their old jobs, and is likely to remain so. Consequently, there is a need for private policies which protect employed workers and compensate them in the event of job loss. Such policies could remedy a high proportion of the problem. The task is to devise private policies which provide greater individual economic security, but do not maintain obsolete jobs perpetually or for long periods of time. Such policies will certainly not be costless. However, considering their concern for economic security, workers would probably be willing to devote a part of their rising income to changes in work rules and fringe benefits which would insure them against severe economic dislocation.

Greater protection of established employment relationships hinges on a widening of the seniority unit, which is often confined to select departments or divisions of a firm. The narrowness of seniority units means that senior employees can be laid off in one division, while considerable hiring is occurring elsewhere in the firm. Interplant transfer systems are, however, receiving increasing attention, and have already been formally established in autos, in steel, in meatpacking, and in railroad clerical work.[21] The importance of this trend is accentuated by the fact that most workers are employed in multiplant firms.

[20] The degree of security which such policy can provide is illustrated by the celebrated Railroad Arbitration Board decree, and the Kaiser Steel-United Steelworkers and the West Coast Longshoreman's agreements, all of which provided quite extensive employment or income guarantees for workers whose jobs were subject to elimination. These private policies tend to minimize and at times to eliminate the adjustment burden by shifting it to younger workers and new entrants.

[21] The complexities of company-wide seniority units are described in Arnold R. Weber, "The Interplant Transfer of Displaced Employees," in Gerald G. Somers, Edwin L. Cushman and Nat Weinberg (eds.), *Adjusting to Technological Change* (New York: Harper and Row, 1963).

The fullest and most effective implementation of wider seniority rights would require a number of additional fringe benefit programs; most particularly, (1) providing additional education and inplant training to upgrade displaced workers even in instances when such investment is not economically advantageous to the employer, (2) limiting the number of paygrades a transferred employee could be downgraded,[22] and (3) moving and relocation allowances within the company domain (benefits which are rare outside of the automobile and railroad industries).

Such widening of the seniority unit would reduce the number of permanent layoffs affecting long tenure workers, but would not eliminate vulnerability in single establishment firms, particularly small ones, and in industries experiencing sharp declines in labor requirements. The economic and psychic losses involved could, however, be offset at the time of displacement if pension rights were vested in displaced workers, and if adequate severance pay were provided. Severance pay programs have been growing and today about 40 percent of workers covered by major collective bargaining contracts are eligible for benefits, generally graduated according to prior length of service. Benefit payments, however, are often inadequate compensation for income losses involved in displacement from a long-held job. Further, the majority of the labor force remains uncovered. Extended coverage of severance pay programs, and provision of larger payments, provide the surest way of protecting workers from income losses due to technical change.[23] Indeed, unless private

[22] Such programs might be criticized as involving potentially expensive open-ended commitments, or infringements on the ability to efficiently operate a plant. These problems can be resolved, however, by limiting the company commitment to so many cents per hour to be paid into a fund. Management could continue to make training and job assignments on the basis of efficiency criteria, while pay and training supplements for eligible employees who did not meet these criteria were financed from the fund.

[23] Lump sum severance payments, graduated by length of service, are often criticized on two counts. First, they overcompensate those workers who can transfer laterally to other jobs, and thus reduce funds available for workers actually experiencing income losses. Second, workers receiving large one-time payments sometimes expend them on protracted vacations. This may be the form of compensation for income loss most preferred at the moment, but it does not prepare workers for the ultimate and perhaps difficult confrontation with the labor market.

The suggested alternative to a lump sum payment is the providing of displaced workers with education, retraining and relocation allowances, and paying the difference, or some portion of the difference, between the workers' new weekly earnings and his previous weekly earnings, up to some maximum expenditure.

policy accelerates the trend toward vested pension rights and adequate severance benefits, public policy steps may be advisable to encourage, or even force, their establishment.

Public Policy

For the present, the most promising public policy measure would be that of requiring employers to give advance notice of major layoffs and plant shutdowns. The United States Employment Service (USES), the state-federal employment agency, is currently experimenting with a voluntary program of advance notification. Although results are not yet available, it seems unlikely that widespread compliance can be obtained on a voluntary basis, since advance notice will impose costs on employers in terms of adverse publicity, premature loss of employees and lowered productivity of the remaining work force.

Advance notice gives workers more latitude for planning savings and labor market strategies. It permits them to engage in job hunting, to assess their labor market acceptability, and to contemplate whatever adjustments in skill, location, or earnings may be necessary, and to do so while still earning an income and without experiencing a demoralizing exposure to joblessness. The possible benefits of advance notice should not be exaggerated, however, since they pertain only to the more aggressive and mobile members of the work force. Permanent plant closedowns are generally foreshadowed by some years of reduced output, transference of functions, termination of hiring, and major layoffs. Workers do not always heed this type of informal advance notice. Even when plant closedowns are announced, some workers do not regard them as permanent, but cling for protracted periods of time to the belief that circumstances will change and the plant will reopen.[24]

The benefits of advance notice can be considerably increased if public agencies prepare older workers for contact with a labor market from which they have been long insulated, and of whose functioning they may have little knowledge. Interviewing, testing, counseling, placement and retraining[25] services can then be deployed without wasting time or dissi-

---

[24] See, for instance, U.S. Department of Labor, Bureau of Labor Statistics, Bulletin No. 1264, *Impact on Workers and Community of a Plant Shutdown in a Depressed Area* (Washington: Government Printing Office, June 1960).

[25] This would require a revision of the Manpower Development and Training Act to permit the establishment of retraining courses for still-employed workers.

pating morale by unemployment.[26] The mass layoff program of the USES and the recently formed President's Task Force on Community Action are hopeful signs that government policy is evolving in this direction, but a far more sizeable effort is needed. Workers affected by plant closedown should have a priority call on the limited resources available for labor market purposes.

This may require a reorientation of the federally financed retraining program, which is currently focused on reducing overall unemployment by remedying skill shortages, and hence on retraining younger workers.[27] A higher proportion of retraining resources could be devoted to long tenure workers who are displaced, or about to be displaced, and whose generally low position in the hiring queue seems socially undesirable. Placing a higher social premium on improving the prospects of these workers would serve to offset the fact that they may have greater than average difficulties in assimilating training, or in being placed, or will have a shorter working span over which to amortize the costs of training. An explicit equity orientation would also involve retraining programs for a wide variety of skills, and provide longer training periods where necessary, to retrain displaced workers for jobs which pay wages comparable to those previously received. The restoration of the workers' previous income status will not always be feasible, but retraining programs should certainly aim in this direction.[28]

[26] Extensive experimentation with relocation allowances would be desirable when plant closedowns affect small, geographically isolated areas, or regions where employment prospects are declining secularly.

[27] Only 11 percent of the trainees enrolled in institutional projects started in 1964 under the Manpower Development and Training Act were forty-five years of age or over. Only 25 percent had 10 or more prior years of gainful employment. In contrast, 37 percent were twenty-one years of age or under and 36 percent had less than three years of prior gainful employment experience. U.S. Department of Labor, Bureau of Labor Statistics, *Manpower Report of the President and a Report on Manpower Requirements, Resources, Utilization, and Training*, March 1965, p. 253 (Washington: Government Printing Office).

[28] The positive way to exploit the advantages of advance notice is to refocus retraining resources around plant layoff situations and the problems of the about-to-be-displaced long tenure worker. However, some long tenure workers may be found ineligible even if the retraining program is given an explicit equity orientation, and some may be uninterested in retraining. Some still will be able to find work only by accepting significantly lower wages or less job status, or a different geographic location. Thus, there may be considerable value in counselling to inform people of facts which they might otherwise absorb only as the result of long and expensive experience. In this instance, the Employment Service can best fulfill

Maintaining Aggregate Demand-Supply Balance

Mobile workers, employers disposed to attrition, and enlightened labor market policies do not in themselves assure that rapid technological progress will not bring massive unemployment. Achievement of reasonable balance between changes in labor demand and supply in various industries and occupations is only possible if demand and the size of the willing labor force are in balance for the economy as a whole.

To achieve balance as new technological knowledge is brought into practice and potential output is increased, there must be a corresponding increase in the effective demand for goods and services (or, alternatively, a shorter work week, longer vacations, or earlier retirements). If demand does not increase as rapidly as potential output, inventories will pile up, managers will begin to lay off workers, and growth potential will be dissipated in involuntary unemployment and underutilized capacity. If demand increases more rapidly and resources already are fully employed, it will exceed the output the economy is capable of producing, and shortages, queues, and the host of inequities and inefficiencies associated with excess demand inflation will develop.

The balance of aggregate effective demand and potential output is far from automatic. In the past demand has sometimes fallen far short of potential—the early 1870's and early 1930's are catastrophic examples—and in other periods demand growth has run away from potential output, as in the World War II period.

There is a widely held belief that when technological advance is rapid, potential output tends to run away from demand. However, the opposite may be true: rapid technological advance may tend to be associated with inflationary pressures and a slow rate with tendencies toward slack. To see what is involved, it is useful to examine technological advances that increase productivity in existing product lines; later the analysis will be extended to include new and improved products.[29]

To maintain balance between potential output and total demand for goods and services, total final demand—the sum of household consump-

---

its function by acquainting workers with labor market realities, and by early encouraging more flexibility in the level of wages and type of work which they are willing to accept.

[29] The following analysis is presented more formally in Richard R. Nelson, "Full Employment Policy and Economic Growth," *American Economic Review*, Vol. 56 (December 1966).

tion, private investment and government spending—must increase by the same proportion as potential output.[30] In principle, increases in potential output resulting from increases in per worker productivity could be matched by growth of household consumption alone. The increased productivity could be exactly balanced by increased real wages and profits in the form of higher money incomes or lower prices, and this increased purchasing power would be exactly enough to purchase, in the form of increased consumer goods, all of the output increase that productivity growth permitted. In practice, such a rise in consumption is unlikely. Some portion of the increased real incomes permitted by productivity increases would be retained by business firms, some would be saved by individuals, and some would be taxed away by governments. Other forms of demand thus must expand to fill the savings and tax gap. To maintain the existing ratio of actual to potential GNP, any increases in individual or business savings or government taxes, generated by the increased real incomes permitted by increased productivity at existing employment rates, must be matched by increases in business investment and government spending.

The Private Sector

Abstracting from government spending and taxing, the requirement for unchanged employment rates is that the growth of investment must equal that growth of savings which would be generated by increased real incomes at existing employment rates.

Private savings have two principal components—savings by households and savings by business firms. Past performance indicates that household savings grow as potential output grows, and roughly in pace with disposable income. Similarly, gross business savings grow with gross business earnings, the proportion of savings to earnings being partially responsive to the finance requirements of planned investment. Savings should remain a roughly constant fraction of GNP as long as the investment-potential GNP ratio remains constant. If the investment GNP ratio rises, the ratio of savings to actual GNP may also rise, although not as much, and the principal effect would likely be a balancing of actual investment and actual savings at a higher ratio of actual to potential GNP—at a lower level of unemployment and slack.

Tendencies toward inflation or slack then hinge largely on what hap-

[30] Also included here should be net exports. These are small for the United States.

pens to the investment-potential GNP ratio. Here it would appear that rapid technological advance provides a strong stimulant.

As pointed out in Chapter 2, an absence of technological advance would sharply limit the pace at which physical capital could be expanded profitably; indeed the rate of growth of the capital stock probably could not exceed that of the labor force for long without sharp declines in the rate of return on new investment. Up to a point this might be compensated by declines in the cost of borrowing. Sooner or later an interest rate floor would be reached, and thereafter the capital stock could grow no faster than the labor force.

With technological progress, increases in the capital labor ratio need not lead to declines in the rate of return on new investment. Indeed, under certain assumptions the capital stock and investment can grow just as fast as potential GNP grows without a decline in the rate of return on capital.[31] The faster the pace of technological progress, and hence the growth of potential output, the faster the capital stock can grow without depressing returns. Since more rapid capital growth requires a higher ratio of investment to GNP, faster technical progress means the fraction of GNP allocated to investment can be larger without causing a decline in the rate of return on capital. Thus, given any existing dynamic equilibrium, an acceleration of technological progress, unless offset by a rise in interest rates, means business firms will find it profitable to invest not only more, but more as a fraction of potential GNP. If the savings schedule does not shift equally, and it is unlikely to, even though both potential output and savings will now be growing faster, equality of savings and investment now will occur at lower, not higher, degrees of slack and unemployment rates.

When the fact is recognized that technological progress usually involves new final products as well as increased productivity in producing old ones, the implications are reinforced. It is possible that new product innovations will stimulate people to spend more and save less. There is some evidence that the early buyers of television financed their purchases partly through decreased savings or increased borrowing.[32] On the

---

[31] One set of sufficient conditions is—a linear homogeneous production function, a unitary elasticity of substitution between capital and labor, and technological advance which results in an equal proportional increase of the marginal productivities of capital and labor. Another set is—a linear homogeneous production function and technological advance which is equivalent to an increase in the labor supply.

[32] See Thomas Dernburg, "Consumer Response to Innovation: Television," in *Studies in Household Economic Behavior* (New Haven: Yale University Press,

other hand, if people did not buy TV's, they might go out more to the movies or buy more of other consumer durables. Thus, the effect of technological advance on consumption propensities is an open question. However, an addition to the range of consumer products does not require the increase in total spending that an increase in productivity does. Even if consumers respond to the availability of new products by spending the same amount, there is no offsetting increase in savings to balance the increased business investment in facilities to produce the new products.[33]

Schumpeter long ago recognized the expansive impact of rapid technological progress. He pointed out that periods of rapid technical change generally have been associated with high investment and low unemployment. The mid-nineteenth century boom was associated with technical progress and investment in railroads and steel, another in the 1920's was associated with the automobile, chemical and electrical industries, and during the early 1950's the economy was spurred by further advances in chemicals and electronics. On the other hand, the depressions of the 1870's and the 1930's were associated with a slowdown of technological progress.

These conclusions could be reversed if technological advance were particularly capital-saving, or if business firms responded sluggishly to new investment opportunities and slack was permitted to develop before investment was stimulated, or if consumers responded slowly to rapidly rising disposable incomes so that their consumption percentage fell. While rapid technological progress is likely to spur the growth of potential output, it may sometimes have the opposite effect.

Fiscal and Monetary Policy

In any case, both experience and theory indicate that the spending, taxing and money-creating powers of the federal government are sufficient

---

1958). For a theoretical discussion see James Duesenberry, *Income, Saving, and the Theory of Consumer Behavior* (Cambridge: Harvard University Press, 1949).

[33] In part, what is happening here is an optical illusion resulting from the inadequate valuation of new final products in the GNP calculations. Because the new final products enter the GNP series with a price weight less than what people would be willing to pay for them, constancy of consumption and of disposable income at accounted prices masks an increase in real consumption (in terms of consumer satisfaction) and an equal increase in real disposable income. Thus, if "correct" price weights were used for new products, and if consumers responded to "better" television sets offered at the same price as older ones by buying the same number and spending the same amount, real consumption, and consumption as a fraction of disposable income, have increased.

to generate any level and rate of growth of money demand. Government taxes, as well as private savings, drive a wedge between income and consumption demand. Government spending, as well as private investment, serves to fill that gap.

The dramatic reduction of unemployment rates during the Korean War and World War II demonstrated the power of government spending. But government dollars have no magic; the 1964 tax cut showed that the government could directly spur private spending. Through its financial operations, the government can influence the relative supplies of money and interest bearing assets, otherwise loosen or tighten credit availability, and increase or reduce the attractiveness and ease of financing investment in new physical capital.

The obvious capabilities of federal fiscal and monetary policies make it important to examine the requirements imposed upon stabilization policy by differing rates of technological progress. The direct effects of technical advance on the aggregate balance of demand and supply and on the level of employment are less important, since they can be compensated for by suitable policies.

In an economy where potential output is growing, the task of stabilization policy is to maintain a ratio between actual and potential output that avoids long spells of high unemployment or sustained inflationary pressures. If it appears that private saving will outrun private investment at full employment, the government can run a counterbalancing deficit to help fill the savings gap, or reduce interest rates to stimulate private investment. If investment promises to outrun savings, the government can run a surplus or tighten credit. This task can be more or less difficult, depending upon the strength and stability of the other forces that determine growth of demand. There is no convincing evidence that rapid technical progress seriously complicates the task, and there is some reason to believe that it may make the task easier.

Rapid technical change has two advantages for the policy maker working within the constraints of the current political and social environment: it tends to reduce both the need for an expansionary monetary and fiscal policy, and the rate of price increase associated with any given unemployment rate.

As pointed out earlier, accelerated technical change probably spurs private investment more than private savings. For a given employment rate target it thus permits higher taxes or higher interest rates, or both. To the extent that the responsiveness of investment to interest rates is limited, maintaining full employment with slow technical progress may require a larger government deficit as a fraction of GNP. With a higher rate of technical progress, full employment may be possible with smaller deficits or even a surplus. This would be of minor significance except for the existence of political obstacles to sustained deficit financing or tax reductions in times of budget deficit. Relatively rapid technical progress reduces the need to confront this prejudice by reducing the need for large, continuing deficits.[34] If fiscal policy needs prove smaller, they may be more attainable. The 1964 tax reduction came several years after it was obviously warranted; had the government deficit been smaller, the cut almost certainly would have come earlier.

In addition, unemployment rate targets may be lowered without running into strong inflationary pressures in times of rapid technical progress. Such progress results in the shifting of final demands and frequently in a heavy concentration of demands in some sectors of the investment goods industries. Labor reallocation is required and demands may rise for skills with long preparation times. These factors in themselves should stimulate higher average price levels, considering the asymmetry of price responses, but ultimately they are likely to be outweighed by the cost reducing impact of rapid productivity growth. This, in turn, means that prices can be reduced, or, more realistically, that a more rapid rate of money wage increase can be accommodated while maintaining stable overall prices.[35]

If there are limits on the size of the government budget or deficit, and pressures on policy to prevent price increases, rapid technological advance may not be a threat to full employment, but a prerequisite for it.

[34] This assumes that the budget and deficit are measured relative to GNP. This assumption of rational perception may be an unwarranted excursion in benevolence. If Congressmen and their constituents think in absolute numbers, more rapid technical advance could compound stabilization problems.

[35] Defeatists maintain there is a learning process. In a full employment economy, unions will successfully and successively raise wage demands until they activate public resistance to price rises and deflationary policies. Productivity acceleration would then provide only a temporary breather, soon to be offset by wage acceleration. It is curious theory. If true, our current institutions and policy goals are quite incompatible.

7

False and Real Concerns About
Technological Progress

In concluding that labor markets are inherently quite flexible, and that technological advance normally tends to stimulate aggregate demand by at least as much as it increases productivity, Chapter 6 presented a basically optimistic summary of the relation between technical change and employment. While the record of adjustment in the past has been marred by unemployment and income losses, now the means are at hand to mitigate these difficulties. The new and pronounced willingness to use fiscal and monetary measures and labor market policy promises to inaugurate an era in which unprecedented income and employment security may be compatible with rapid technological changes.[1]

[1] The recent National Commission on Technology, Automation and Economic Progress Report, published since this manuscript was written, also appraises the relationship between technological change and employment. The Commission found: 1.) that appropriate use of fiscal-monetary policy could ensure a continuing compatibility between rapid technological progress and high levels of employment; 2.) that there was no evidence that the increasing demand for highly educated and skilled workers was generating structural imbalances in the labor market, and; 3.) that the evolution of private and public policies had done much to reduce the cost of adjustment for individual workers, but that there was considerable room for further progress. The Commission's recommendations in this area merit reading and serious consideration. See *Technology and the American Economy*, Vol. 1 (Washington: Government Printing Office, 1966).

A Historic Divide?

Some argue that such optimism is unwarranted; that in the future technical change will be radically different, thus creating a need for major new policy departures. Specifically, they predict that consumer desires will not keep pace with the rise in potential income, or that technological change is likely to take a sharply labor-saving direction, or that the amount of structural readjustment required by technological change will increase sharply.[2] This chapter will investigate and appraise these issues.

Satiation

So long as consumers continue to spend a relatively high proportion of their additional income on goods and services, generalized expansionary fiscal monetary policy can effectively stimulate output and employment. It would be quite a different matter if wants for goods and services were so well satisfied at existing income levels that latent demands were weak or nonexistent. If government fiscal actions were then to provide individuals with more income, the impact on real demand and hence on employment would be small. If private wants are approaching satiation,[3]

---

[2] William Fellner in his *Trends and Cycles in Economic Activity* (New York: Henry Holt & Co., 1956), and in other works, is concerned with the possibility that technological progress may become very capital saving (as well as with the possibility of too sharp a labor saving bias). A shift to capital saving bias would cause the same kinds of troubles as a slowdown of technological advance generally—a slowing down of the rate of growth of investment opportunities profitable at any given interest rate. The preceding chapter pointed out that this kind of difficulty can be dealt with effectively by fiscal-monetary policy, if consumption wants are not satiated.

[3] For instance, Charles C. Killingsworth states: "Look across the whole range of consumer goods and you will see that our mass consumption society has done a highly effective job of supplying the wants of the great majority of consumers. About 99.5 percent of the homes that are wired for electricity have electric refrigerators; 93 percent have television sets; 83 percent have electric washing machines; and we have even more radios than homes. The only sharply rising sales curve in the consumer durables field today is that of the electric can opener industry. The electric toothbrush and electric hairbrush industries are starting to grow rapidly too. But the growth of employment in these new industries will not offset the declines in the older, larger consumer goods industries.

"The doctrine that machines make jobs, to the extent that it rests on research

and if technical progress continues to raise potential output, it will then be necessary to heed those voices crying for a massive expansion of the public sector, or for a drastic shortening of the work week, or for a moratorium on technical change itself.[4]

But this would not appear a problem of the present or near future. Even though the American economy has been characterized as affluent, 1965 per capita annual disposable (after tax) income was only about $2,400. The average family had a money income of $6,900. This permits an unparalleled standard of living, but one which still falls considerably short of that retailed by the *Ladies' Home Journal,* or the other taste-makers of our society. It also falls short of permitting the cultivated and cosmopolitan life advocated by the critics of *Journal* culture. The continuing intensity of consumption desires is attested by the fact that consumers today spend more than 90 percent of their incomes on goods and service, a somewhat higher proportion than in the 1870's, although per capita real consumption has increased fivefold over the period.[5] If present income levels still leave many wants unmet for the average citizen, the gap is much greater for those with below-average incomes. Nor is there any reason to believe that individual wants will be satiated by income growth over the next few decades. Even if growth in output per man hour increased from its present rate of 3.0 percent a year to 4.0 percent a year (and if none of the benefits were taken in the form of ad-

rather than faith, is drawn primarily from studies of the periods 1899-1937 and 1899-1953. These were mainly years when the growth potential of most markets for goods was still very great. I think it is a major source of error to assume that the markets of our great mass-production industries will grow at the same prodigious rate in the second half of the 20th century that they achieved in the first . . . consider the basic causes for the booming prosperity which most of Western Europe and Japan are now enjoying. These countries are in the early growth stages of the mass-consumption society. . . . At their present rates of growth it will be several decades before they achieve our degree of saturation of markets. So automation is having a different impact there. "Automation, Jobs, and Manpower: The Case for Structural Unemployment" in Garth L. Magnum (ed.), *The Manpower Revolution: Its Policy and Consequences* (New York: Doubleday and Co., 1966).

[4] For an argument for the need for such policy departures, see Donald N. Michael, *Cybernation: The Silent Conquest* (Santa Barbara: Center for the Study of Democratic Institutions, 1962).

[5] *Annual Report of the Council of Economic Advisers* (part of *Economic Report of the President, January 1966*) (Washington: Government Printing Office, 1966), pp. 216, 227-28; and Simon Kuznets, *National Product Since 1896* (New York: National Bureau of Economic Research, 1946), p. 119.

ditional voluntary leisure), it still would take twenty years before average family income reaches $15,000.[6]

In the far future, preferences between leisure and goods may be very different. Annual family incomes will reach $50,000 in about seventy years at present rates of productivity growth, or sixty years at a 4 percent growth rate. For such a society, satiation of desire for material goods would be a definite possibility, but still far from a certainty. In any case, the society where wants are satiated, and additional output has little value, is currently far beyond reach.

Technical Advance and Real Wages

The increasing sophistication of production systems has inspired the vision of a world in which man cannot compete successfully against the machine, or can do so only by adopting rickshaw tactics and lowering his wages.[7] This will not transpire simply because technical advance reduces the cost or increases the productivity of machines. Historically, technical change has done just this, but so long as aggregate demand grew sufficiently to absorb the output produced by the labor force equipped with the new machines, the result was increased output, high returns to capital, and secularly rising real wages. Assume that the demand satiation problem is not present and fiscal and monetary measures prevent generalized excess supply. Then the fear of man succumbing economically to the machine will be realized only if technical change stimulates such a sharp substitution of machines for men that there is a decline in the demand for labor at existing real wage rates, even when demand is sufficient to keep the expanded and modernized capital stock fully utilized. The result will be either a fall in real wages, or unemployment, because at full employment the marginal productivity of labor would fall short of the wage rate, or both.

Assuming that with appropriate fiscal-monetary policy actual demand

[6] The average annual rate of increase in output per man hour in the private sector between 1955 and 1966 was computed on the basis of establishment data. Source: *Annual Report of the Council of Economic Advisers, January 1966, op. cit., p.* 245.

[7] For instance, Norbert Wiener states: "Let us remember that the automatic machine, whatever we think of any feelings it may have or may not have, is the precise economic equivalent of slave labor. Any labor which competes with slave labor must accept the economic conditions of slave labor." *The Human Use of Human Beings* (Boston: Houghton Mifflin Co., 1950).

grows in pace with potential output, whether or not the real wage rate compatible with full employment would be permanently depressed, depends on whether the physical quantity of capital expanded rapidly enough to offset the fact that each unit of capital is used with progressively less labor. Reductions in the marginal productivity of labor would persist only if the relative advantage of machines over labor grows more rapidly than the number of machines. If this happens, there would be a rise in the profit rate for new capital; if real wages fall, the profit rate must rise. Such a combination of events in unlikely to be long lived. If the interest rate is held constant and if investment is sufficiently responsive to differences between the rate of return on new investment and the interest rate, the economic system would, over the long run, respond to even very labor saving technological advance with a rapid growth in the number of machines, rather than with a fall in real wages or unemployment.[8]

But achievement of an adequately high machine-labor ratio might take a long time. In the interim, fiscal-monetary policy would have to cope with three tasks, somewhat similar to those facing underdeveloped economies which lack enough production facilities to employ their urban labor forces. First, sufficient demand would have to be maintained to secure full utilization of the existing capital stock, and of that portion of the labor force which it would use. Second, the expansion of capital must be encouraged, for only growth in the number of machines will permit full absorption of labor in the private sector. Third, employment would have to be found for excess labor; this would require government sponsored or subsidized programs of an extremely labor-intensive nature, like leaf raking.[9]

---

[8] It is assumed that technological advance results in an increase in potential output for any factor combination, and that the production function always is convex. Technological advance that permits output increases only at certain factor ratios, or which introduces non-convexities into the production function, would be consistent with lower real wages even when the capital stock expanded sufficiently to drive down the rate of return on capital to the preinnovation level. However, in general, technological advance should result in an outward shift in the factor price frontier for all factor proportions. See Paul Samuelson, "A New Theorem on Non Substitution" in Hugo Hegeland (ed.), *Money, Growth, and Methodology* (Lund, Sweden: C.W.K. Gleerup Publishers, 1961).

[9] However, even if the marginal product of labor falls off sharply on machinery currently in use at the existing number of shifts, an unprecedented rash of labor-saving innovations is still unlikely to make direct federal hiring of labor an absolute prerequisite for full employment. The existence of standby facilities in continu-

To date there has been no tendency for the situation just described to develop. The technical history of the past two centuries is largely the story of the substitution of machines for men in specific jobs. But with continuous growth in the amount of plant and equipment and in the level of demand, this substitution has occurred with rising real wages and without rising unemployment. There is no evidence that recent technical changes have differed from their generally benign predecessors. Recent decades have been marked by innovations like electronic control systems, high-speed cash registers, and the automatic cotton picker, which substitute machinery for labor. But there have also been innovations which have sharply reduced the amount of machinery needed to produce a unit of output, while having a lesser effect on labor requirements. Examples include the oxygen fuel converter, the installation of the electric motor in machine tools, the carbide tipped machine tool, microwave relay stations, and the use of the transistor in computers.

Thus, there is little reason to believe that computers are outcompeting people for jobs. However, since World War II, society appears to have institutionalized the expectation that real wages will rise annually and by at least several percent. Such expectations mean that a certain minimum pace and factor bias of technical change are now necessary for social and economic harmony. If technical change proceeds at the same pace, but becomes more laborsaving, it will produce more friction between workers and employers over wage increases, or unemployment, or inflation (or, more likely, all three).[10] The same thing will occur if technical change becomes slower, but continues to have the same laborsaving effect. Thus, technical change has become a necessary condition for low-friction collective bargaining.

---

ous process industries, and the ability to employ additional shifts in other industries, would seem to provide a buffer of important dimensions. But it would be necessary to generate enough demand to make the operations of second and third shifts profitable, and this would certainly entail considerable inflation.

[10] Under these circumstances, the wage-price guideposts of the Council of Economic Advisers, which are based on a moving average of average labor productivity, can give quite the wrong signal. If innovations become more labor saving, the profitability of new investment will increase. Profitability will be further augmented if real wages increase by the same rate as the average product of employed labor (which will be increasing more rapidly than the marginal product). The resulting substitution of capital for labor will raise the average product of employed labor still further. The guideposts will then allow for still higher real wage increases.

Technical Change and Structural Unemployment

Technical change can raise the marginal productivity of the overall labor force, but in an uneven and disruptive manner. The productivity of labor with certain types of education, skill, or experience can be sharply increased at the same time that the demand for other workers is being reduced. This worsened mismatching between workers and jobs is commonly characterized as a rise in structural unemployment.

If employer demands for different labor skills change rapidly, and if relative wages are not adjusted accordingly, there will be two major consequences. First, unemployment rates will be high among those workers whose skills have become unnecessary. Second, employers currently in the market for additional labor will generally have more difficulty finding the skills they need. Under these circumstances, overtime can be increased for currently employed workers, or wages can be raised to attract qualified workers from other firms, or from outside the labor force. Employers also can hire less qualified workers, either increasing training expenses or allowing quality standards to decline. Or, at some cost, jobs can be redesigned and simplified to make use of available skills.[11] Whatever approach employers follow in augmenting their work force, unit labor costs will rise. The higher costs involved in employing unsuitable labor, and in adopting other adjustments to localized shortages, are the heart of the structural unemployment problem.

A rise in structural unemployment is unlikely to require the extreme policy departures which might be needed if consumer satiation develops, or if technical change sharply reduces the marginal product of labor and creates capital bottlenecks. Higher structural unemployment can usually be remedied either by pursuing a more expansionary fiscal-monetary policy, or by increasing expenditure on labor market policy. Indeed, under virtually all conceivable circumstances, expansionary fiscal-mone-

---

[11] The dilution of job content in response to rising wage differentials or the protracted persistence of vacancies is nicely illustrated in the hospital industry. Rising work loads for resident physicians have resulted in greater responsibilities being assigned to interns. Some of the functions previously performed by interns were then transferred to professional nurses. This intensified an already rising demand for nurses. As a result, the traditional tasks of the professional nurse are now being performed by practical nurses or nursing aides, with the professional nurse functioning to a considerable extent as a foreman. Donald Yett, *"An Economic Analysis of the Nursing Shortage,"* mimeo.

tary policy by itself will be adequate. The expansion of demand will stimulate employers to incur the expenses of simplifying jobs and upgrading workers. As demand increases, incomes would rise most rapidly in labor shortage occupations, attracting new workers, encouraging others to retrain themselves, and motivating employers to expand training efforts. Changes in relative wages and prices would encourage the use of production techniques and the sale of products which employ high proportions of labor types which are in excess supply. Given public aversion to inflation, however, it may frequently be preferable to attack higher structural unemployment with a combination of fiscal and monetary measures and labor market policy.[12]

During the past decade there has been considerable concern that a rise in structural unemployment might in fact have occurred. This has been based on the recognition of two separate but related problems. The first concerns the difficulties confronting displaced blue collar workers in adjusting to a period of job expansion centering in white collar and service type activities.[13] The second is related to generally rising education-

[12] The exact mix of policy instruments will depend on the aversion of the society to inflation, and on the social rate of return on labor market policy. Increases in structural unemployment would be likely to result in significantly higher permanent levels of unemployment only if the society had little tolerance for price rises, and if the productivity of labor market policy were low.

In assessing policy choices, it is important to differentiate between permanent and "one-shot" increases in structural unemployment. A permanent rise in structural unemployment will increase the rate of change in labor costs per unit of time associated with any unemployment rate. This presumably will increase the rate of price change per period of time, and call for a compensatory policy mix consisting both of more expansionary fiscal-monetary policy and more labor market policy. In contrast, a "one-shot" rise in structural unemployment will affect the increase in labor cost experienced along the time-path to any lower unemployment rate, but will not affect the rate of change in labor cost normally associated with that unemployment rate. Fiscal-monetary policy will then be the preferred and normally the exclusive policy instrument, since it can remedy the situation at the cost of only a "one-shot" rise in prices. Most of the concern over higher structural unemployment has involved "one-shot" occurrences. See Edward D. Kalachek, "The Composition of Unemployment and Public Policy" in R. A. Gordon and Margaret Gordon (eds.), *Prosperity and Unemployment* (New York: John Wiley & Sons, 1966).

[13] See, for instance, "Statement of William McChesney Martin, Jr., Chairman, Board of Governors of the Federal Reserve System" and subsequent questioning and submissions in U.S. Congress, *January 1961 Economic Report Of The President And The Economic Situation and Outlook,* Hearings Before the Joint Economic Committee, 87 Cong. 1 sess. (Washington: Government Printing Office, 1961), pp. 462-501.

al requirements,[14] which raise the possibility that increasing shortages of highly educated or trained workers might coexist with growing surpluses of uneducated and low skilled workers.[15] These questions have been subjected to a number of statistical investigations, but little evidence has been found to indicate that structural unemployment has risen: indeed, there has been much evidence to contradict its occurrence.[16] More pragmatically satisfying is the evidence provided by the economic expansion which began in 1961. When unemployment fell in 1962 and again in 1964 and 1965 under the impact of expanding demand, blue collar workers, low skill workers, and those with relatively little educational background benefitted, and more than proportionately. By the spring of 1966, the unemployment rate was around 4.0 percent, below the 4.3 percent average for 1955-57, and unemployment of structurally vulnerable workers was generally about the same or lower than in 1955-57.[17]

The Education Problem

Higher structural unemployment, then, is not a contemporary problem. But the teasing question remains: in the future, are educational require-

[14] See, for instance, Charles C. Killingsworth, "Automation, Jobs, and Manpower: The Case for Structural Unemployment," in Garth L. Magnum (ed.), *The Manpower Revolution: Its Policy and Consequences* (New York: Doubleday and Co., 1966).

[15] In contrast, it is possible to argue that the major structural adjustment problems of the American economy are behind us. Today's most serious adjustment problems to a considerable extent represent the last stages of transition from a rural to an industrial and urban society. The Negro laborer and the white subsistence farmer, ejected from farming by advancing technology or attracted by higher urban incomes, bring with them a heritage of low educational attainment, nonexposure to industrial discipline, and lack of pecuniary attainment values. Their high job turnover and proneness to continuous bouts of unemployment may be due more to lack of flexibility and work orientation than to specific skill deficiency. Taking a long view, these problems may diminish as the farm-nonfarm shift is completed, as the country becomes more geographically integrated and as a higher proportion of its workers come within the orbit of urban educational systems and work values.

[16] See, for example, Edward D. Kalachek, *Higher Unemployment Rates, 1957-60; Structural Transformation or Inadequate Demand,* Subcommittee on Economic Statistics of the Joint Economic Committee, 87 Cong. 1 sess. (Washington: Government Printing Office, 1961); and Otto Eckstein, "Aggregate Demand and the Current Unemployment Problem," in Arthur M. Ross (ed.), *Unemployment and the American Economy* (New York: John Wiley & Sons, 1964).

[17] Data obtained from *Manpower Report of the President, March 1963* (Washington: Government Printing Office), and U.S. Department of Labor, Bureau of Labor Statistics, *Employment and Earnings,* Vol. 12, No. 7 (January 1966).

ments likely to outrun educational achievements, resulting in a seriously mismatched labor force? The preponderance of empirical evidence and theory both indicate that this is unlikely.

To begin with, the nation is experiencing a continuing rise in educational achievement of significant magnitude, proceeding, according to Denison, at 1.6 percent a year.[18] The young are increasingly spending longer periods of time in school. New labor force entrants average three and one-half more years of education than retirees. As a result, the median educational attainment of adult male labor force members has risen from slightly less than grammar school graduation in 1940 to slightly less than high school graduation in 1957, and to slightly more in 1964. At present only about 10 percent of the work force have college degrees.[19] During the next decade, perhaps 20 percent of new entrants will be college graduates. It would be unfortunate, indeed, if these highly educated workers could not find challenging jobs.

In contrast, the evidence on educational requirements is ambiguous. The advance in educational attainment cannot be fully explained by the growing importance of occupations which require advanced educational backgrounds. Eckaus estimates that changes in the occupational composition of the work force between 1940 and 1950 required only a 4 percent rise in average educational attainments, much less than the rise that was actually experienced.[20] Rising levels of education have primarily resulted in better educated workers in every occupation.

[18] More specifically, he estimates that the average total number of days of school attended by males twenty-five years of age or older will increase by 17.6 percent between 1960 and 1970. Edward F. Denison, *The Sources of Economic Growth in the United States and the Alternatives Before Us* (New York: Committee for Economic Development, 1962), p. 73.

[19] Denis F. Johnston, "Educational Attainment of Workers, March 1964," *Monthly Labor Review,* Vol. 88 (May 1965). U.S. Department of Labor, Bureau of Labor Statistics, Special Labor Force Report No. 53.

[20] Eckaus worked with Bureau of Employment Security data which summarized for 4,000 jobs the judgment of experienced labor market specialists on the amount of general educational competence required for average performance. He translated educational competence into conventional school years and the 4,000 jobs into 200 Census occupational categories (Richard S. Eckaus, "Economic Criteria for Education and Training," mimeo.). Working with nine major occupational categories, and with white males ages thirty-five to fifty-four, Folger and Nam found that about 85 percent of the rise in educational attainment between 1940 and 1950, and again between 1950 and 1960, could be attributed to increased educational levels within occupations. Only 15 percent could be attributed to shifts in the occupational structure from occupations requiring less to occupations requiring more education. John K. Folger and Charles B. Nam, "Trends in Education in

Such a pervasive rise in educational attainments is in large part a supply phenomenon. Jobs are being filled with better educated people simply because such people are available and are cheaper to train or otherwise more desirable than people with less education. Thus, average educational attainment rose for many occupations between 1950 and 1960, in the absence of any obvious increase in skill requirements.[21] Indeed, case studies of transitions to a new technology do not suggest any sharp or pervasive rise in requirements. These studies indicate that there are many innovations and many degrees of automaticity, which have quite different effects on labor requirements.[22] They are consonant with an overall rise in skill requirements, but one which is modest and not pervasive.[23]

Surely this, rather than revolutionary changes, is what should be expected. Knowledge of a process, and the need for knowledge to operate it, are often inversely related. As seen in Chapter 5, the introduction and early operation of new processes require highly trained and gifted people capable of decision making in an environment of uncertainty and imperfect knowledge. But the growth of understanding about particular processes, and the learning experiences of early use, ultimately lead to specialization of function and subdivision of labor. As knowledge progresses, it results in routinized and mechanized processes capable of being easily operated. The early ranks of computer programmers included a high proportion of Ph.D. mathematicians; today, high school graduates are being hired. During the early stage of transistors chemical engineers were required to constantly supervise the vats where crystals

Relation to the Occupational Structure," *Sociology of Education,* Vol. 38 (Fall 1964).

[21] For instance, the median number of school years completed by glaziers rose from 9.7 to 10.6 and by railroad switchmen from 9.9 to 11.1. *Ibid.,* p. 32.

[22] See, for example, Kenneth G. Van Auken, Jr., "Personnel Adjustments to Technological Change," and William A. Faunce, "The Automobile Industry: A Case Study in Automation," in Howard B. Jacobson and Joseph S. Roucek (eds.), *Automation and Society* (New York: Philosophical Library, 1959); U.S. Department of Labor, Bureau of Labor Statistics, *Impact of Automation,* Bulletin No. 1287 (Washington: Government Printing Office, 1960); and James R. Bright, *Automation and Management* (Boston: Harvard Business School, Division of Research, 1958).

[23] Even a gradually rising skill level could ultimately result in a situation where the least skilled job available required education and training exceeding the genetic capacities of a substantial portion of the labor force. But there is no reason to believe that point is near; nor need it ever be reached if teaching skills improve rapidly enough.

were grown. As processes were perfected, they were replaced by workers with less education. All along, then, the development of new processes will be raising skill requirements while the perfection of old ones will be lowering them.

Additionally, following the principles discussed in Chapter 2, growing relative shortages of highly skilled labor and surpluses of unskilled labor will encourage technical changes which reduce skill requirements. James Bright observes, "Machinery manufacturers cannot sell equipment on any large scale if extraordinary skills are required to operate or maintain it. . . . Thus, there is continual effort by the machine designer to simplify the operation and maintenance requirements of complicated machinery and there is an unpredictable but steady downgrading of operator skill requirements through machinery improvement in many instances."[24]

It is thus quite reasonable to expect that workers with less than a high school education will be readily able to obtain jobs in the future, if an adequate level of overall demand is maintained. As always, workers with less than average educational attainment will continue to earn less than average incomes, and experience above average unemployment whenever overall demand is deficient. If the nation is concerned with achieving higher relative incomes for the poorly educated, direct or indirect income transfers must be instituted to achieve that objective.

Technological change, then, is unlikely to pose any severe long-range problems. The nation may have reached a historic divide, but not one at which the effects of progress will become more pernicious. Rather, it is likely that a set of policies and a general economic flexibility have been achieved which are capable of reconciling rapid and uneven technological progress with a high degree of personal economic security.

There remain, however, real reasons for concern about the adequacy of the nation's adjustment to technological advance, but the difficulties are of a different sort than those usually stressed.

Technical Change and the Social Framework

Adjustment to technical change involves far more than the reallocation of capital and labor, and the maintenance of adequate effective demand. If properly designed, political and social institutions can remain unchanged for centuries, so long as technology is constant also. But new

---

[24] *Ibid.,* p. 189.

products and new processes give rise to new problems and require new legislation, public functions, and modes of thought. It frequently is not appreciated that technical change requires a continuing reappraisal of the laws and institutions by which a society governs itself.

The requirement for labor flexibility, and the sensitivity of the economy to changes in aggregate demand-supply balance, are largely the results of technological change. A century and a half ago, families and communities were much more self-sufficient than today. A typical family provided a significant share of its needs directly with its own labor and most of the rest was provided through sale of products or service to the local community, or through employment in a small business firm selling to the local community. Incomes were used mostly to buy locally produced goods and services. This way of life was ended by technological advances which required a far greater division of labor and specialization of firms and regions.

Today the typical American earns his livelihood working in a large impersonal organization that sells its products on a geographically large —often national—market, and spends his income on products produced in all corners of the country and the world. In contrast with a century and a half ago when a man's ability to earn a livelihood depended almost totally on the value of his effort in his local community, today his livelihood is in considerable part dependent upon the demand for goods and services—and hence for labor—in the economy as a whole. While formerly a local community had the economic wherewithal, and the economic autonomy, to take care of its own, this is no longer the case. The need for social security, unemployment compensation, compensatory fiscal and monetary policies, and similar programs follows directly from these developments, though the appropriate institutions and ways of thinking evolved quite slowly.

While the evolution of social policies and institutions now has gone a long way toward making personal economic security consistent with rapid technological progress, other kinds of institutional adjustment have lagged badly.

Innovations Create Problems

Often the full potential of an innovation cannot be exploited without new legislation or institutions. It may have side-effects on health, safety, convenience or aesthetics which can be treated only by community action. For example, the invention of the automobile required social decisions on the mechanisms and institutions by which suitable roads would be built; the market system could not deal with that problem. The building of roads upset the status quo everywhere, and created a new host of policy problems. Mechanisms for the establishment and enforcement of speed limits, safety standards, and other regulations had to be developed to ensure safety of communities through which the automobile traveled. Land use patterns were greatly altered, creating the need for policies which would reconcile the general desire for rapid automobile transportation with the goals of preserving attractive natural areas and maintaining pleasant living environments. The nation has only begun to appreciate the magnitude of these problems and the necessity for working out effective solutions.

With the development of new construction materials and designs, certain building codes which once served to protect against shoddy construction have become obstacles to improved or lower cost housing. The development of sophisticated chemical products has created the need for public agencies to investigate their direct and indirect impacts, regulate their use, and ensure public awareness of hazards. The airplane brought in its wake the need for protection against the intrusion of offensive noises. The technologically-induced increase in life expectancy has combined with the technologically-induced isolation of older people and now poses serious problems for the elderly who face, on the average, over a decade of retirement often spent alone, and at reduced incomes. Only recently have increased social security payments and medicare been instituted to deal with the financial side of this problem. The psychological aspect still is untouched.

Although it is sometimes convenient to specify certain dimensions of performance as "economic" and others as "non-economic," this split is highly arbitrary. The production of automobiles, houses, insecticides and airplanes can be quantified in dollar terms and registered in the market place. The losses which result from ignoring aesthetics in land use, noisy environments, the failure of consumers to understand the hazards of some chemicals, and the lethargy with which society deals with the less pleasant consequences of longer life spans, are less susceptible to quantification, but are equally real. An economic system should be judged by how it affects the lives of its citizens, and not by how well it maximizes money profits or measured output.

The record of institutional adjustment is spotty. It has been best when public policy action has been required to permit the full private exploitation of profit opportunities opened by technical advance. Highways have been built, airports established, and building codes altered, albeit somewhat slowly.

Adjustment has been far less satisfactory in dealing with the personal insecurities and external diseconomies generated by technical change, and with all those factors not readily quantifiable into private pecuniary profit. In part this has been due to a readily understandable failure to predict not easily predictable occurrences. In part, it is also due to a lethargy in response, and a naively fatalistic belief that the destruction of amenities is the price of progress. But it is also due to the fact that strong interest groups generally are connected with particular products, and there are few effective lobbies for the general non-pecuniary welfare. Only after a long lag were the dangers of insecticides investigated by the government and communicated to the public. While much progress has been made, in many areas industrial plants still are permitted to manufacture smog, and highway engineers still select road routes on the basis of minimum land costs. The noise problem generated by airplanes is still largely ignored.

Institutional flexibility is as important as labor or capital flexibility in determining the costs and benefits of technical advances. Unfortunately, social institutions have proved less flexible than tangible resources. American society has not learned how to rapidly update its control mechanism so as to better reconcile technical advance and the quantifiable aspects of progress with other facets of the good and safe life. To an alarming extent, society is not even aware of the problem.[25]

[25] Hopefully the report of the National Commission on Technology, Automation, and Economic Progress, op. cit., is a sign of a newly developing public and governmental appreciation of the problems and opportunities resulting from technological change, and consequently may indicate a shortening of the lag in adjusting social institutions to new technologies. Among other things, the Commission advocated that we cope with the current lag by allocating increased resources, particularly research effort, to the unmet "human and community" needs associated with growing urbanization. Further, and perhaps more importantly, its proposals for developing a social accounting system which takes cognizance of externalities, and for establishing "some national body of distinguished private citizens . . . concerned with 'monitoring' social change, forecasting possible social trends, and suggesting policy alternatives to deal with them" would treat with the generalized lag problem.

PART III

Policy Issues

8

Existing Public Policies and Institutions

The stage now is set for an examination of public policy. This chapter considers the arsenal of governmental institutions and programs that influence the rate, direction, and effectiveness of technological advance.

Present governmental policies are vast and heterogeneous. Most prominent are the R&D spending programs of the various government agencies, listed in Table VIII-1. In addition there are many programs supporting technical information services, and the education and training of scientists, engineers and technicians; the Atomic Energy Commission (AEC), National Science Foundation (NSF), National Aeronautics and Space Agency (NASA), and the Departments of Defense, Health, Education and Welfare, Commerce, Interior, and Agriculture all have such programs. Other policies and programs are intended to structure the system of constraints and incentives which face private organizations and individuals in the technological advance process: for example, the patent system and certain aspects of the tax code. Still others, such as support of general education or regulatory actions, also influence inventors and innovators, although this is not their principal objective.

In trying to influence technical advance, the government has had two broad objectives. The first is to create advances needed by governmental agencies in performing specific functions. The second is to stimulate progress to benefit either a particular private sector or the economy as a whole.

151

TABLE VIII-1. *Federal Expenditures on R&D, Fiscal 1964*

(In millions of dollars)

Agency and Subdivision	Expenditures
Total, All Agencies	13,649.8
Department of Agriculture, Total	178.4
Agricultural Research Service	98.4
Cooperative State Research Service	41.5
Economic Research Service	9.8
Farmer Cooperative Service	.7
Forest Service	27.4
National Agricultural Library	*
Statistical Reporting Service	.5
Department of Commerce, Total	53.4
Area Redevelopment Administration	.7
Bureau of the Census	1.8
Bureau of Public Roads	4.2
Coast and Geodetic Survey	2.2
Maritime Administration	7.5
National Bureau of Standards	23.3
Office of Business Economics	2.0
Patent Office	.6
Transportation Research	.9
Weather Bureau	10.2
Department of Defense, Total	7,432.9
Department of the Army	1,394.8
Department of the Navy	1,715.1
Department of the Air Force	3,917.9
Defense Agencies, n.e.c.	384.0
Departmentwide Funds	21.1
Department of Health, Education, and Welfare, Total	746.9
Food and Drug Administration	6.3
Office of Education	12.7
Public Health Service	705.5
National Institutes of Health	638.0
Saint Elizabeth's Hospital	.3
Social Security Administration	1.8
Vocational Rehabilitation Administration	15.8
Welfare Administration	4.5

Source: National Science Foundation, *Federal Funds for Research, Development, and Other Scientific Activities*, Vol. 14 (Washington: Government Printing Office, 1965), pp. 78–79.
n.e.c. Not elsewhere classified.
* Less than $50,000.

TABLE VIII-1. (*continued*)

Agency and Subdivision	Expenditures
Department of the Interior, Total	92.3
Bonneville Power Administration	.3
Bureau of Commercial Fisheries	18.5
Bureau of Land Management	.4
Bureau of Mines	25.5
Bureau of Outdoor Recreation	.1
Bureau of Reclamation	1.8
Bureau of Sport Fisheries and Wildlife	11.6
Geological Survey	21.9
National Park Service	1.5
Office of Coal Research	2.4
Office of Saline Water	8.3
Office of Water Resources Research	
Department of Labor, Total	7.2
Bureau of Apprenticeship and Training	.1
Bureau of Employment Security	1.0
Bureau of Labor Standards	.3
Bureau of Labor Statistics	2.3
Office of Labor Management Policy Development	.1
Office of Manpower, Automation, and Training	2.1
Wage and Hour and Public Contracts Division	1.1
Women's Bureau	.2
Post Office Department	7.1
Department of State, Total	3.2
Departmental Funds	.1
Agency for International Development	3.0
Department of the Treasury, Total	2.2
Bureau of Engraving and Printing	.4
United States Coast Guard	1.8
Other Agencies, Total	5,126.3
Advisory Commission on Intergovernmental Relations	.2
Atomic Energy Commission	1,236.0
Civil Aeronautics Board	.1
Civil Service Commission	.1
Federal Aviation Agency	62.7
Federal Communications Commission	.3
Federal Home Loan Bank Board	.1
Federal Trade Commission	.2
Housing and Home Finance Agency	.1

TABLE VIII-1. (*continued*)

Agency and Subdivision	Expenditure
Library of Congress	.1
National Aeronautics and Space Administration	3,637.2
National Science Foundation	140.7
Office of Emergency Planning	.3
Peace Corps	.3
Small Business Administration	.4
Smithsonian Institution	4.5
Tennessee Valley Authority	5.1
United States Arms Control and Disarmament Agency	5.0
United States Information Agency	.6
Veterans Administration	32.3

Technology for the Public Sector

The largest of the government R&D spending programs are primarily intended to provide new or improved technology for public sector functions. In 1964 more than 75 percent of the federal R&D budget of roughly $13.7 billion was spent through the Department of Defense (DOD) to advance technology relevant to national security.[1] The AEC and NASA together accounted for 15 percent more, much of it related to national security. Other R&D programs seek to improve government provisions for veterans, protect the public health, protect the public from impure foods and dangerous drugs and medicines, support the construction and maintenance of public facilities, like roads and airports, improve air safety, and run the postal system. In all of these areas, the government is charged with performing a function, and research and development is undertaken to permit it to perform more efficiently.[2]

The need for government undertaking or supporting this kind of R&D was recognized early.[3] Responsibility to establish standards for weight

[1] National Science Foundation, *Federal Funds for Research, Development, and other Scientific Activities,* Vol. 14 (Washington: Government Printing Office, 1965). Unless otherwise noted, all government R&D expenditure figures cited in this chapter are from this source.

[2] For a discussion of government R&D programs see National Science Foundation, *Federal Organization for Scientific Activities, 1962* (Washington: Government Printing Office, 1963).

[3] The basic background history of the evolution of policy is A. Hunter Dupree, *Science in the Federal Government; A History of Policies and Activities to 1940* (Cambridge: Belknap Press of Harvard University Press, 1957).

and measures written into the Constitution obviously implied, and soon led to, a small research effort in the Treasury Department. Coast and inland surveys and explorations were financed or undertaken by the Navy and Army to enable them better to protect the country. The army arsenals engaged in R&D on new weapons. Responsibility for public health and for the health of the armed forces soon led to medical research at the federal maritime and army hospitals. But as late as 1935 total federal expenditures on R&D amounted to less than $125 million, only a quarter of the national total. The dominant role of public sector R&D dates from the defense needs of World War II.[4]

Internal Versus External Sources of R&D

Of course, the fact that a federal agency has a responsibility for a function does not mean that it must conduct or support all of the R&D relevant to its needs. The government is in much the same position as a business firm which produces goods and services. In some instances it must conduct or finance its own R&D. In other instances, suppliers or potential suppliers will finance it, motivated by the expectation of selling the results to the government.

Outside the defense related areas and the nuclear energy field, the government relies heavily on its suppliers to finance the relevant R&D. While there are many non-defense public sector R&D programs, most of them are quite small. In 1963 the total federal expenditure on them was roughly $1 billion, about half of this in the field of health. State and local government R&D spending was negligible. Yet federal, state, and local expenditures on goods and services for non-defense functions amounted to some $70 billion, the major items being education, public health, safety and sanitation, highway and public utility construction and operation, and natural resource development and management.

The low level of R&D spending by the non-defense public agencies has many aspects in common with most consumer goods industries. In both cases, many inputs are purchased from other sectors which are more R&D intensive. A high proportion of the products and materials utilized by the non-defense public sector, such as building materials, typewriters, automobiles and trucks, are not specialized to it and are

[4] Nestor Terleckyj, *Research and Development: Its Growth and Composition* (New York: National Industrial Conference Board, 1963).

purchased on competitive markets. To the extent the government is a discriminating consumer with a sharp eye to relative cost and quality of competing products, government demand, like private demand, provides incentive for private R&D.

However, as in the private sector, a government agency cannot rely totally on its suppliers and other sources of R&D. In certain cases the public agency or the business firm must do or support the R&D itself, even if it has strong suppliers.

With new, technically complex products, being a discriminating consumer generally requires research both for evaluation and for identification of profitable uses. The General Services Administration and the National Bureau of Standards provide this kind of service for federal government agencies, but some carry on their own research efforts to make them more effective consumers.

If the agency needs confidential or specialized information, it must finance or do work itself. Since information is an awkward commodity to sell, private companies have little initiative to do the R&D on their own. The Food and Drug Administration conducts research relevant to determining drug and food safety and effectiveness. The Bureau of Public Roads conducts research on highway design. The need for specialized knowledge blurs into the more general motivation of many government agencies to advance knowledge in fields of their interest more rapidly than would otherwise occur; the R&D grants by the National Institutes of Health on various public health problems and the programs of the Forestry Service on soil chemistry are good examples. Here, government agencies have been unwilling to rely on such R&D as would be done without federal support and have supplemented the external R&D with their own programs.

Finally, where quite specialized equipment is needed or where there are considerable gains to be made from significantly modifying general purpose equipment for special governmental uses, the government usually has to provide much of the funds for R&D. While being an aggressive and receptive consumer will stimulate some private effort, private suppliers naturally are reluctant to invest in an uncertain and expensive project which, if successful, will have only a single and often capricious potential buyer. Further, in many such cases the government agency has a better perception of its needs than a supplier, and this itself warrants a closer guidance of the direction of R&D. Thus, the Post Office supports

R&D on postal sorting equipment, the Office of Saline Water on various desalinization systems, and the Federal Aviation Agency on air safety equipment. The major examples, however, are in the field of defense and space.

As with a business firm, the extent to which a government agency can count on others to support the R&D it needs, and the extent to which it must do the conducting or supporting itself, varies from case to case. Apart from the national security and health areas, however, government decision makers explicitly or implicitly assume that the needs of the public sector for new products and processes generally are similar to those of the private sector, and that where they are dissimilar, private R&D organizations have incentive to try to meet them. With few exceptions, government R&D is limited to small in-house applied research programs to keep the agency up to date and to deal with special problems. Recently there have been strong suggestions that in many public sector areas the premises on which this minimum scale policy are based are faulty, and that the government should support R&D in the same spirit and with the same vigor as in defense, although, of course, on a smaller scale.[5]

The Polar Case of Defense

Before World War II, national security research needs were met in much the same way as in the rest of the public sector. Government defense R&D spending was low—less than $100 million in 1935—and a considerable portion of the work was undertaken in army arsenals and navy facilities.[6] The primary effort was obtained by stating requirements to stimulate business firms to invest their own funds in the hope of selling the device or component or system to a service. The Army Air Corps had a policy of avoiding direct financing of R&D in private companies wherever possible, and buying privately developed aircraft and engines.[7] Today in-house facilities still play an important role, and some

[5] See Richard R. Nelson, "The Allocation of Research and Development Resources: Some Problems of Public Policy," *Economics of Research and Development* (Columbus: Ohio State University Press, 1965), and *Report of the Committee on the Economic Impact of Defense and Disarmament, July 1965* (Washington: Government Printing Office, 1965).

[6] Terleckyj, *op. cit.*

[7] For a discussion see Robert O. Schlaifer and S. D. Heron, *The Development of Aircraft Engines and Fuels* (Boston: Harvard University Graduate School of Business Administration, Division of Research, 1950).

military R&D still is drawn through the demand route, but the bulk is achieved through DOD contracts with business firms. The AEC, which conducts both military and civilian oriented research, utilizes a hybrid—government owned facilities operated under contract by non-profit institutions and business firms.

The special characteristics of defense requirements account for the predominance of government support. Since World War II the payoffs from rapid advances in defense hardware have become very high, and the costs of not possessing the advanced equipment potentially catastrophic. The sharply intensified pressure for major advances has greatly increased the expected R&D costs and the risks of failure; the development of the Atlas missile cost over $3 billion.

At the same time, defense-related hardware has become so highly specialized that DOD is the sole, or at least the overwhelmingly dominant, buyer. Even if a private company succeeds in developing a first-rate product on its own, the product might not fit current defense needs as perceived by the DOD, and would have little or no civilian value.

As a result, the Department of Defense has been forced to finance its R&D input. DOD has utilized contractors rather than government laboratories partly because the very size of the R&D budget raises political resistance to a substantial expansion of government employment and partly because of belief in the innate advantages of private operations. NASA and AEC are in comparable positions of requiring specialized R&D which is financed from agency funds. NASA has relied on contractors though its own laboratories (inherited from NACA and the Army) have played an important role. The AEC has utilized contractors to operate government owned facilities.

These agencies also have had to finance a large share of the more fundamental research in fields that underlie the technology of their systems. Thus DOD, AEC, and NASA account for over 60 percent of total basic research support provided by the federal government. The achievement of rapid and major advances in systems performance would be impossible in the absence of forced feeding of the relevant sciences.

Support of General and Private Sector R&D

Several important federal programs, although in part designed to create technology for use in the public sector, also seek to stimulate technological advance for general or private sector use. The NASA program and the civilian applications programs of the AEC are the most prominent examples. In addition, there is a small but important sub-group of government programs, which have little to do directly with public sector technology. The R&D support programs of the National Science Foundation and the Department of Agriculture cannot be justified on the grounds of government responsibility to provide a particular service. The patent system or the treatment of the proceeds of sales of patents as capital gains cannot be so justified.

These public policies recognize that, for certain kinds of activities essential to technical progress, external economies and uncertainties tend to drive a wedge between private incentive and social return, and for others scale requirements may dwarf the capabilities of unaided private initiative. To compensate, policies have evolved to increase private incentives, or to increase private capabilities. In a few cases the government itself has taken responsibility for a large share of the R&D effort to stimulate technological advance for general or private sector use.

Increasing Returns to Invention and Innovation

In the absence of some public policy mechanism, the private returns to invention and innovation in many cases would tend to be far less than the social returns. If imitation were inexpensive and could proceed quickly and without legal hindrance, as soon as the innovating firm had designed, developed, and introduced a new product, other firms would be able to produce identical products and quickly drive down the profit. The same conditions that reduce incentive also reduce pressure. A firm need not fear that other firms will make its product obsolete through R&D, if it can quickly and cheaply imitate their designs.

Of course, in many cases imitation is not costless; effective imitation, just as the original R&D, may take considerable money and time. Often the information carried by the product itself is far from sufficient to permit imitation. Much of the relevant knowledge may pertain to production processes; this was true of nylon and the transistor. Often this kind of knowledge can be kept secret for a considerable time. Sometimes, even if the knowledge is easily available to a competing company, considerable time and expense will be required to train labor, obtain the relevant capital equipment, and gain effective access to the market. The cost of imitating relative to the cost of the original R&D obviously varies from case to case, as does the lead time of the innovator. However, if a head start defended by secrecy were the only advantage, in many instances there would be little incentive for invention and innovation.

A variety of instruments of public policy can enable a firm to capture a larger share of the benefits it creates through invention and innovation, and thus tip the balance towards initiating rather than imitating. For example, Alexander Hamilton proposed that the federal government award grants or prizes for important inventions.[8] While occasionally the U.S. has granted funds to inventors for demonstration and tests of their inventions (Morse and the telegraph is a good example), the problem of how to select inventors and inventions has scotched serious consideration of this idea as a general incentive mechanism. Similarly, proposals that business tax rates be lowered on the profits from products invented or introduced by the company have not been adopted because of the difficulty of defining new products and separating such profits from others.

The patent system has been the principal social device for increasing the returns to invention and innovation. The grant of a temporary monopoly right to the inventor goes far back in history and was carried to the American colonies from England. The Constitution makes specific provision that, "The Congress shall have the power . . . to promote the progress of science and useful arts, by securing for limited times to authors and inventors the exclusive rights to their respective writings and discoveries." Congress responded by passing a patent act in 1790. Subsequent legislation has revised and codified the system and precedent and practices have evolved but the basic mechanism has not changed significantly.

The patent system raises the returns to invention and innovation by increasing the cost and difficulties of imitation. It makes private property out of what otherwise would, in the absence of secrecy, be in the public domain.[9]

The prospect of a patent, however, provides greater incentive for certain kinds of R&D than for others. It probably adds little to a company's

---

[8] See Dupree, *loc, cit.*

[9] For a survey of economic analysis regarding the patent system see Fritz Machlup, *An Economic Review of the Patent System, Study of the Subcommittee on Patents, Trademarks, and Copyrights of the Senate Committee on the Judiciary,* 85 Cong. 2 sess. (Washington: Government Printing Office, 1958).

incentive to improve its own processes or make its existing products more attractive. Improved processes often can be kept secret for some time, and even with the possibility of patenting it often is difficult to find out and prove that other companies are using a particular process. Furthermore, the cost of doing the original R&D for minor product improvement may not greatly exceed the cost of imitating.

The prospect of being able to block imitation, however, undoubtedly greatly raises the incentives for major new product invention and innovation. It is difficult to conceive of Goodyear spending as much time and effort trying to improve rubber, of Edison pushing as hard his expensive work on the electric light system, or Du Pont spending money so fast on the development of nylon, if the only advantages to be won were a place in history and the temporary financial advantages of being first.

The stimulus provided by the patent system to inventive activity varies with the institution doing the work. Without patent protection, the gains to a large manufacturing company from inventive activity in the fields of its marketing and production competence would be smaller. However, if the work is relatively cheap or permits a significant head start, strong incentives would still exist. According to Scherer a high percentage of executives of large companies said that even without the prospects of patents, there still would be considerable R&D in their product lines.[10] However, for an independent inventor or for a small company that can produce or sell only at a limited rate, the legal property right on an invention may be the only thing that enables a profit to be made. An inventor cannot interest a company in using his invention unless he partially discloses it, but this disclosure may be sufficient to permit the company easily to re-invent his invention. A small company may have a head start, but if it can only build up production and sales slowly this may not provide much profit before vigorous competition begins. The major role played by private inventors and small companies in many fields was described earlier. In many instances, this group did the original work and then sold or licensed patent rights. This broadening of the incentive to invent is one of the most important social benefits of the patent system.

These benefits do not come without cost. Like any other policy to increase the returns to invention and innovation—for example, the

[10] Frederic M. Scherer, *et al., Patents and the Corporation* (Boston: J. J. Galvin, 1958).

granting of prizes or tax credits—the patent system involves a transfer of income from the general public or a subgroup of the public to successful innovators. However, unlike the financing of prizes out of tax revenues, the transfer of income is hidden. Rather than tapping public tax revenues, the patent system effects the income transfer by granting the inventor a monopoly right. While the public treasury is short-circuited, the transfer of income is just as real, although it may come from potential competitors or subgroups of consumers rather than the public at large. There are additional costs as well, because the patent holder generally has the opportunity to charge higher prices or otherwise restrict use. Knowledge of how to make a better product, or use a better production process is intrinsically a public good. Unlike the use of the time of a skilled laborer or of a machine, use by one person of knowledge does not mean that some other use necessarily must be foregone. It is in the social interest that existing knowledge be free for use wherever it may be of positive social value. In contrast, it is in the interest of a particular producer to limit the use of knowledge so as to give it a scarcity value. But society would be better off if it could award the inventor a prize, comparable to the profits from the patent, in return for unrestricted use. Granting a private right to exclude inherently is a socially inefficient way to reward the creation of a new public good.

The inefficiencies and, indeed the dangers, of granting private monopoly rights are particularly great if an individual, a company, or a small group of companies, gain a stranglehold on a major field of technology. Such a development may frustrate the very purposes of the patent system by negating its two most important benefits: stimulating major product innovation and broadening the sources of invention. If a patent position becomes so strong that potential competitors despair of being able to compete in the future, the result may be not just a monopolist, but a monopolist with little competitive pressure and limited outside sources of ideas. Discussion with several prominent private inventors, and with presidents of technically progressive small firms, has revealed a great reluctance on their part to try to invent in areas where the market is limited to one or two firms. Thus, over the long run, the effect of a dominant patent may be to slow significantly the pace of technological progress.

Despite its inherent limitations, no realistic total substitute for the patent system has yet been proposed. The principal debate regarding the patent system has been in terms of how it should be revised to work better.[11] A presidential commission has been appointed to explore this question.

Government Support of Science and Technology

The patent system is not the only string in the government's bow; over the years the patent system has been supplemented in many ways and for many purposes.

The early ventures of the federal government into the support of activities creating knowledge of widespread use were associated with a public sector need.[12] While the Lewis and Clark expedition and, later, the Coast Survey were motivated in large part by the needs of the Army and Navy, they resulted—and were intended to result—in knowledge of widespread use. Out of these early surveys grew the present continuing Coast and Geodetic Survey. In the 1830's and 1840's the government financed research and experiments on safe construction of boilers and, later, a Naval Observatory was established. Again, while a principal motivation was military need and public safety, these programs were expected to and did create knowledge of general utility—the information provided by the Observatory enabled significant reductions in merchant ship voyage time. From these beginnings have come today's institutions and programs where a general public interest or private sector need is strong or dominant.

If we look at current institutions we find three main groups differentiated by motivation and scope. In the first are programs and institutions trying to achieve rapid rates of technological advance in certain

[11] For a provocative proposal see Michael Polanyi, "Patent Reform," *Review of Economic Studies,* Vol. 11 (Summer 1944).

[12] During the Constitutional Convention there were proposals for a national university to provide, among other things, education in the sciences, and for laboratories and institutes to support and undertake scientific research and to disseminate technical and scientific information. These were to complement and supplement the patent system, increasing the capability for invention and innovation by subsidizing the inputs. Such ideas failed to gain a place in the final constitution. While the power of Congress to allot funds to the support of science and education was not excluded—indeed, some thought it was implicit in the broad mandate to advance the general welfare—it was not explicit; and, with the establishment of the patent system, federal policies to advance the scientific and technical base of the nation developed slowly and haltingly.

The principal reference is Dupree, *loc. cit.*

fields where the public interest is believed to transcend private incentives; health and aviation are good examples. These areas tend to lie in the grey region between private and public sector. In the second are policies designed to support R&D in industries like agriculture, where smallness of firm size is judged to result in weak capabilities. The third includes programs aimed at broad scale support for certain kinds of activities, like basic research and scientific education, instead of being focused on a particular area of technology or an industry group.[13]

The most important programs in the first group are those of the Public Health Service, NASA, and the civilian applications programs of the AEC. The support of medical and biological science and technology by the Public Health Service was originally justified by the obvious public mandate to prevent the spread of communicable diseases and gradually broadened into a responsibility to conduct and support basic and applied research in health and medicine across the board, as well as support of university training and education. During the 1930's these trends culminated in the establishment of the National Institutes of Health (NIH). In 1964 NIH undertook over $100 million of research in its own laboratories, and provided over $500 million in grants, mostly for basic research at universities, often at medical schools. It was the dominant source of R&D support in the field of health, spending more than double the outlays of the drugs and medicine companies. Clearly, the judgment has been made that the socially desired quantity and scope of health and medical research cannot be brought forth by private incentive and philanthropy alone.

In 1912 the National Advisory Committee on Aeronautics (NACA) was created to spur and facilitate the development of American aviation. During its heyday in the thirties, NACA operated laboratories and facilities that played a major role in the development of civil as well as military aviation in the United States. NACA pioneered in the development and operation of R&D facilities for general use—wind tunnels, for example—in information collection and dissemination, and in basic research and exploratory development. It undertook major work on aircraft streamlining, design of parts of engines, properties of fuels,

[13] The following discussion draws heavily on Dupree, *loc. cit.*; NSF, *Federal Organization for Scientific Activities, loc. cit.*; and Don K. Price, *Government and Science, Their Dynamic Relation in American Democracy* (New York: New York University Press, 1954).

structural aspects of aircraft design, building and testing all kinds of experimental hardware.

With the growing R&D effort of the Air Force after World War II, and the consequent major expansion of the R&D facilities of private companies, NACA was no longer the primary supporter and undertaker of far-reaching R&D in the field of aviation. In 1958 it passed out of existence as a separate entity and became a nucleus for the new National Aeronautics and Space Administration, whose mission included space and space exploration, as well as aviation. The shift from the mission of NACA to that of NASA involved a larger scope and a major increase in the size and complexity of the research program. The relevant research fields which can be justified as permitting or facilitating space exploration are as broad as the entire spectrum of science. As a result, by 1962 NASA was by far the largest government supporter of basic research, providing nearly half of the federal total. It spent three times more on basic research than the second largest supporter, the Department of Defense. It provided four times more basic research funds than the National Science Foundation. However, while NSF funds for basic research went principally to universities, NASA's funds were spent largely in industry, or in special research centers.

In 1946 the Atomic Energy Commission was established to advance the nuclear sciences and technologies for military applications and public use. The AEC supports work ranging from the creation of prototype peacetime power reactors and research on the uses of radioactive isotopes to basic research in physics, chemistry, and biology. It also provides a large number of scholarships and fellowships and assists colleges and universities to improve their educational programs in relevant fields, and serves as a major technical information center. The AEC is far and away the largest federal supporter of basic research in physics.

These three major R&D programs—NIH, NASA, and AEC—account for over 80 percent of non-DOD R&D spending. Each is aimed at providing strong stimulus and support for the rapid advancement of a particular area of technology. Part of the motivation is to stimulate technology relevant to a public sector, such as the prevention of epidemics or defense; part is the recognition that major advances in product performance and quality in the fields yield benefits that transcend private profit calculations.

In the second group are a smaller set of programs which are motivated more by the weakness of R&D capabilities in certain industries than by the potential significance of social returns. The federal program of support of agricultural R&D typifies this group.[14] Support of agricultural research, experimentation, and information dissemination long preceded the establishment of a Department of Agriculture. During the 1830's and 1840's a limited amount of work, including the operation of an experimental farm, was undertaken under the auspices of the patent office. The passing of the Morrill Act in 1862 and the establishment of the Department of Agriculture led to a vast expansion of federal stimulus. A complex and comprehensive program has developed, including research by Department of Agriculture scientists in intramural laboratories and field stations, substantial support of agricultural research conducted by the states through their experimentation stations, and a comprehensive program of collection and dissemination of scientific and technical information through departmental facilities and bulletins, and through matching fund support of the Federal-State Agricultural Extension Service.

Federal support of technological advance in agriculture originally could be justified simply on the grounds that the individual production units of the industry—individual farms and farmers—did not have the resources to engage in an efficient research effort. At the time the program developed, there were few supplying industries to do R&D. Further, the program was pervaded by the philosophy that all farmers ought to be able to use freely new and improved practices—in sharp contrast with the rationale of the patent system, which sought to create a monopoly for the inventor. As the set of supplying industries began to evolve, and some of the chemical companies entered the fertilizer and insecticide business, need for public financing of certain kinds of R&D diminished. But there are still aspects of farming that are not reflected in obvious markets for these companies. Aside from the farmers, no businesses

[14] While to date no really satisfactory history of NIH, NACA-NASA, or AEC has been written, there are a number of good histories of federal R&D in agriculture. A recent study is U. S. Department of Agriculture, *State Agricultural Experiment Stations*, Misc. Publication No. 904 (Washington: Government Printing Office, 1962). For a more detailed and sophisticated study (although less up-to-date) see A. C. True, *A History of Agricultural Experimentation and Research in the United States, 1607-1925*, U.S. Dept. of Agriculture Misc. Publication No. 251 (Washington: 1937). See also Vernon W. Ruttan, "Research on the Economics of Technological Change in American Agriculture," *Journal of Farm Economics*, Vol. 42 (November 1960).

exist which are interested in better irrigation techniques, or better ways to raise cattle. Companies that produce equipment used in irrigation, or feed for cattle, are interested in improving and making their products more attractive, but generally are not interested in the broader problem. Farmers themselves generally cannot engage as individual units in an R&D program of efficient size.

Other major government R&D support programs aimed at specific industries include those of the Office of Coal Research, the Bureau of Commercial Fisheries, and the Department of Commerce's recent program of textile technology.

The NSF is one government agency whose mandate for the support of science and technology extends beyond the confines of a particular public sector function, or technological field, or industry. Its creation in 1950 marked the culmination of long-standing pressures to institutionalize federal responsibility for general support of basic research and science education. Its mandate was to "initiate and support basic scientific research, to correlate such programs with those undertaken by individuals and by public and private research groups . . . to strengthen scientific research potential including the support of activities designed to improve education in the sciences throughout the United States . . . " The NSF supports basic research in almost every area of science through grants to individuals and educational and research institutions, and it supports large scale endeavors like the Mohole project. The Foundation also is charged with developing and recommending ideas for national science policy.

The rationale for the National Science Foundation is the external economies generated by basic science generally. Its primary mandate contains no specific practical objectives, although it is charged by statute with weather modification research. Indeed, in most fields, the NSF has tended to shy away from projects which have a clear-cut practical application.

Despite its widespread association with basic science support, the NSF accounts for only about 15 percent of federal spending on basic research, and spends far less than such mission oriented agencies as NASA, DOD, AEC, and NIH. Yet this 15 percent may be pivotal. History is clear that prior judgments of practical promise tend to screen out some of the ultimately most fruitful basic research projects. Because of its mandate to support science for science's sake with the premise that scientific advance benefits all, the NSF ranks as one of the most important institutions of science policy.

Other Policies and Programs

While the patent system and government spending programs discussed above are the principal direct mechanisms by which public policy affects the rate and direction of technological advance, a host of other policies and programs affect incentives and capabilities for R&D and innovation. In some cases this is the principal objective, in other cases not.

Federal policies regarding education clearly are of very major importance. Many of the agencies discussed earlier in this chapter support scientific education, as well as research. The National Defense Education Act is just one example of the wide concern of the federal government generally with higher education. In recent years the federal government also has been playing an increasing role in supporting education below the college level.

The federal tax law obviously affects incentives for R&D. One provision was introduced explicitly for this purpose; proceeds from the sale of patents may be treated as a capital gain, even if the person is a professional inventor and presumably in the business of creating and selling patentable inventions. Other aspects of the tax code, like the ability to expense outlays in the year incurred, rather than depreciating them over a number of years, provide extra incentives for R&D as compared with physical investment, but were not instituted specifically with that objective.

The enforcement of the Sherman and Clayton Acts cannot help but influence the attitude of a large company with respect to certain kinds of R&D, for these laws affect such matters as compulsory licensing, the setting of royalties, and merger activity. The requirements for FHA loans can be set so as to facilitate or hinder the introduction of new housing components, materials, and designs. The Civil Aeronautics Board, by encouraging competition in service rather than price, encourages technological advances that lead to faster flights rather than lower costs.

More generally, the tone established in the economic system as the result of fiscal and monetary policies can have a profound impact on technological progress. If inadequate policy results in unutilized capacity and unemployed labor, it will diminish incentives to introduce and re-enforce worker resistance to labor saving innovation. On the other hand, if aggregate demand is kept strong and the labor market is tight, incentives for productivity increase will be high, and resistance smaller.

The Ferment for Change

In recent years there has been growing ferment for reform of public policy towards technological progress. Three separate, but related, concerns can be identified.

The first relates to the greatly expanded federal programs in the fields of defense and space, and their absorption of such a large share of the nation's design and development talent.[15] Fears have been expressed that R&D resources are being used to the neglect of other high priority or promising fields of pure and applied science. More generally, there is concern about the development of a defense-fed "big science" lobby, and the possible stranding of many scientists and engineers if defense needs taper off. Questions have been raised about the high cost of the defense and space R&D programs, and suggestions made regarding their more efficient management.[16]

Second, stimulated by such writers as Galbraith, many people have become concerned about the small amount of resources allocated to meeting many non-defense public sector wants. In particular, it is argued that such fields as low income public housing, education, mass transport, urban services, and the whole set of regulatory problems relating to environment—smog and pollution control, noise abatement, etc.—have been short-changed on R&D.[17]

Third, a new interest has developed in stimulating economic growth as a means of better meeting public wants and eliminating poverty.

[15] In the late fifties there was also fear of a defense oriented slant in higher education. See Charles Kidd, *American Universities and Federal Research* (Cambridge: Belknap Press of Harvard University Press, 1959). But the increasing role of NSF and HEW in supporting campus research has meant DOD by 1966 was estimated to provide only a quarter of the federal R&D funds spent in universities.

[16] Burton H. Klein, "A Radical Proposal for R and D," *Fortune* (May 1958), and Merton J. Peck and Frederic M. Scherer, *The Weapons Acquisition Process: An Economic Analysis* (Boston: Harvard University Graduate School of Business Administration, Division of Research, 1962), are examples.

[17] See the references cited in footnote 5 of this chapter.

Under the auspices of the Department of Commerce, a number of new federal programs to stimulate technological advance have been started or proposed. At the same time new programs of manpower training and retraining have been initiated, largely justified by the belief that more rapid technological advance is making, or would make, them necessary. A Presidential Commission on Automation and Technological Advance has proposed new federal programs to stimulate technological progress and to facilitate adjustment to rapid progress. A presidential commission on patent reform has been established.[18]

Overlapping these three sources of ferment has been a growing concern with the organization of government policy. Government policies and programs have grown like Topsy. In some cases, several agencies are supporting R&D in a particular area, such as space. In other areas, like mass transport, no agency has accepted responsibility. The terms of grants and contracts differ from one agency to another. The policy making and coordinating machinery is tangled and involved. Clearly, no effective machinery exists for evaluating the allocation of R&D resources as a whole. For example, a Department of Science to rationalize and centralize the existing structure has been recommended.

The following chapter deals directly with only a small subset of these issues. The proposals that are presented are concerned with increasing the effectiveness of the resources allocated to advancing technology. The principal objective motivating the proposals is increasing the rate of economic growth. However, several of the proposals have relevance to other areas of concern; in particular, more efficient management of government R&D, and more effective delineation of the government's role in stimulating R&D relevant to the public sector.

[18] Much of this discussion has been summarized in the *Annual Report of the Council of Economic Advisers, January 1962* (Washington: Government Printing Office, 1962), ch. 2.

9

Public Policy Proposals

Technical change has done well by Americans. It has contributed mightily to the improvement of health, the spread of leisure, and the enrichment of life generally. If results be the standard, the institutions of the American economy that foster and adjust to technical change have been remarkably effective. They have been so because the inherent abilities of a profit-oriented economy to initiate, diffuse, and adjust to technical change have been supplemented by government policies and regulations in many areas where private market incentives alone were not adequate to achieve satisfactory results.

As is traditional with government programs, existing policies and institutions in this field have evolved in response to the recognition of specific opportunities and problems. Such a pattern of evolution almost inevitably leads to an incomplete portfolio of policies.

This chapter proposes five additions to the present policy portfolio: (1) a federally supported National Institute of Technology to sponsor research and experimental work in the middle ground between academic science and product development; (2) a limited number of government supported R&D programs on large, technically advanced systems; (3) a limited number of continuing government R&D programs relevant to specific industries; (4) the use of government procurement to stimulate early experimental use; and (5) an industrial extension service to promote diffusion of new technology.[1]

[1] The industrial extension service does not represent a new policy. The State

171

The Analytic Basis for the Proposals

These five proposals are not intended to bring about comprehensive reforms which would achieve optimum resource allocation to and among the different activities generating technological advance. The present state of knowledge is not strong enough to permit quantitative determination of the average or marginal rate of return in the different activities, and thus does not permit policy recommendations to be derived from optimization principles. It is not possible objectively and confidently to determine whether too little or too many resources are being devoted to R&D as a whole, either absolutely or relative to investment in education and physical capital. The authors believe that too little is being invested in R&D, but their proposals are not based on this guess.

Market Failure as a Policy Guide

While the present state of knowledge is not strong enough to permit derivation of quantitative rates of return, or optimal allocations of resources, it is strong enough to suggest that for certain kinds of activities there are serious market imperfections. Private individuals and firms determine whether or not to engage in an activity, and the extent of their effort, on the basis of expected profitability. When there are significant external economies—unsupplemented private initiative is unlikely to support work to the extent that is socially optimal.

Where government policies already exist which provide added incentive or reduce private costs, or which supplement effort directly, it is difficult to say whether the latent tendency toward underallocation of private effort has been compensated. However, where policies do not exist, where incentive modifications appear minor relative to the gap between private and social returns, or where direct supplements appear small relative to the scope of socially desirable work (clearly a matter of judgment), a presumption exists that further allocation of resources

---

Technical Services Act became law in 1965. Because the concept is new and untested, and because certain major modifications are believed desirable, a discussion of this program is included under the proposals.

would yield a higher than average rate of return, and that government policies to achieve such an expansion are in the public interest.[2] The proposals rest on the analysis in Part I which aimed to identify areas where the market cannot be expected to work well, and on the survey of existing policies in the preceding chapter.

Sequential Experimentalism as an Approach to Specific Policy Formulation

While identification of current market failure problems can provide guidance for direction, it cannot provide guidance as to the size or kind of program which would be most appropriate. The analysis of market failure together with some imaginative thinking regarding the broad nature of a program that might deal with the problem can provide a policy maker with an idea of how to start, but somehow he must acquire additional information to determine exactly what direction and distance is most desirable.

Under such circumstances the most fruitful way to proceed is sequentially and experimentally; neither doing nothing because knowledge is less than perfect nor leaping farther than necessary in a prejudged direction. Government policy making presently has a tendency to vacillate between these extremes. There is a tendency to delay for a long time the introduction of a new program because of uncertainties, and then suddenly to jump in fully with a large commitment to a prescribed program, with no better knowledge base than before, when political pressures for doing something become strong. Once proposed or initiated, the program is then popularized among the public and in the Congress as a sure antidote, rather than as a promising probe of the environment.

This knowledge myth, which forces dedicated public servants to engage in charlatanism, seriously impedes the development of public pol-

---

[2] It is assumed implicitly that the other activities of the economy do not have such market failure problems, or that these problems are being met by existing policies. Otherwise, this kind of analysis sometimes can lead one in the wrong direction. This problem is discussed extensively in the literature on the economics of the second best. See, for example: K. Lancaster and R. G. Lipsey, "The General Theory of Second Best," *Review of Economic Studies,* Vol. 24 (1956), and E. J. Mishan, "Second Thoughts on Second Best," *Oxford Economic Papers,* Vol. 14 (London: Oxford University Press, October 1962).

It also should be stressed that the criteria is higher social return than the resources would attain in other uses, not just positive returns.

icy. The channeling of large sums of money into programs predetermined on the basis of sketchy information narrows the range of alternatives that can be tried, and thus reduces the range of policy instruments that have been tested. Further, it deters useful experimentation, since all programs are action programs. It places a high premium on actions likely to yield simple-minded quantitative indexes of immediate success. For instance, government social welfare programs have generally achieved popular support because of concern over instances of severe personal hardship. Frequently, however, these programs, once instituted, skim the cream off the top, devoting their efforts to groups whose problems are most readily susceptible to alleviation while scrupulously avoiding the hard-core cases.

Conditions of great uncertainty call for imaginative and flexible probings, not vacillation between inaction and commitment. Indeed, the way uncertainties are dealt with in the R&D process would appear an applicable model. As described in Chapter 5 the typical R&D strategy of the business firm is to avoid major financial commitments to untried ideas; rather, it seeks to obtain knowledge and thus to reduce the uncertainty surrounding the idea by investing relatively small sums in additional research. At each stage in the process, the company spends money to generate the knowledge necessary for deciding whether to proceed or retrench. As the idea proceeds from design concept to laboratory experimentation to prototype construction to production of limited batches, the investment becomes larger, and is undertaken only if the evidence increasingly points to the probability of profitable production.[3]

The policy proposals discussed here are modeled on this strategy. The operational implications can be summarized as follows: (1) In situations where the payoff from proposed programs is highly uncertain—quite possibly very high, but also, possibly negligible—or where the nature of the most effective program is uncertain, decision with respect to establishing the program on a large scale should be postponed unless there are reasons to think that time is of the essence. Instead, efforts should be made to resolve key uncertainties, and in many cases the most effective way to do this is to initiate a pilot or experimental program. (2) These

[3] Two case studies of R&D decision making at the Bell Telephone Laboratories which illustrate these points are Thomas A. Marschak, "Strategy and Organization in a System Development Project" and Richard R. Nelson, "The Link Between Science and Invention: The Case of the Transistor," both in *The Rate and Direction of Inventive Activity* (Princeton: Princeton University Press, 1962).

pilot programs should, where possible, be instituted on a modest scale and should be viewed as having two objectives—some alleviation of the problem the program is designed to deal with, and creation of the data necessary to make a better analysis of the merit of the program and its most fruitful nature and size. A large part of the program design should involve a data collecting scheme. (3) Procedures and criteria for evaluation and consequent redirection should be fully integrated with the action program, rather than appended as an afterthought.

It is not implied that policy making in this complex area can be fully formalized with mechanical evaluation procedures and sequential decision rules. Even with the greatest foresight regarding data collection, and with sophisticated analysis to draw inferences from data and experience, a considerable element of non-formalized judgment will be necessary. But judgment can be greatly facilitated by careful prior consideration of the major uncertainities surrounding the program, the most fruitful ways to acquire knowledge to reduce or resolve these uncertainties, the nature of the decisions that should be made at some later point on the basis of the knowledge acquired in the course of the program, and the decision making machinery suited to make these decisions effectively and without bias.

Policies and programs differ intrinsically in the extent to which they are amenable to a sequential decision approach. Specific research and development projects and programs directly financed by the government are well suited to this strategy. The early decision can be in terms of a small scale commitment to undertake research on the key uncertainties, and to undertake experimental development of critical but uncertain components. Decisions regarding larger scale financial commitments and the details of the design, if development is to be pressed, can await better estimates of costs and product attributes.

At the other extreme, regulatory or administrative changes, such as patent reform, or the integration of appropriate agencies under a Secretary of Science and Technology, are much more difficult to undertake sequentially and, to the extent that a step by step approach is feasible, much more difficult to evaluate. In between these two cases lies a range of government programs where some sequentialism is possible and where it is possible to construct a partial objective criteria of success, relying heavily on control samples, planned program diversity or variation, and multivariate analysis. But the chances of making an effective evaluation hinge heavily on whether a well conceived data collection program is integral, and whether evaluation mechanisms are established in advance.

It is not suggested that government agencies have not learned by doing and have not acted upon what they learned. Nor is experimentalism totally alien to government decision making. Demonstration projects are being increasingly employed in imaginative ways, particularly by the Housing and Home Finance Agency (HHFA) and in the retraining and poverty programs, which are also making some use of statistical evaluation techniques. However, the number of government programs which have been influenced by this approach is quite limited. Still more limited are the instances where conscious environment-probing was an integral aspect of the program, and where subsequent developments and extensions were based on the evaluation of data generated by the pilot program.[4]

Each of the proposals presented in the following sections is directed to an activity or facet of the technological advance process where the analysis of Part I suggests strongly that a significant degree of market

[4] The approach to public policy here advocated may be clarified by comparing and contrasting it with the concept of disjointed incrementalism developed by David Braybrooke and Charles E. Lindblom in *A Strategy of Decision: Policy Evaluation as a Social Process* (New York: The Free Press of Glencoe, 1963). The authors have proceeded by isolating uncorrected market imperfections and inadequate or improper focuses in government policy, and then recommended corrective action on an experimental basis. This corresponds closely with their preferred strategy of moving against specific social ills, rather than seeking comprehensive reforms and the achievement of global optima. However, we do not eschew general equilibrium analysis, since it frequently provides valuable qualitative guidelines. For instance, it indicates, other things constant, that as the percentage of the economy's human and material resources working in a particular industry changes, the percentage of the nation's R&D effort directed toward attempting to increase productivity in that industry should also change in the same direction. This suggests, for example, that as agriculture declines in relative importance, government R&D resources should shift similarly.

More to the point, it is agreed that limitations on the information available to decision makers generally means that the preferred policy strategy is an incremental one. Exploratory, serial, and reconstructive policy action is the heart of disjointed incrementalism and also of sequential experimentalism. The difference is that Braybooke and Lindblom find policy formulation to be exploratory, serial, and reconstructive, and applaud it as such. In contrast, the authors find that the incremental nature of decision making reflects political hesitancy, more than experimental philosophy. And the value of serial and reconstructive activity is considerably limited, because only a small portion of the information potentially available from incremental policy change can be tapped. Sequential experimentalism then proposes a rationalization of policy formulation which would make it more efficiently exploratory, serial, and reconstructive.

failure exists which is not remedied adequately by the policy instruments and institutions discussed in the preceding chapter. For each of the areas it appears possible to design an experimental program which, without massive commitment of resources, can probe the problem and feed back information that will help improve judgment regarding whether any kind of program at all is likely to have net payoff, and if so the kind and scope of the program. While formal evaluation procedures cannot substitute for judgment, careful planning of data collection and analysis can help to make judgment somewhat less capricious.

While the proposed experiments have been worked out in enough detail to make evident the rough outlines of a program, the kinds of data it should aim to explore or collect, and a sketch of evaluation criteria and important future decisions, much more thought and research and planning should go into the design of any of these proposed programs before they are implemented as an experiment.

These proposals are not strictly original, and other analysts undoubtedly would come up with a somewhat different list. There is a strong oral tradition among people interested in this area (if a weak written tradition of well articulated proposals) and a large number of proposals have been discussed in large and small groups. The proposals described here may not be the best ones, but they are presented without prejudice to other proposals, and in the spirit that there is little to be lost and much to be gained from an experimental probe of the possibilities.

A National Institute of Technology

A National Institute of Technology should be established to provide grants for research aimed at building the scientific underpinnings of various areas of technology, and for experimental development to test the feasibility and broad-scale attributes, advantages, and problems of advanced designs.

The Nature of the Gap

Much of the thinking about research and development implicitly draws a sharp distinction between basic research and product development. Basic research is viewed as work conducted largely by academic scientists, motivated by the desire to advance academic science, and highly diffuse in its benefits. Product development is viewed as work conducted by business firms or private inventors aimed directly at a new product design, and whose value to society is almost exclusively incorporated in a patentable product. Yet the preceding analysis has stressed the importance of kinds of R&D that fit neither of these categories.

One very important kind of R&D is research aimed at placing the technology of an industry on a stronger scientific footing. Another is experimental development to test the feasibility and broad attributes of radically new products and process designs. Much of the R&D supported by NACA in aviation was of these sorts, as is the work supported by the Department of Agriculture. Thus NACA supported research to enable better understanding of air flow over different shapes, and built and tested engine cowlings and wing models to test promising designs that the research suggested. The Department of Agriculture financed research on the mating habits of various insect pests, and built and tested traps based on scents and sounds that the research revealed as important.[5]

As pointed out in several of the preceding chapters, technology-motivated basic research and experimental development may be the key to efficient rapid technological advances. Yet in the absence of strong government support, this often is not the kind of work that academic scientists are interested in: while some of it is basic research, it largely concerns specific practical problems. The research supported by Agriculture was on insect pests rather than on insects that were particularly convenient to study, or which were particularly interesting from the point of view of the traditions of genetics. While in certain fields, such as medicine and agriculture, and recently defense and space, universities do focus their work to make a contribution to applied problems, the kind of R&D done somewhat depends on the kinds of grants and contracts available. In recent years the Departments of Defense and Agriculture, NASA, the AEC, and HEW, have been the overwhelmingly dominant source of research funds for the universities and nonprofits, accounting

---

[5] Note that the distinction between research aimed at understanding a phenomenon potentially relevant to a technology, and building and testing interesting design concepts, is not razor sharp. One looks to understand what is, the other to explore something that might be useful, but often, as in the cases above, one leads into the other. But they need not be tightly linked. NACA's work leading to the area-progression rule did not lead to any particular follow-on hardware test program. The experimental development of computer controls for machine tools undertaken during World War II did not stem directly and immediately from any particular nonhardware research project.

for more than 90 percent of the federal funds received. It would appear that only a small proportion of the work at universities and nonprofits is aimed at the broad domain of civilian industries and product fields.

Nor, in the absence of special policies, is there strong incentive for business firms to undertake this kind of work, *at least not up to the levels of public interest in its accomplishment.* Chapter 4 indicated that the payoffs tend to be highly uncertain, and that the value of the work is likely to transcend anything that is directly, or ultimately, patentable. Thus, the major payoff from army-supported R&D on programmed machine tools was not the specific configuration which resulted from the program, but rather the demonstration of general utility of its concept and approach. The work intrinsically tends to generate knowledge that others can use without compensation. Moreover, the gap between private and social returns transcends the problem of one firm being able to use (without compensating payment) the knowledge created by the R&D of another. Even if the results were fully patentable and the patent fully enforceable, the "consumer surplus" problem would remain. To the extent that basic research and experimental development pave the way for major advances in certain performance attributes—and this often is their intent—many purchasers will gain value far in excess of the price they must pay. At the consumer good level, this is reflected in the undervaluing of new products in the GNP calculations. At the producer good level, it is reflected in high profits that certain firms can make as a result of new materials and equipment created by their suppliers.

Despite these factors driving a gap between social and private profit, business firms do undertake some basic research and some experimental development. In many cases an exploratory project may appear so promising that even a small share of the benefits amounts to a handsome profit. In the science-based industries the combination of a good knowledge base and of purchasers valuing highly new products and responding quickly to their introduction (with consequent major payoffs to a head start) stimulate a considerable amount of this kind of R&D. Science-based industries are the minority, however, and even here private benefits are only a portion of social benefits. Thus, while private firms do carry on some of this work, there are a large number of projects with a high social rate of return which fail the private profitability criteria.

The preceding chapter discussed a few sectors in which public programs have evolved to finance this kind of R&D. The important examples are health, aviation, and agriculture, and in these areas technological progress has been extremely (sometimes embarrassingly) rapid. The federal government should support this kind of R&D across the board.

Functions and Characteristics of the Institute

There are two possible models for such a program. One would be to follow the example of the National Advisory Committee on Aeronautics and conduct the research in government facilities. The second would be to follow the example of the National Science Foundation and work principally through support to outside organizations. (The National Institutes of Health and the Department of Agriculture research support programs are somewhere in between.) Greater flexibility suggests the second approach, though the organization will need some in-house capability to evaluate proposals. One possibility would be to link the Institute with the National Bureau of Standards. The balance between in-house research and grants can be worked out as experience accumulates, but the Institute would probably be primarily a grant-giving agency. It should be willing to take the initiative to point out promising areas to which it would give priority.

To stress the analogy to the National Science Foundation and to the National Institutes of Health the proposal is called a National Institute of Technology. The mission of this organization is to support research and experimental development meeting three criteria:

1. The proposed research or experimentation, if successful, would produce knowledge which could be exploited to yield significant increases in the performance or efficiency of a class of products or processes.
2. There should be a reasonable chance of success at a level of funding commensurate with a high rate of return, if successful.
3. It should be established why business firms presently are not undertaking projects of this kind despite the high expected social rate of return.

There are some extremely difficult questions regarding whether the Institute should aim principally to support work done by business firms and private inventors, or work in the universities. It is quite possible that the former would yield the greatest payoffs—that the Institute should aim to stimulate proposals from imaginative engineers in business firms, and to provide encouragement and financial assistance to freelancers. There would, however, be serious problems regarding dispositions of any resulting patents. Business firms or private inventors would probably not accept government support for ideas they thought exciting if the price of such support was abandonment of patent rights, and while the useful knowledge created usually would transcend the patent rights, a privately held patent might obstruct others from capitalizing on the knowledge created.

While some kind of a patent licensing arrangement could be worked out, it is suggested that the objective of the grants should be viewed as knowledge for general use in the public domain. Any resulting patents should vest with the public, and there should be full publication and publicity of results. This would mean that the bulk of the grants would go to colleges and universities (principally engineering departments) and nonprofit organizations. However, grants for research conducted in the facilities of business firms should not be precluded. For certain kinds of projects, industry facilities and participation may be very important.[6]

The research support program of the Institute undoubtedly would overlap the scope of the engineering sciences support program of the National Science Foundation, and in some cases the basic research program of mission-oriented government agencies like the DOD. For experimental hardware projects there would be some overlap with mission-oriented government agencies, if not with the National Science Foundation, although this should not present a problem. Presumably the Institute would avoid projects where other financing was readily attainable and, in any case, multiple alternative sources of support for this kind of work are to be highly desired. When the National Science Foundation was established there were major alternative sources of government basic research support, and the NSF continues to be a small-scale sup-

[6] Under these circumstances, the following conditions might be imposed to assure that the knowledge entered the public domain. The project must be run jointly by a university and a business firm or group of firms with a university person in at least joint project directorship. The research project should be separated physically from any proprietary work to assure that there are no constraints on visiting and observing. Finally, the academic group would have authority over the project write up and reporting. However, setting these restrictions might preclude certain useful projects, and an agreement that results be fully published and that patent rights vested with the public may be sufficient.

porter of basic research relative to such organizations as the DOD, NASA, AEC, and HEW. The principal distinguishing function of the Institute, like the distinguishing characteristics of the NSF, would be the responsibility for across-the-board support of a particular class of activity. While the NSF is concerned with advancing the frontiers of science, the Institute would be concerned with advancing the frontiers of technology.[7]

An Experiment

It is extremely difficult to judge in advance the social payoffs from such a National Institute. They might be large or they might be small. Ultimately it might be desirable to have such an Institute supporting a large share of the research undertaking in engineering schools with an annual budget of between $100 million and $500 million, or it might turn out that the useful scope for such an Institute is very limited. The following seem to be major kinds of questions that must be resolved before the merit and role of such an institute can be determined.

What kinds of research and experimental development projects would be proposed? Would they be those not otherwise undertaken (or not as intensively) in the absence of such a grant program? To what extent would the requirement for public vesting of patent rights deter worthwhile proposals? Is the university focus the right one, or would it be better to support R&D in business firms, or by private inventors? To what extent would R&D, which proved successful in creating and testing new

[7] The Institute proposed has no direct precedent either here or abroad. The closest analogy is with the National Research Development Corporation of Great Britain, but the differences are as important as the similarities.

The National Research Development Corporation (NRDC) was established in 1948 with the objective of developing and achieving commercial utilization of the inventive ideas resulting from government R&D, and also of worthwhile inventions and ideas submitted to it by private sources. Like the NRDC, the National Institute would be concerned with supporting attempts at major technological advances. But unlike the NRDC, the National Institute would view its objective as that of generating data, theory, and knowledge about the characteristics of advanced design concepts so as to facilitate follow-on development by the private sector, rather than achieving directly a usable and profitable product or process design. Thus, while the NRDC tends to judge projects for selection on the basis of commercial promise, and to evaluate its success in large part in terms of royalties on licenses, the National Institute would tend to judge projects on technological promise, and evaluate success in terms of stimulus of product development efforts that make use of the knowledge and concepts created.

design concepts, prove a stimulus to further product and process development?

These questions can only be answered on the basis of experience. To that objective, the Institute should be viewed initially as an experiment of five years length, and with annual funding limited to roughly $15 million. This budget should be sufficient to support approximately ten experimental development projects, each involving perhaps twenty professional scientists and engineers, and twenty smaller scale research projects at about a five-man level. To those used to DOD research projects, such project sizes may seem too small-scale to be effective. Yet the key experimental development work on radar and television was conducted by much smaller groups. Large development projects aimed at practical hardware—not experimental evidence of feasibility, problems, and merit —often are not much larger. The project sizes permitted by the proposed budget are relatively large considering the nature of the work. The principal question is whether the size of the proposed experimental budget permits enough projects to be financed to fully test the concept, considering that far-reaching R&D always has its failures. The level of funding seems sufficient, but this requires further study.

There is also a question of the time period for the initial experiment. The fruition of this kind of R&D requires considerable time. One should not expect to have much information even on the narrow technical merit of the projects for at least five years. Evaluation of economic impact will take longer. At the end of five years it should be possible to begin to answer some of the questions above. Then, if several of the projects have led to interesting technical results, and there is a large number of grant applications with considerable merit, there would be a case for expanding the program significantly.

Selected Support of Large Scale Development Projects

Support provided by the National Institute generally would carry R&D on a particular process or product only to the stage where feasibility and broad scale attributes were demonstrated. The program is not designed to bring the technology to the point of operational utility; that is left to private initiative. However, occasionally it is in the public interest for the government to carry R&D through the expensive middle and late stages of development. The National Institute should be authorized to help support such work under special circumstances.

The Problem and Its Scope

Even when the most significant uncertainties have been resolved by prior basic and experimental R&D (of the sort the National Institute would support), in some cases development opportunities of high social return may be deterred because of the cost and scope relative to the financial and technical resources, and market interests, of private firms. There is some tendency for firm size in an industry to adjust itself to the size of R&D opportunities, and for the large supplying firms to lend a hand, but from time to time the cost and scope of certain worthwhile development projects may swamp existing private capabilities and interests.

Perhaps the most important kind of situation where this will occur is when an important advance can be achieved most efficiently through integrated redesign of a large number of components—each produced by a different industry—to exploit opportunities for complementarity or trade-off. Even if a firm knowledge base is established, the fact that multiple components are involved may make this work expensive, and technical competence and market interest may be too fragmented for private cooperation to be possible without a helping hand. Thus, the R&D capabilities and incentives of existing firms may fail to define the scope of the design and development task broadly enough.

In military R&D there is almost a fetish about defining broadly the system to be designed and developed. There are advantages in so doing. Thus a modern missile "systems" development aims to design the airframe, the guidance equipment, aspects of the engine, the fuel subsystem, and the launching equipment as a package. By viewing the design and development task this broadly, the analysts and engineers are able to consider the alternative of developing a larger engine to power a larger airframe in order to accommodate a larger guidance subsystem versus designing an especially compact guidance system, or the alternative of designing tanks in the missile for storing fuel for long periods of time versus developing fuel storage capacity, plus rapid fueling equipment as part of the ground installation, and so forth. If the design and development tasks were viewed more narrowly, as being constrained to accept the current stock of engines plus the current set of engine developments as given, or to accept current fuel pumping equipment as given, these alternatives would be foreclosed.

The supersonic transport, low cost housing, and an inter-urban rail system, among others, have been cited as civilian cases in which a broad scale systems view of the design and development task might have high payoff. It is argued that in these cases private business organizations will not be able or motivated to take a broad enough systems approach. The R&D cost of trying to achieve a supersonic transport, for example, given that a large number of necessary components do not exist and would have to be designed for the aircraft, would strain the financial resources of private aircraft companies. In the housing case, it is not so much that better housing is not feasible without a broader system approach, or that it is particularly costly to try to design a house as a "system"; rather, the problem is that there are unexploited opportunities in designing components to fit together as a system and the costs of exploiting these are large relative to the financial resources of the general contractors who build and sell houses as a system. The companies with large financial and technical capabilities—the materials suppliers—are interested in only their part of the "system." The rail transport case has elements in common with both above; costs are high, and the organizations with the R&D capabilities and resources—the engine and car manufacturers and the rail manufacturers—are interested in just a part of the system. The railroads—who presumably are interested in the total system—seem incapable on their own of getting such a system designed and built.

These examples, and the fact that major advances in military hardware have been achieved in systems development projects, suggests to many a great shortage of large systems development in the civilian economy. It has been suggested that in the civilian economy, in contrast with the military, technological progress is piecemeal and haphazard, and that a vast number of great opportunities to exploit interdependence fall through the cracks. This view is probably grossly exaggerated. While there almost certainly are cases in which important systems development opportunities are being missed, the problem probably is nowhere nearly so generic and widespread as many believe.

It is true that there are many systems in the civilian economy, where a system denotes a complex of components or products and the design of one influences the optimal design of others. Furthermore, it is true that different companies produce different parts of a system. But this does not necessarily mean that systems matching is ineffective. Automobiles, gasoline, and roads are clearly a system; so are spinning machines and weaving machines. These groups of products are systems in that the design of one, in certain important respects, is sensitive to the design of the others. But how far should the boundary of a system be pushed? A pencil itself is a system composed of a lead, eraser, and a wood integrating shell. Pencils and paper comprise a more broadly defined system. Should desks be included in the pencil and paper system? Clearly there are some design interdependencies (thick paper can compensate for rough desks, and the size and hardness of the pencil lead should depend on the thickness and texture of the paper).

As these examples indicate, the boundaries of a system are somewhat arbitrary. Furthermore, while different manufacturers produce different parts of the systems above, the parts all work together. Well matched systems do not depend on integrated design efforts. Automobile companies are able to accommodate and to influence the gasolines that are developed by oil companies, and vice versa.

Advances in components and materials have had a strong impact on stimulating redesign of products which could use them as inputs. More generally, advances in one component of a system have tended to stimulate changes in the other components needed to make for a better overall system. For example, Schlaifer and Heron have documented the interrelation of advances in aircraft engines and in aircraft fuels.[8] Better recording technology has stimulated R&D on better sound reproduction systems.

Where the lags involved have been great, leaving major unexploited opportunities for better systems integration, companies have tended to expand the scope of their own systems. Thus, many electronic companies have produced hi-fi packages, as well as individual components. By and large, product boundaries (the complex of interacting components put together and sold as a unit by companies) tend to be defined in such a way as to contain the most important interactions, and the residual interdependencies are worked out quite well between companies, if with a time lag.

[8] Robert O. Schlaifer and S. D. Heron, *The Development of Aircraft Engines and Fuels* (Boston: Harvard University Graduate School of Business Administration, Division of Research, 1950).

While recognizing that almost all products are systems and often quite complex ones, the fact remains that in civilian R&D the scope of a product design and development effort usually is defined much more narrowly than in military projects. Far more components are assumed as given; thus the size of the R&D efforts generally are much smaller. While in military R&D a systems development effort may involve over 1,000 professionals and annual expenditures of $50,000,000, in civilian R&D the projects involving more than 50 people are rare. The TH system at Bell Labs involved about 90 technical people and an annual expenditure rate of about $4 million. Total expenditures were about $15 million, and this was one of the largest and most complex non-military systems R&D efforts ever undertaken.[9] The TH system was a large systems development in the sense that a large number of components and subcomponents were either specifically designed or significantly modified for the system. But in contrast to some military efforts, a large share of the components, elements, and materials were taken off the shelf. Bell Labs could have viewed the systems development task in a larger context, and redesigned its whole telephone system—not just its long range relay system—but it obviously chose not to.

Why do systems developments tend to be much smaller in scope and staffing in the civilian economy? The principal reason is greater concern for R&D and total cost, and a significantly smaller premium on the somewhat higher performance which could be achieved through better subsystem matching. The broader the systems development task is defined, the higher the R&D costs; further, the greater the percentage of the old system that is made obsolete and so the greater the changeover cost. For the military a small performance difference in such a factor as aircraft speed may determine success or failure in air-to-air combat; for most civilian products marginal improvements are seldom crucial. Hence the Air Force used to spend $2 billion dollars every five years in building the best possible fighter and even vaster sums in totally reoutfitting its squadrons. It certainly would not be rational for society every five years to tear up all of the roads and build new ones because a slightly different road design is made optimal by changes in vehicle design.

In short, expanding the scope of the system to be developed is one way to achieve major advances. However, it is not the only way. Over

[9] See Thomas Marschak, "Strategy and Organization in a System Development Project," *loc. cit.*

the long run, and in most cases, supporting a wide range of research and experimental development projects is probably a more efficient approach. To the extent that research and experimental development permit and stimulate companies to improve their products—which are part of larger systems—system performance can and will be improved without requiring large scope systems development projects. Marginally redesigning a number of other components to accommodate better a radically improved new component probably is not beyond the capability of most medium sized companies in most industries. If the redesign is not too great the companies that produce these components often can be induced to do the job.

The question of public support for systems R&D thus is largely a question of when a higher performance system is to be achieved, and the most efficient way to achieve improved systems. It would appear that public support is warranted only when there are major gains to society from an advance sooner than would result without such support, and where support of systems R&D is an efficient way to hasten the advance.

Circumstances Warranting Government Support

The special circumstances would appear to be of two sorts, generally. The first is the kind of situation discussed in Chapter 4, in which a particular industry, because of lack of a strong internal R&D capability, is unable to redesign its products and processes to take advantage of a specific opportunity or class of opportunities afforded by new materials and equipment, and none of the suppliers has a strong interest in reaching its R&D forward. The individual housing unit case is a good one. Here it may be useful for the National Institute of Technology to be willing to support a research and development aimed at exploring new housing designs beyond the stage where its support usually stops, and to carry support of the work to the point where little further development is necessary.

The second situation is when there appear to be significant public benefit aspects to the development of the system in question, or where public benefits reside from having the new system sooner than would result from private initiative alone. Mass transit systems may be an example. Under such circumstances support of systems design and development by the appropriate public agencies would appear warranted. However, outside the fields of defense and space, public agencies seldom have taken a strong and active role in supporting the development of systems relevant to their domain. In the absence of a radical change in the R&D policies of the several government agencies, it would appear that a National Institute of Technology working in concert with the relevant agencies could play a useful role in supporting R&D for the public sector beyond the research and experimental development stages.

Industry Research Programs

General support of technology-instituted basic research and experimental development, plus selected support of R&D on large and expensive systems of high social value where private initiative alone cannot be expected to do the job, should go a long way toward filling the important gaps in the present national R&D effort. Neither of these policies represent a long term commitment of federal funds to a particular industry. However, in an extremely limited number of cases such a long run committal of government funds may be justified.

Limitations of Industry Research Programs

Organizing government support for civilian technology through industry research programs is more common in other countries than in the United States.[10] Yet, there are special programs of this sort here, as for example, the programs of the Department of Agriculture and the coal research program of the Department of the Interior. Such an industry focus can be tailored to fit well specified technical needs and potential users can be brought early into the R&D process. Such advantages prompted the proposal of industry research programs when U.S. economic policy began in 1963 to emphasize the government promotion of civilian technology.[11]

Despite these advantages, the inherent limitations of industry-oriented

[10] For a discussion of the Department of Scientific and Industrial Research in England—perhaps the most important example of an industry research support program—see U.S. Congress, Joint Committee on Atomic Energy, *Scientific Research In Great Britain* (Washington: Government Printing Office, 1960), and Charles Carter and Bruce Williams, *Science In Industry; Policy For Progress* (London: Oxford University Press, 1959).

[11] See *Economic Report of the President, January 1963*, and the accompanying *Annual Report of the Council of Economic Advisers* (Washington: Government Printing Office, 1963), pp. 63-65. In both fiscal years 1964 and 1965, the Department of Commerce proposed research support programs for textiles, building and machine tools. The total funds requested were small (under $5 million annually). Congress appropriated only a small part of the program for textiles.

research programs should give such programs a very limited role. There is, first of all, the question of which industries are to receive research support. One possible criterion would be to select those with a low R&D to sales ratio. The simplicity of this criterion is matched only by its irrationality. There is nothing sacred about the R&D to sales ratio: indeed, an economy in which R&D allocations were optimized by an all-knowing and perfectly rational computer would display wide variations in the ratio, simply because R&D is much more productive in some industries than in others.

Another possible criterion is to limit research support to the so-called sick industries, that is, those suffering from low profits, unemployment, and a declining demand. But R&D aimed at increasing productivity is as likely to hurt profits and employment as to help them.[12] While R&D on new uses for the industry's product would be more likely to aid employment and profits in the industry, it may have very low social payoff and transfer problems to other sectors. To use research support to deal with the problems of industries in trouble would be likely to be ineffective. At best it would force economic growth to meet the existing distribution of resources, rather than to be responsive to relative returns and costs.

Even if these problems of the choice of industry could be solved,[13] some of the advantages of industry focus are likely to be simultaneously disadvantages. The closeness of the research organization to existing firms in the industry means that the program would be guided by the well-being of these firms. Thus, there is likely to be resistance to R&D which might seriously change the existing status quo, even though this might be where the big payoffs lie. Furthermore, the R&D program is likely to be focused upon developments that increase the industry's demand at the expense of other industries. Economy-wide gains here may be small. (The Department of Interior coal research program, for example, emphasizes projects that will expand coal consumption at the expense of other energy sources.) Finally, once the government research program becomes part of the industry's establishment, it is difficult to discontinue even though the payoffs from continued work may fall con-

---

[12] This, of course, depends on the elasticity of demand.

[13] The criterion of relative social rates of returns on R&D investment in various industries meets the objections discussed above. It is not presently an operational concept.

siderably. (Department of Agriculture research illustrates this point all too well.)[14]

General support of technology-motivated basic research and experimental development, plus selective support of specific systems R&D projects beyond the financial capability and market scope of existing firms, should cover most of the gaps in the existing R&D spectrum for most industries. In view of the significant inherent problems of programs representing a long run committal to a particular industry, in contrast with support of particular projects judged on their merits without prejudice for or against the industry most affected, industry support programs should be undertaken only if very strict criteria are met.[15]

[14] Don K. Price, *The Scientific Estate* (Cambridge: Harvard University Press, 1965), points out that the same kind of problem resides in government programs aimed at areas of technology, like atomic energy.

[15] The authors would be mildly sympathetic to partial government aid for industry cooperative research associations in whatever industry they are formed. Such a program might involve giving governmental support to the formation of industry organized research cooperatives either through tax credits or government grants that match the contributions from the firms in the industry. All industries might be made eligible so that the problem of industry selection is by-passed. The limits on these programs is industry willingness to put up funds.

As Chapter 3 enumerated, many cooperative research organizations are already in existence. Most, however, are small and none has government aid. In contrast, they are a more major factor in the United Kingdom research scene (with the fifty-three largest industry associations accounting for 4 percent of U.K.'s 1963 industrial research). Here the government provides about one-quarter of their expenditures, with industry providing the remainder.

The English experience indicates that the cooperatives have been useful in performing applied research on industry-wide problems like the maintenance of equipment, or common manufacturing problems. They have been useful in testing and evaluating materials and in distributing technical information. But as an effective source of far reaching developments they have proved a disappointment. Furthermore, the cooperative research association suffers from the limitations of government supported industry research programs; namely, narrowness of scope and unwillingness to upset the status quo. The various evaluations of English experience point out that the cooperatives concentrate upon work with a relatively immediate and certain payoff. This is to be expected for the cooperative depends on continued industry support which is forthcoming more freely for short-run efforts.

For these reasons, the higher priority has been assigned to the National Institute of Technology. The authors regard the industry cooperative as a device that may earn its keep and justify some government support. It is not, however, likely to be a major policy instrument in promoting technical change and, accordingly, it is not incorporated in the higher priority policy proposals.

Special Situations Justifying Industry Support

The following criteria are proposed:

1. The industry must have both a low level of R&D activity and a low rate of technical progress. If industry R&D activity is already at a significant level, the business firms are likely to be exploiting the most attractive alternatives. If, despite low in-house R&D effort, technical progress still is relatively rapid, suppliers and independent investors are probably picking up a large share of the most promising projects.

2. The industry must have institutional barriers that are deterring R&D by private firms. These barriers can include a predominance of firms too small to undertake an efficient sized R&D program (as in agriculture), lack of a strong organization responsible for integrating the final product (as in housing), or government laws and restrictions (as again in housing where it is alleged local building codes have this effect).

3. The industry should be one where the value of more rapid technical progress is high. This usually means that the industry is a large sector of the economy, or that there is another special social interest in its output.

These three criteria taken together serve as a proxy for a social rate of return. When they are met, there would appear a significant probability that government support of R&D beyond basic research and experimental development and beyond the selection of a few specific systems projects might yield significant social benefits. When the first two criteria are met, there would be evidence that the industry is not capable on its own of conducting the follow-on work needed to reach the point of practical applications, and that there might be a considerable number of projects with high social returns. Where the last criterion is met, as well, the gains to society from helping the industry on a long term basis might be high.

Criteria Applied: Contrasting Cases of Construction and Textiles

These criteria may be illustrated by application to two industries—textiles and construction. Both have been leading candidates for industry research programs; the Department of Commerce, for instance, included them in its proposed civilian technology program in 1964 and 1965. Congress approved a small scale textile program and rejected the building construction research program. This was precisely the wrong decision; construction research should have been supported and textile research should not.[16] Consider how each industry meets the three criteria.

Turning to the first criterion, both textiles and construction show relatively low rates of research intensity, but construction meets this part of the criteria better. The R&D to value added ratio was .12 for construction and .28 for textiles;[17] by comparison the figure for the economy as a whole was .43. Construction lagged even more noticeably in productivity advances. Between 1899 and 1953 output per manhour increased annually by 1.1 percent in construction, compared with 2.0 percent for the

[16] One troublesome problem at the outset is the definition of the two industries. Textiles as used here include the apparel industry; at least, that is how the Department of Commerce has interpreted its program. Construction includes heavy construction (roads and airports), as well as housing, even though the former has benefited from advances in earth-moving equipment. Construction is used here, however, since most of the data is on that basis. The differences between the industry as a whole and its component subsectors are troublesome to define throughout. Most of the research in the combined textile and apparel sectors is in textiles. As a result, a small scale research program in apparel might be highly productive.

[17] Data is for 1956 and is taken from Edward F. Denison, *The Sources of Economic Growth in the United States and the Alternatives Before Us* (New York: Committee for Economic Development, 1962), pp. 241-42. Unfortunately the NSF surveys, Denison's source, do not treat construction separately. In absolute amounts this was $23 million for construction and $24 million for textiles. Each industry had only small amounts of publicly financed R&D.

Research intensity may be much less meaningful than, say, capital intensity. As pointed out earlier, research is a public good par excellence; that is, one firm's use of the results of research does not preclude another from its use. On the other hand, the larger an industry, the greater is the likelihood of diversity in its output and thus the need for more research effort to achieve the same results. Furthermore, the greater the size of the industry, the more research effort may be needed to speed up the diffusion process since that process often depends on close linkage of research units to production management. Finally, the larger the industry, the greater the effects on the economy of research in that industry. For these reasons ratios of R&D to value added are used even though these are imperfect measures.

A closely associated difficulty is the investment in technical change which is not reflected in the R&D statistics. Occasionally architects and engineers carry out in their day-to-day activities what in manufacturing would be counted as R&D and mechanics in textile mills have been inventors. Yet considering such activities would probably not alter the research-poor character of these two industries.

private domestic economy as a whole. Textile productivity over this period actually grew faster than the national average, at an annual rate of 2.5 percent.[18] According to Meyerson, Terrett and Wheaton, the average consumer in 1929 could buy more housing than his 1955 counterpart despite an increase in real purchasing power of over 50 percent. Since 1955, the difference, they say, is widening.[19] In contrast, the real price of clothing has fallen continuously, even apart from the quality gains of artificial fibers.

The second criterion is an institutional organization that is likely to impede research by private firms. Both textiles and contract construction often are thought of as industries composed mostly of firms too small to conduct R&D programs. Yet in 1958 textile firms averaged 287 employees,[20] and there were more than fifty firms in the textile industry employing over 1,000 people and conducting R&D programs. These large firms account for a large share of industry output; the twenty largest firms in 1958 accounted for 54 percent of cotton textile shipments.[21]

Firms in contract construction tend to be much smaller, averaging only twelve employees per firm, with the few multi-million dollar firms accounting for only 4 percent of the contract construction and these firms concentrated in the non-housing portion of the industry.[22] In construction, the problem of small firm size is reflected in and compounded by fragmentation. The production process itself is fragmented among many distinct types of trades and subcontractors, assuring that some R&D falls between the cracks. According to Meyerson and his associates, "The housing industry . . . . is not a clear-cut entity like steel making or textile manufacturing, in which the operations of any single firm are under continuous management control. It is, in fact, a heterogeneous aggregation of more or less related industries, government bodies, financial

[18] Data from John W. Kendrick, *Productivity Trends in the United States* (Princeton: Princeton University Press, 1961), pp. 148-49.

[19] Martin Meyerson, Barbara Terrett, and William L. C. Wheaton, *Housing, People, and Cities* (New York: McGraw-Hill Book Co., 1962).

[20] Data from U.S. Bureau of the Census, *Concentration Ratios in Manufacturing Industry, 1958*, a report prepared for the Subcommittee on Antitrust and Monopoly of the Committee on the Judiciary, U.S. Senate (Washington: Government Printing Office, 1962).

[21] *Ibid.*

[22] Joe S. Bain, *Industrial Organization* (New York: John Wiley & Sons, 1959), p. 97.

institutions, and labor unions."[23] While textile production process also is divided among firms, fragmentation would appear to be far less, and there are many integrated firms.

The final criteria relate to a high social gain from a faster rate of technical progress. One aspect is significant industry size. Both textiles and housing meet this criterion, with construction representing about 8 percent of the economy, and textiles and apparel about 3 percent, although obviously construction is the more important. The more elusive aspect is a special social interest in technical gains in the industry transcending the well being of the industry or the alternative uses of its resources.

Since the thirties an increased concern with the quality and cost of housing has been expressed in the extensive public housing programs and governmental loan guarantee. To be even more current, a reduction in housing costs would be a significant contribution to the anti-poverty campaign and to efforts to create a more attractive urban environment. All these considerations reflect a belief that housing conditions have a major impact upon people's social and psychological characteristics. There would appear to be no equivalent condition regarding textiles.

To summarize—housing meets all three criteria; textiles partially satisfies only one. Nevertheless a prudent man would insist on a full-scale industry study before deciding on the merits of an industry research program for either textiles or housing.

A Proposed Housing Research Program

Such a full-scale study is likely to confirm the view that a housing research program would meet the criteria for industry research support. The following considerations should be general guidelines for the research program:

1. The priorities should be on-site construction and housing units as a whole, aspects where R&D is negligible. A low priority should be assigned to research on building materials and mechanical components. Here there are often major manufacturers in glass, precast cement, and so forth, each with research programs, even though they are counted in the data for other industries.

2. The research program should be composed of a number of relatively small scale projects, rather than a few massive aerospace sys-

[23] Meyerson, *et al., op. cit.*, pp. 104-05.

tem type efforts. The latter is both the inappropriate and expensive way to advance technology, for reasons discussed earlier.

3. The research program should not accept the existing structure of the industry or the housing codes as given. Indeed, some part of the research program should specifically be earmarked to examine the rationality of existing housing codes.

4. Finally, early liaison should be established with housing research abroad. The Dutch, for example, have a system of housing experiment stations and the United Nations has several regional housing research centers. The High Authority of the European Coal and Steel Community has already launched an experimental program involving 1,000 units. Housing research, perhaps more than other kinds of research needs, tends to be shaped by local conditions. However, in the absence of a research tradition in either the industry or government, research experience elsewhere has not been capitalized upon in the United States. In general, one important feature of such research groups is that they serve as listening posts for research elsewhere.

In line with the experimental approach, such a research program would have an initial lifespan of five years. The annual appropriation should be between five and ten million dollars. While this seems small by normal government standards, such an amount would represent a significant increase in housing research and development expenditures. Furthermore, this amount should flow primarily into the R&D effort itself; construction of housing should be for experimental purposes rather than demonstration. More wide-scale testing could be provided by public housing. Since it is outside local building codes, on-base military housing may provide particularly useful laboratories.[24]

A federal housing research program has been proposed before, and precedents are not lacking. The pre-World War II Federal Housing Administration included a Technical Division which carried on some housing research up to World War II. The Public Housing Act of 1949 specifically authorized a housing research program which operated only one year—hardly a fair trial—when it was curtailed and then eliminated

[24] There is already an HHFA Low Income Demonstration Project involving a $237,600 contract to the Pratt Institute to design an improved cost-reducing multi-level apartment building with no restriction as to building codes. The design would be erected on a military base.

by appropriations actions.[25] Congress has never voted to renew this program and, as a result, in 1960 the Housing and Home Finance Agency was spending less for housing research than the Department of Agriculture was spending on the development of chicken coops.[26]

The quick demise of the 1949 housing research program was due to industry opposition. Brick manufacturers and associated crafts were afraid the program might develop materials and procedures that would discourage the use of brick. Lumber firms and associated crafts were afraid the program might develop materials and procedures that would discourage the use of lumber, and so on through all the crafts, sub-contractors, and types of materials. This poses a dilemma: the very fragmentation that discourages research by private firms also creates opposition to research by the government. In such successful instances of government-industry research as the National Advisory Committee of Aeronautics, the industry was aircraft manufacturers interested in the entire airplane. One can imagine quite a different history had there been separate firms, trade associations, and unions organized around wood struts and fabric fuselages.

Louis Winnick has observed that: "There must be a restoration of concern over the 'real' side of housing: building costs, techniques and industrial capacity, subjects which drew much attention during the thirties and forties, but which have been neglected since 1949 in favor of manipulating mortgage terms. . . . The time is ripe to embark on a full-scale effort to bring down building costs, for which the prospects are better than they have been in a long time."[27] Congress must decide which interests shall dominate: that of consumers in better housing, or that of producers in the existing division of the market.

Other Industry Research Programs

There may be other industries that meet the criteria for an exception from the general rule against industry research programs. For example,

---

[25] Meyerson, *et al.*, p. 231.

[26] Meyerson, *et al.*, p. 340. $15,000 is the 1960 figure Meyerson reports. By 1965 more research was currently undertaken by HHFA but the agency generally avoids the term research. The biggest source of research is in the Low Income Housing Demonstration Program where about $940,000 has been granted to devise new techniques and build experimental housing units for low income groups.

[27] In Nelson N. Foote and others, *Housing Choices and Housing Constraints* (New York: McGraw-Hill Book Co., 1960).

urban mass transit may now, and more likely in the future, fall into this category. Little research is now done; the industry is a large one, and the efficient movement of people about the city is an essential condition for the functioning of urban areas. The consumers are local transit authorities and the suppliers are largely in the business of furnishing individual components; hence, it may be that there are institutional obstacles to technical change. Finally, the major technical change in urban transit—the combination of automobile and super-highways—may now be imposing high social costs in terms of land use and the more intangible destruction of urban amenities. Similar conditions may prevail in local governmental services generally—from police protection to trash removal. To test the desirability of research programs in such fields requires considerably more research than is feasible for this volume.

An Experimental Procurement Service

The fourth proposal is to use federal purchasing power in civilian markets to accelerate the process of technical change for the wide range of products in which the government is a big consumer. For such a reorientation of purchasing procedures, an Experimental Procurement Service should be established within the General Services Administration (GSA), the central purchasing agent for the federal government. The new service would promote the procurement of new products and the use of performance standards, a method of purchasing that favors technical change.

The Problem

Chapter 5 identified the key role of the early experimental users of a new product or process. Their trial, and the information acquired with respect to the merits and difficulties of the new invention, provides an important input into the decision processes of the rest of the potential users. Early use is risky, and generates external economies of information. These are key characteristics that suggest that private initiative, guided by the profit motive, will not draw sufficient resources unless supplemented by active public policies.

Of the many ways that the federal government could act to enlarge the ranks of early users, among the most promising is for it to become an early user itself. Seven and one-half billion dollars worth of unspecialized goods are now bought each year by the federal government: $1.5

billion in GSA Federal Supply Service purchases, $5 billion in defense purchases of civilian type goods and $1 billion in direct procurement by civilian executive agencies.[28] This is a major share of the shipments of many industries. Even where the share is small, as in clothing and textiles, the federal government is still the largest single purchaser because the remaining sales are split between thousands of wholesale and retail shipments.

Present purchasing practices tend to work against the government being an early user in three ways. First, many products are specified by procurement orders in exact physical terms, thus precluding the introduction of new products. Second, there is tendency to reduce the number of different catalog items in any one category, thus discouraging product diversity.[29] Technical change, however, is facilitated by product diversity, for new products are often initially superior in a limited spectrum of the ultimate uses, so that the early diffusion stage requires both the new and old product. Third, the present policy emphasizes price competition, as in the advertising for sealed bids and awarding the order to the lowest responsible bidder.[30] Yet often the advantages of new products are in better performance rather than in a lower price, so that the emphasis on price discourages their introduction.

It is not easy to turn existing procurement practice around, nor should the emphasis on low prices be abandoned. Hence, a parallel organization to the Federal Supply Service is proposed—an Experimental Procurement Service.

This organization, with a relatively small annual budget of approximately $15 to $20 million, would still be part of the GSA. As a result, it might influence the Federal Supply Service which would be

[28] Author's estimates for fiscal year 1964.

[29] The Federal Supply Service has a standardization service engaged in such activities as reducing the number of types of teletypewriter ribbons from sixty-two to two. See *Report of the Administrator of General Services, 1964* (Washington: Government Printing Office)—henceforth cited as *Administrator's Report*. On the other hand, the tendency towards standardization is limited by a "customer orientation" that allows scope for using agency preferences. The GSA's origins as a centralized procurement service in 1949 involved accommodating individual agencies with a procurement tradition. Yet the emphasis on standardization for large volume procurement necessarily has made the GSA hostile to individual agency experimentation.

[30] See Dickson Reck, *Government Purchasing and Competition* (Berkeley: University of California Press, 1954).

doing the larger part of federal purchasing. The new service would also need to establish close relationships with the DOD, since the largest volume of unspecialized products is direct purchases by the Defense Department. Here, however, the task would be simplified by the fact that defense buying often follows the product schedules of the GSA, so that its acceptance ensures defense procurement. Furthermore, the trend is to shift the non-specialized purchasing from Defense to the GSA. In 1964, for example, GSA began purchasing for the DOD all its paint and hand tools.[31]

Specific Tasks of the New Service

The first task of the Experimental Procurement Service would be the purchase of new and relatively unproven products. It would buy such items in limited quantity, concentrating on items used by several agencies and likely to be used generally throughout the economy.

Once purchased, the new products would be distributed to agencies, and the experience with their use would be carefully monitored. The Service would write up the experience, making the reports publicly available. In this way the private sector could learn directly from federal experience. This would in itself be an innovation, for according to Dickson Reck's pioneering study of federal procurement, "The General Services Administration does not attempt to make such (purchasing) information available for the good reason that it is responsible for government purchasing and not for supplying information to other buyers."[32] The objective of a general acceleration of technical change requires making the information available to other buyers. There is some evidence of interest in such purchasing information: a National Association of Purchasing Agents Survey showed 31 percent of the companies used federal specifications in their own buying, such specifications being the one kind of purchasing information which must be disclosed in the invitations to bid.[33]

Where the initial experience warrants, the Experimental Procurement

---

[31] *Administrator's Report.* Another reason we would place the new service within GSA is that in a quiet way the GSA has been an innovator. For example, in 1964 the GSA pioneered in the application of computers to freight rate auditing and the use of new movable interchangeable office partitions.

[32] Reck, *op. cit.,* p. 214.

[33] *Ibid.,* p. 87.

Service would urge the inclusion of new products as standard items in the Federal Supply Schedule. Once in the schedule, the new product's salesmen can be relied upon to familiarize agencies with the item.

The second major task of the Service would be the development of performance standards for government procurement. As noted above, a central feature of the government procurement is product specification in exact physical terms, as, for example, the gauge of steel to be used in filing cabinets or the chemical composition of paint. In contrast, performance standards would state what kind of punishment the filing cabinet should be able to endure or how long the paint should last. Performance criteria are more favorable to technical change, in that a new product of a different composition (the usual case) can meet performance criteria, whereas physical specifications practically rule out new products. Even apart from the effects on technical change, performance criteria have the obvious advantage of stating directly the users' objectives in the product specification. Physical specifications are used only because performance is difficult to observe directly and such specifications are cheaper to develop.[34] Furthermore, physical specifications are cheaper to administer. Visual inspection often suffices and, where it does not, only simple laboratory tests are necessary. To establish whether a product meets performance specifications may cost thousands of dollars.

Given these relative costs and the need for thousands of specifications, it is not surprising that the standardization group of the FSS has placed relatively little emphasis on performance standards. The resources of the Experimental Procurement Service will redress the balance. It will not start from scratch; the National Bureau of Standards, with long experience in developing performance criteria, has already under way two important projects to devise performance standards—a $150,000 annual effort on roofing materials and a $500,000 annual effort on data processing systems.[35] Probably a good part of the Service's funds here can be used by contracting with the National Bureau, but the Service should

[34] The average cost of developing new FSS specifications is about $1,000. This is roughly estimated from appropriations data in the hearings on the fiscal year 1966 budget (Independent Offices), and data in the *Administrator's Report*. In contrast, the National Bureau of Standards tire testing program to develop performance standards cost roughly $300,000 (Reck, *op. cit.*, pp. 195-96).

[35] U.S. Department of Commerce, *Hearings Before a Subcommittee of the Committee on Appropriations for 1965, House of Representatives*, 88 Cong. 2 sess. (Washington: Government Printing Office, 1964).

be free to use other government laboratories, universities, or private companies.[36] The resulting performance standards, and the reports on new products, should be made public.

Evaluating the Experiment

The title, Experimental Procurement Service, is intended in two senses; it will experiment with new products, and, like all the proposals, it is itself an experiment. Accordingly, a five year limit is suggested for the life of this service; then the merit of continuance or expansion would be evaluated.

There are two different dimensions to be considered: benefits to the government in its own operations, and benefits from more rapid diffusion generally. One might measure the pattern of federal and private adoption in those products where the Service is active relative to those products in which it has played no role. The speed-up in diffusion can then be weighed by the gains in productivity, utility, and so forth, that the new products represent over the products they displace. This would give a crude measure of the crucial question: how much does the Service add in stimulating new product adoption in the federal government and the economy generally?

[36] Closely related to the development of performance standards is the study of whether some sort of "systems" cost encompassing maintenance and operations as well as initial cost could be used in awarding orders. Many technical changes involve the substitution of capital for labor, or in terms of government procurement, a higher initial price, and a lower operating and maintenance cost. Some new products, like an electric typewriter, become a separate item in the supply system, but for less sharp breaks in technology the problem of a bias against high initial costs may be of some importance. This difficulty could be met by some use of a DOD practice of comparing weapons systems, not on initial cost, but on a five-year total system cost which includes initial cost and operations, maintenance, and personnel training for five years. Systems with advantages in operating cost then obtain credit for such advantages. This method of procurement was blessed in effect by Congress in legislation establishing the GSA. Instead of requiring the award to the lowest responsible bidder, the law provides, "Award shall be made . . . to that responsible bidder whose bid, conforming to the invitation for bids, will be most advantageous to the Government, price and other factors considered." (June 30, 1949, Chap. 288, Title III, sec. 303, 63 Stat. 395, 41 USCA 253 [b].) The intent was to allow a trade-off between product qualities and price in making awards. In fact, "other factors" are seldom used because they are difficult to administer and justify. A study of the use of system costs by this new service for a few selected items may be one way of introducing more flexible trade-offs between quality and initial price than now exists, thus making the procurement system more receptive to technical change.

Note, however, that great success in itself would be suspicious. The easy way to operate this Service would be to pick off products that had begun to be adopted widely in the private sector and were on the threshold of adoption by the federal government. The Service should do more than this—it should reach far back in the adoption process and hence experience some conspicuous failures.

Some Political Problems

The economic calculus of total benefits and costs represent, however, only part of the impact of the Service. If it is successful, it will have distributional aspects; that is, some individuals will be hurt and some will gain. These specific impacts will lead to political difficulties.

The political difficulties center first on the publication of reports of early use. Some of these will be negative, and there is a long-standing tradition that government agencies do not make negative statements about the products of manufacturers. The initial reluctance of the Public Health Service to take a stand on smoking, the limitation of the Food and Drug Administration to questions of the safety rather than the effectiveness of new drugs until very recently, and the furor which occurred when the Bureau of Standards labelled a battery additive as useless, are all expressions of this tradition.[37] On the other hand, reports on early use will lose their creditability if only the positive ones are published.

Second, the Experimental Procurement Service, if it succeeds, will tilt government purchasing in the direction of new products and, as a result, will favor one kind of manufacturer over another. Congress has displayed a preference for keeping federal purchasing in line, and not ahead of current commercial practice, simply to insure that all existing manufacturers have a chance to participate in federal sales. The preference for a passive role for government procurement is manifested in the early years of GSA by the limited funds for commodity research and the fact that "for many years Congress struck out from appropriation bills budget requests for purchasing program research."[38] But one cannot have it both ways: it is impossible to keep government procurement open to all established manufacturers, and at the same time use it to

[37] A major exception is the Department of Agriculture whose research bulletins have indicated certain kinds of products were worthless although brand names have not been mentioned. Perhaps, because it is so long-standing, there has been little objection.

[38] Reck, *op. cit.,* p. 211.

stimulate the development of new technology. The small-scale experiment proposed here will shift federal procurement toward the latter direction. The potential gains make the experiment well worth attempting.

An Industrial Extension Service

In 1965 the Congress passed the State Technical Services Act[39] which created, under the direction of the Department of Commerce, a program to support universities in providing technical assistance to small and medium sized business firms to accelerate the diffusion of technology. Since the program is so promising and so new, and since to a considerable degree it is being undertaken as an experiment along the lines suggested in this study, some discussion of it is warranted.

The Nature of the Gap

As the frontiers of new technology are pushed ahead, industrial practice and production follow, sometimes pressing close on the leaders, sometimes lagging behind, the gap varying from industry to industry and firm to firm. A stimulus to economic growth can come from bringing the technology in general use closer to frontiers, as well as from advancing the frontiers. The Industrial Extension Service is motivated by the hypothesis that some, but certainly not all, of the lag in the adoption of new technology by many small firms reflects their inability to comprehend and evaluate available technical information.

Any business firm, large or small, has available to it a flood of literature on new products and materials in the form of technical magazines and advertising brochures. However, as pointed out in Chapter 5, some new developments have a built-in set of strong advocates—in particular new products and materials produced by profit oriented business firms. Others, like new processes not associated with profits for a supplier, generally do not have advocates. For these developments the business firm generally must take initiative on its own. For its evaluation the firm has access to the technical literature and the advisory services of suppliers, government agencies like the Small Business Administration, and consultants. But a significant number of firms are unable to understand and evaluate the technical literature, unacquainted with and untrusting

[39] State Technical Services Act of 1965. Public law 182, 89 Cong. 1 sess. (Washington: Government Printing Office, 1966).

of the assistance of professional consultants, and even unaware that technical problems have solutions and that there are better ways of doing things.[40]

The problem area concerns largely small business firms without a strong inhouse technical competence—generally this will mean without an R&D staff. In 1959 more than 99 percent of all business firms, and more than 90 percent of all manufacturing firms, employed less than 100 persons. These small firms accounted for about 40 percent of total business employment, and about 20 percent of manufacturing employment.[41] And in any manufacturing industries the percent of employment accounted for by small firms was significantly higher than the 20 percent national average. In lumber and wood products, apparel and related products, printing and publishing, and furniture, the figure is above 40 percent. For stone, clay and glass products; food and kindred products; and fabricated metal products the figure is about 35 percent. Thus, the small firm sector is important outside of manufacturing, comprises one-fifth of manufacturing employment, and more than one-third of manufacturing employment in a number of major industries. Prior to the State Technical Services Act of 1965, what was missing was a service that could bring the advantages of different processes to the attention of this class of firm in a convincing way, help develop their competence to evaluate new inputs, and help them effect the switchover to new methods. In short, what was missing is an analogue to the type of service provided to farmers by the cooperative federal-state extension service.[42]

The social benefits of such a service, if effective, could be substantial. The costs of low productivity are only partly reflected in a lower rate of profits for the owners; often they are reflected in lower wages for employees and in higher prices and lower quality products for consumers. Competition with more progressive firms for labor and customers tends

[40] For a discussion of the availability of technological information see S. Herner and R. S. Meyer, *How Smaller Firms Solve Problems and Keep Abreast of Technical Development* (Washington: Herner and Company, 1957).

[41] *U.S. Census of Manufacturers: 1958*, Vol. I, *Summary Statistics* (Washington: Government Printing Office, 1961).

[42] For a history of agricultural extension, at least in its early days, see A. C. True, *A History of Agricultural Extension Work in the United States, 1785-1923*, Dept. of Agriculture, Misc. Pub. No. 15 (Washington: Government Printing Office, 1928). For analysis, see Vernon W. Ruttan, "Research on the Economics of Technological Change in American Agriculture," *Journal of Farm Economics*, Vol. 42 (November 1960).

to mitigate this situation, but not eliminate it. The costs of a large gap between average and best practices, and the benefits of reducing that gap, are likely to be widely shared.

It is possible, of course, that such a service might reduce the incentives for individual firms to maintain their own in-house technical evaluation capability. It is doubtful that this will be significant, however. The effect is more likely to be the opposite. Increasing the competitive strength of small and medium-sized companies may spur the more progressive ones to greater efforts. One of the more important effects of such a program might be to improve the general competitive tone of the economy by reducing the advantages of large firms with large technical staffs.

The Nature of the Services

The bulk of the work of an effective Industrial Extension Service probably should be dissemination of information about best practice through short courses, conferences, and demonstrations. Consultation with firms which come in with questions and problems, and dissemination of information as to where specialized consulting or other help can be obtained, should be provided. But the effectiveness of the Service will depend largely on how well it is able to identify fields and classes of firms where actual practice is lagging significantly, contact and convince them that the advantages of adopting new practices are great, and help them make a change. Much of the activity of an effective Service undoubtedly should involve visiting, observing, and proselytizing in the field. Some research should also be done to identify the kinds of practices and techniques where the payoffs from adoption would be greatest.

This is much in the spirit of the Agricultural Extension Service. However, this analogy is far from perfect. In its heyday the Agricultural Extension Service of a state usually dealt with a relatively homogeneous group of clients. Further, at that time a well-trained extension agent could be familiar with most aspects of agricultural technology. In contrast, an Industrial Extension Service must deal with a highly diversified set of clients and a considerable degree of specialization would be required. Another important difference is that individual farmers seldom view others as competitors. In manufacturing, an improvement in one firm's productivity and sales may be at the expense of other firms.

The most fundamental problem will be delineating the group of prospective clients. Although in practice county agents concentrated upon the most receptive farmers, agricultural extension services took all farmers into their domain. In industrial extension some hard decisions must be made as to who are the appropriate clients. While no one would consider sending an industrial extension agent to call on Du Pont, it is still hard to isolate the groups for which the pay-off from industrial extension would be greatest. They include small and medium manufacturers without a technical staff of their own, but this group is large and diverse, including both the progressive and the backward. Some narrower group must be delineated.

The problem here is much like the allocation of attention in manpower retraining programs. Just as the easiest persons to retrain and reemploy are not necessarily the ones for whom retraining makes the greatest difference, the firms which are easiest to persuade to adopt technology are not necessarily the ones for whom the Extension Service makes the biggest difference in their productivity.

The problems of isolating prospective clients of the Service, and finding the best methods to reach them, can be resolved only by experimentation designed to yield cost-benefit information about different classes of clients. The following are a small sample of relevant questions:

1. To what extent will business firms using backward practices be willing to listen to and be persuaded by an industrial extension agent from the state university? Can such persuasion take place in short courses and conferences to which business firms are invited to send representatives, or must the Extension Service more aggressively reach out and force its attention on the firms most in need of help. If the latter proves to be the case, the cost of the Service per firm influenced will be greater.

2. To what extent does useful advice depend on intimate knowledge of the specific problems of a particular firm, in contrast with more general knowledge of the best practices and typical practice in the industry? If the former, again a much more costly Service will be required, or the advice will be of much less value and relevance.

3. Will the costs, in terms of increased need for personal consultation, be significantly larger for the backward firm with almost no in-house technical competence than for the average or just sub-average firm, with perhaps a greater facility to learn from more impersonal and formal presentations? If the backward firms are extremely expensive to

reach, then perhaps the Service should focus its efforts on the sub-average firm rather than the most backward ones.

4. To what extent will the industrial extension agents displace existing private consulting firms, thus making little net contribution to improving technology? The Service should complement rather than compete with such services. At the same time, many firms outside the business mainstream should be reached, and they may require individualized consulting services. It may be possible to set up referral procedures to increase the demand for private consulting services.

Answers to such specific questions will not only guide the organization of the Service; they also will determine the principal question about the Industrial Extension Service concept as a whole. Will such a program have the high rate of return that its parallel with the Agricultural Extension Service and the foregoing analysis of the diffusion process suggest? The answer requires actual experience.

An explicit experimental focus is particularly important because many states now have such programs, yet by and large they have not been collecting the relevant data.[43] To be sure, the services of several of these programs appear to be much in demand, and in some cases business is an enthusiastic supporter. However, political support of a program that gives something for nothing scarcely is a reliable index of rate of return.

The Program as an Experiment

Some criticisms of the State Technical Services Act are suggested by the way it appears to be taking shape. One is that the formal statement of the program lays more stress on preparing and disseminating written reports, and serving as a reference service, and less stress in identifying, testing, and evaluating possible improved practices, than may be desirable. But the major problem with the program as presently conceived is that it is far less of a controlled experiment than it might be.

It does not make provision for encouraging specific kinds of diversity in the various states. Nor does it require the kind of statistical reporting that would collect data relevant to the most important unresolved ques-

---

[43] Twenty-eight states now have some kind of information and/or research service for business firms run through universities. Georgia, North Carolina, Pennsylvania, and Iowa all have medium-sized to large programs, with Georgia's annual budget for work of this kind running to $500,000 a year, but most of the efforts are small—involving a staff of half a dozen professionals or less.

tions listed above. For example, comparison of changes in average practice over a five-year period between one region with such a Service and one without would have been useful, but the initiation of the program in all states precludes this. Data could still be collected to compare large and small programs. The establishment of the program on a fifty-state level, with no attempt to sponsor different approaches in exploring questions of this sort, makes it more difficult to answer these questions. However, there should be enough natural diversity among the states to obtain some answers if the questions are posed and the statistical reporting procedures are established early.

Without an early orientation to experimentation, data collection, and analysis, little more will be learned about the impact of industrial extension than is now known from the experiences of the recent state programs. In the absence of such an orientation, the proposed evaluation in future years may not be able to provide a firm recommendation supported by empirical quantitative evidence. Indeed, it might be able to do no more than recommend further experimentation.

A Concluding Note

The five proposals presented in this chapter are designed to deal with the major failures in the structure of private incentives and capabilities not already dealt with by existing public programs. The National Institute of Technology is addressed to the most important unmet problem—the uncertainties and externalities involved in technology-motivated basic research and experimental development. The proposal for selective support of major systems development aims at a different problem—that of stimulating more applied R&D of larger cost and scope than existing business firms can support. In special cases, where conditions of market failure with respect to R&D in an industry are chronic, special industry research support programs are recommended. The proposal to make government procurement more progressive and experimental is designed to enlarge the ranks of early users, where external economies of information useful to later prospective buyers may be great. The Industrial Extension Service, recently instituted under the State Technical Services Act, aims at the other end of the diffusion process; it seeks to spur the laggards.

These proposals are aimed principally at making the process of technological advance more efficient in the sense of getting more output from the resources invested. If implemented, they will certainly have greater impact in certain sectors than others, but their objective is greater efficiency across the board. Except in cases relating to sectors where the existing institutional structure is particularly adverse, or to applied R&D that yields public benefits, the proposals have not been purposefully oriented toward changing the direction of technological advance.

The proposals, however, are consistent with a major shifting of the direction of technological advance. In guiding allocation of attention and resources for any or all of the programs, one of the criteria must be the value society places on the likely resulting technical advance. Everyone has his own set of values. For example, many people, including the authors, would assign a valuation significantly greater than market price to technological progress which promised directly or indirectly to improve the quality of the environment by reducing smog, noise, or congestion, or which would increase the quality or reduce the cost of low income housing. If R&D projects of high promise are available, the authors would like to see a significant increase in the quantity of resources allocated to the nondefense public sector generally, and particularly R&D aimed at enabling urban governments to perform their functions more effectively and at making urban areas more pleasant places in which to live.

However, other people have different values. Furthermore, it is not clear that strongly slanting R&D toward meeting specific social wants is the most effective policy approach. Many people believe it important that large cities establish good mass transit systems. One way to move toward this objective is to invest in more R&D on mass transit. But it can be argued that present technology is quite adequate for the design of much more swift and attractive mass transit than is presently available; that mass transit is needed now, and that there are few research possibilities which promise quickly to lead to significant increases in performance or reductions in cost. Hence, proper policy calls for building mass transit systems now in the cities that most need them, based on existing technological knowledge, with perhaps a small continuing R&D program so that in later years the new systems can be better than the old. But even when the eye is on the future, rather than investing large sums in R&D on mass transit, investment in increasing productivity in certain important manufacturing sectors where the promise of R&D is particularly great might be more efficient, for this increased wealth could then be used to subsidize mass transit. Because of the existence of these kinds of options, proposals must be judged on their likelihood of achieving significant technical advances, as well as on the value society places on those advances.

Policy toward technological advance should be viewed as one among a wide range of public policy instruments, all together molding the allocation and effectiveness of resources. There are some instances where it is important to aim R&D precisely at a high priority objective. In most obvious cases existing technology does not provide a satisfactory solution, even if massive resources are invested using currently existing techniques; thus, to find a cure for cancer, or to go to the moon, significant R&D is needed. But for objectives like gaining a significantly improved urban transport system, or renovating central cities, or eliminating poverty in the U.S., it is not at all clear that a massive dose of directly aimed R&D is the best approach; techniques already exist that can deal with these objectives if resources are allocated to them. With the exception of cases where existing technology is inadequate to the task, public policy toward technological advance should be viewed as providing generally exploitable increased economic potential, aimed at the areas where opportunities are greatest for expanding potential output, and leaving for other policy instruments the marshalling of resources to meet specific social objectives. Whatever the goals, affluence helps.

Bibliography

Abramovitz, Moses. "Resource and Output Trends in the United States Since 1870," *American Economic Review,* Vol. 46, No. 2 (May 1956).

Adams, Leonard P., and Aronson, Robert L. *Workers and Industrial Change; A Case Study of Labor Mobility* (Cornell Studies in Industrial and Labor Relations, Vol. 8). Ithaca: Cornell University Press, 1957.

Alchian, Armen; Arrow, Kenneth J.; and Capron, William. *An Economic Analysis of the Market for Scientists and Engineers.* The RAND Corporation, Santa Monica, RM-2190-RC, June 1958.

Allen, Francis R., and others. *Technology and Social Change.* New York: Appleton-Century-Crofts, Inc., 1957.

Ames, Edward, "Research, Invention, Development and Innovation," *American Economic Review,* Vol. 51, June 1961.

Ames, Edward, and Rosenberg, N. "Changing Technological Leadership and Industrial Growth," *Economic Journal,* Vol. 73, March 1963.

Anderson, C. Arnold, and Bowman, Mary Jean (eds.). *Education and Economic Development.* Chicago: Aldine Publishing Company, 1965.

Anthony, Robert N. *Management Controls in Industrial Research Organizations.* Boston: Harvard Business School, Division of Research, 1952.

Arrow, Kenneth J. "The Economic Implications of Learning by Doing," *Review of Economic Studies,* Vol. 29, June 1962.

Asher, Harold. *Cost Quantity Relationships in the Airframe Industry.* The RAND Corporation, Santa Monica, R-291, July 1956.

Ashton, Thomas S. *The Industrial Revolution, 1760-1830.* London: Oxford University Press, 1964.

Bain, A. D. "The Growth of Demand for New Commodities," *Journal of the Royal Statistical Association,* Vol. 126, Series A, 1963.

Bain, Joe S. *Industrial Organization.* New York: John Wiley & Sons, Inc., 1959.

Baldwin, William. "Contracted Research and the Case for Big Business," *Journal of Political Economy,* Vol. 70, June 1962.

Bancroft, Gertrude and Garfinkle, Stuart. "Job Mobility in 1961," *Monthly Labor Review,* Vol. 86, August 1963.

Barber, Bernard. *Science and the Social Order.* New York: The Free Press of Glencoe, Inc., 1952.

Barnett, Homer. *Innovation; the Basis of Cultural Change.* New York: McGraw-Hill Book Co., 1953.

Baxter, James P. *Scientists Against Time.* Boston: Little, Brown and Company, 1946.

Becker, Gary S. *Human Capital; a Theoretical and Empirical Analysis, with Special Reference to Education* (National Bureau of Economic Research). New York: Columbia University Press, 1964.

Bello, Francis. "The World's Greatest Industrial Laboratory," *Fortune,* November 1958.

Blank, David M., and Stigler, George J. *The Demand and Supply of Scientific Personnel.* New York: National Bureau of Economic Research, 1957.

Blaug, M. "A Survey of the Theory of Process-Innovations," *Economica,* Vol. 30, February 1963.

Braybrooke, David, and Lindblom, Charles E. *A Strategy of Decision: Policy Evaluation as a Social Process.* New York: The Free Press of Glencoe, Inc., 1963.

Bright, Arthur Aaron, Jr. *The Electric-Lamp Industry: Technological Change and Economic Development From 1800 to 1947.* New York: The Macmillan Company, 1949.

Bright, Arthur Aaron, Jr., and Maclaurin, W. Rupert. "Economic Factors Influencing the Development and Introduction of the Fluorescent Lamp," *Journal of Political Economy,* Vol. 51, October 1943.

Bright, James R. *Automation and Management.* Boston: Harvard Business School, Division of Research, 1958.

Brode, Wallace. "The Growth of Science and a National Science Program," *American Scientist,* March 1962.

Brown, Gilbert, "Characteristics of New Enterprises," *New England Business Review,* June 1957 and July 1957.

Brown, Murray, and De Cani, John S. "Technological Change and the Distribution of Income," *International Economic Review,* September 1963.

————. "A Measure of Technological Unemployment," *Review of Economics and Statistics,* Vol. 45, November 1963.

Brown, William H. "Innovation in the Machine Tool Industry," *Quarterly Journal of Economics,* Vol. 71, August 1957.

Brozen, Yale. "The Economic Future of Research and Development," *Industrial Laboratories,* December 1953.

_____. "Invention, Innovation, and Imitation," *American Economic Review,* Vol. 41, No. 2, May 1951.

_____. "Research, Technology and Productivity," in L. R. Tripp (ed.), *Industrial Productivity.* Madison, Wisconsin: Industrial Relations Research Association, 1951.

_____. "Technological Change, Ideology and Productivity," *Political Science Quarterly,* Vol. 70, December 1955.

Bruton, Henry. "Innovations and Equilibrium Growth," *Economic Journal,* Vol. 66, September 1956.

Bush, George P., and Hattery, Lowell H. (eds.). *Scientific Research: Its Administration and Organization.* Washington: University Press of Washington, D.C., 1950.

Bush, Vannevar. *Science, The Endless Frontier.* Washington: U. S. Government Printing Office, 1945.

Butterfield, Herbert. *The Origins of Modern Science: 1300-1800.* New York: The Macmillan Company, 1957.

Carter, Charles F. *Investment in Innovation.* London: Oxford University Press, 1958.

Carter, Charles F., and Williams, Bruce R. *Industry and Technical Progress: Factors Governing the Speed and Application of Science.* London: Oxford University Press, 1957.

_____. *Science in Industry; Policy for Progress.* London: Oxford University Press, 1959.

Cohen, I. Bernard. *Science, Servant of Man.* Boston: Little, Brown and Company, 1948.

Coleman, James, Katz, Elihu, and Menzel, Herbert. "The Diffusion of an Innovation Among Physicians," *Sociometry,* December 1957.

Comanor, William S. "Research and Competitive Product Differentiation in the Pharmaceutical Industry in the United States," *Economica,* Vol. 31, November 1964.

Conant, James B. *Science and Common Sense.* New Haven: Yale University Press, 1951.

Council of Economic Advisers. *Economic Report of the President, Together with the Annual Report of the Council of Economic Advisers.* Washington: U.S. Government Printing Office, 1962, 1964.

Denison, Edward F. *The Sources of Economic Growth in the United States and the Alternatives Before Us* (Supplementary Paper No. 13). New York: Committee for Economic Development, 1962.

Denver Research Institute. *The Commercial Application of Missile/Space Technology.* Denver: University of Denver, 1963.

Dernburg, Thomas F. "Consumer Response to Innovation: Television," in *Studies in Household Economic Behavior.* New Haven: Yale University Press, 1958.

Drandakis, E. M., and Phelps, Edmund S., "A Model of Induced Innovation, Growth and Distribution." Cowles Foundation Discussion Paper No. 186, July 26, 1965.

Duesenberry, James S. *Income, Saving, and the Theory of Consumer Behavior.* Cambridge: Harvard University Press, 1949.

————. "Innovation and Growth," *American Economic Review,* Vol. 46, May 1956.

Dunlop, John (ed.). *Automation and Technological Change* (The American Assembly). Englewood Cliffs, N.J.: Prentice-Hall, Inc., 1962.

Dupré, Joseph S., and Lakoff, S. A. *Science and the Nation; Policy and Politics.* Englewood Cliffs, N.J.: Prentice-Hall, Inc., 1962.

Dupree, A. Hunter. *Science and the Emergence of Modern America, 1865-1916* (The Berkeley Series in American History). Chicago: Rand McNally & Co., 1963.

————. *Science in the Federal Government; A History of Policies and Activities to 1940.* Cambridge: Belknap Press of Harvard University Press, 1957.

Eckaus, Richard S. "Economic Criteria for Education and Training," *The Review of Economics and Statistics,* Vol. 46, May 1964.

Eckstein, Otto. "Aggregate Demand and the Current Unemployment Problem," in Arthur M. Ross (ed.), *Unemployment and the American Economy.* New York: John Wiley & Sons, Inc., 1964.

Enos, John L. *Petroleum Progress and Profits.* Cambridge: The M.I.T. Press, 1962.

————. "Invention and Innovation in the Petroleum Refining Industry," in *The Rate and Direction of Inventive Activity* (National Bureau of Economic Research). Princeton: Princeton University Press, 1962.

Evans, W. Duane. "The Production Economics of Growth," *American Economic Review,* Vol. 46, May 1956.

Ewell, Raymond H. "Role of Research in Economic Growth," *Chemical and Engineering News,* Vol. 33, No. 29, July 18, 1955.

Fellner, William. "The Influence of Market Structure on Technological Progress," *Quarterly Journal of Economics,* Vol. 65, November 1951. Erratum. Vol. 66, May 1952.

————. *Trends and Cycles in Economic Activity.* New York: Henry Holt & Company, 1956.

————. "Two Propositions in the Theory of Induced Innovations," *Economic Journal,* Vol. 71, June 1961.

Folger, John K., and Nam, Charles B. "Trends in Education in Relation to the Occupational Structure," *Sociology of Education,* Vol. 38, Fall 1964.

Foote, Nelson N., and others. *Housing Choices and Housing Constraints.* New York: McGraw-Hill Book Co., Inc., 1960.

Frankel, Marvin. "Obsolescence and Technological Change in a Maturing Economy," *American Economic Review,* Vol. 45, June 1955.

Galbraith, John Kenneth. *American Capitalism, the Concept of Countervailing Power.* Boston: Houghton Mifflin Co., 1952.

Gilfillan, S. Colum. "Inventiveness by Nation and State, A Note on Statistical Treatment," *Journal of the Patent Office Society,* Vol. 12, June 1930.

————. "The Prediction of Technical Change," *Review of Economics and Statistics,* Vol. 34, November 1952.

————. *The Sociology of Invention.* Chicago: Follett Publishing Co., 1935.

————. *Inventing the Ship.* Chicago: Follett Publishing Co., 1935.

Glennan, Thomas. "Issues in the Choice of Development Policies." The RAND Corporation, Santa Monica, P-3153, October 1965.

Graue, Erwin. "Inventions and Production," *Review of Economics and Statistics,* Vol. 25, November 1943.

Griliches, Zvi. "Hybrid Corn: An Exploration in the Economics of Technological Change," *Econometrica,* Vol. 25, October 1957.

————. "Research Costs and Social Returns: Hybrid Corn and Related Innovations," *Journal of Political Economy,* Vol. 66, October 1958.

————. "Research Expenditures, Education, and the Aggregate Agricultural Production Function," *American Economic Review,* Vol. 54, December 1964.

Griliches, Zvi, and Schmookler, Jacob. "Inventing and Maximizing," *American Economic Review,* Vol. 53, September 1963.

Grosse, Anne P. "The Technological Structure of the Cotton Textile Industry," in Wassily Leontief and others, *Studies in the Structure of the American Economy; Theoretical and Empirical Explorations in Input-*

Output Analysis (Harvard Economic Research Project). New York: Oxford University Press, 1953.

Gustafson, Eric. "Research and Development, New Products, and Productivity Change," *American Economic Review,* Vol. 52, May 1962.

Habakkuk, H. J. *American and British Technology in the Nineteenth Century.* New York: Cambridge University Press, 1962.

Hahn, F. H., and Matthews, R. C. O. "The Theory of Economic Growth: A Survey," *Economic Journal,* Vol. 74, December 1964.

Hall, Arnold. "Research, Development and Technical Issues," *Flight,* December 28, 1956.

Hall, George R., and Johnson, Robert E. "Aircraft-Co Production and U.S. Procurement Policy." Unpublished manuscript.

Hall, Rupert. "The Scholar and the Craftsman in the Scientific Revolution," in M. Clagett (ed.), *Critical Problems in the History of Science.* Madison: University of Wisconsin Press, 1959.

Hamberg, Daniel. "Invention in the Industrial Research Laboratory," *Journal of Political Economy,* Vol. 71, April 1963.

————. "Size of Firm, Oligopoly, and Research: The Evidence," *Canadian Journal of Economics and Political Science,* Vol. 30, February 1964.

Hayek, Friedrich August von. "The Use of Knowledge in Society," *American Economic Review,* Vol. 35, September 1945.

————. "Economics and Knowledge, *Economica,* Vol. 4, New Series, February 1937.

Herner, S., and Meyer, R. S. *How Smaller Firms Solve Problems and Keep Abreast of Technical Development.* Washington: Herner & Co., 1957.

Hertz, David B. *The Theory and Practice of Industrial Research.* New York: McGraw-Hill Book Co., Inc., 1950.

Hickman, Bert O. *Investment Demand and U.S. Economic Growth.* Washington: The Brookings Institution, 1965.

Hicks, John R. *The Theory of Wages.* London: Macmillan & Co., Ltd., 1932.

Hill, Samuel E., and Harbison, Frederick. *Manpower and Innovation in American Industry.* Princeton: Princeton University, Industrial Relations Section (Research Report Series No. 96), 1959.

Hirsch, Werner Z. "Manufacturing Progress Functions," *Review of Economics and Statistics,* Vol. 34, May 1952.

Hitch, Charles. "The Character of Research and Development in a Competitive Economy." The RAND Corporation, Santa Monica, P-1297, May 1958.

Holland, Susan S. "Long-Term Unemployment in the 1960's," Special Labor Force Report No. 58, Monthly Labor Review, Vol. 88, September 1965.

Holman, Mary A. "The Utilization of Government-Owned Patented Inventions," The Patent, Trademark and Copyright Journal of Research and Education, Summer 1963 and Fall 1963.

Jacobson, Howard B., and Roucek, Joseph S. (eds.). Automation and Society. New York: Philosophical Library, 1959.

Jerome, Harry. Mechanization in Industry. New York: National Bureau of Economic Research, 1934.

Jewkes, John, Sawers, David and Stillerman, Richard. The Sources of Invention. New York: St. Martin's Press, Inc., 1958.

Johnston, Denis F. "Educational Attainment of Workers, March 1964," U.S. Department of Labor, Bureau of Labor Statistics, Special Labor Force Report No. 53, Monthly Labor Review, Vol. 88, May 1965.

Josephson, Matthew. Edison. New York: McGraw-Hill Book Co., Inc., 1959.

Kaempffert, W. B. (ed.). A Popular History of American Invention. New York: Charles Scribner's Sons, 1924.

Kalachek, Edward D. "The Composition of Unemployment and Public Policy," in R. A. Gordon and Margaret Gordon (eds.), Prosperity and Unemployment. New York: John Wiley & Sons, Inc., 1966.

Kamien, Morton I., and Schwartz, Nancy L. "Optimal Induced Technical Change," Pittsburgh, Carnegie Institute of Technology, mimeographed, 1966.

Katz, Elihu. "The Two-Step Flow of Communication: An Up-To-Date Report On An Hypothesis," Public Opinion Quarterly, Vol. 21, Spring 1957.

Keesing, Donald B. "Labor Skills and Comparative Advantage," American Economic Review, Vol. 56, No. 2, May 1966.

_____. "The Impact of Research and Development on United States Trade," Columbia University, mimeographed, April 1, 1966.

Kendrick, John W. Productivity Trends in the United States (National Bureau of Economic Research). Princeton: Princeton University Press, 1961.

Kennedy, Charles. "Induced Bias in Innovation and the Theory of Distribution," Economic Journal, Vol. 74, September 1964.

Kidd, Charles V. American Universities and Federal Research. Cambridge: Belknap Press of Harvard University Press, 1959.

Killeffer, David Herbert. *The Genius of Industrial Research.* New York: Reinhold Publishing Corp., 1948.

Killingsworth, Charles C. "Automation, Jobs and Manpower: The Case For Structural Unemployment," in Garth L. Magnum (ed.), *The Manpower Revolution: Its Policy and Consequences.* New York: Doubleday and Co., 1966.

Klein, Burton H. "The Decision Making Problem in Development," in *The Rate and Direction of Inventive Activity* (National Bureau of Economic Research). Princeton: Princeton University Press, 1962.

_____. "A Radical Proposal for R and D," *Fortune,* May 1958.

Klein, Burton H., and Meckling, William H. "Application of Operations Research to Development Decisions," *Operations Research,* May-June 1958.

Koopmans, Tjalling (ed.), *Activity Analysis of Production and Allocation.* New York: John Wiley & Sons, Inc., 1951.

Kuhn, Thomas S. *The Structure of Scientific Revolutions.* Chicago: University of Chicago Press, 1962.

Kuznets, Simon. *Secular Movements in Production and Prices.* Boston: Houghton Mifflin Company, 1930.

Lancaster, Kelvin. "Change and Innovation in the Technology of Consumption," *American Economic Review,* Vol. 56, No. 2, May 1966.

Lancaster, Kelvin, and Lipsey, R. G. "The General Theory of Second Best," *Review of Economic Studies,* Vol. 24, No. 1, 1956.

Lange, Oskar. "A Note on Innovations," *Review of Economics and Statistics,* Vol. 25, February 1943.

Little, Arthur D., Inc. *Basic Research in the Navy.* Report to the Secretary of the Navy by the Naval Research Advisory Committee. Cambridge, Massachusetts: 1959.

_____. *Patterns and Problems of Technical Innovation in American Industry.* Report to the National Science Foundation, Washington, D.C., September 1963 (A Government Research Report, U.S. Department of Commerce, Office of Technical Services).

Machlup, Fritz. *An Economic Review of the Patent System, Study of the Subcommittee on Patents, Trademarks, and Copyrights of the Senate Committee on the Judiciary,* 85 Cong. 2 sess. Washington: U.S. Government Printing Office, 1958.

_____. "Can There Be Too Much Research?," *Science,* November 28, 1958.

_____. *The Production and Distribution of Knowledge in the United States.* Princeton: Princeton University Press, 1962.

Maclaurin, W. Rupert. *Invention and Innovation in the Radio Industry*. New York: The Macmillan Company, 1949.

_____. "The Process of Technological Innovation: The Launching of a New Scientific Industry," *American Economic Review*, Vol. 40, March 1950.

_____. "Technological Progress in Some American Industries," *American Economic Review*, Vol. 44, May 1954.

_____. "The Sequence from Invention to Innovation and Its Relation to Economic Growth," *Quarterly Journal of Economics*, Vol. 67, February 1953.

Mansfield, Edwin. "Entry, Gibrat's Law, Innovation and the Growth of Firms," *American Economic Review*, Vol. 52, December 1962.

_____. "Industrial Research and Development Expenditures: Determinants, Prospects and Relation to Size of Firm and Inventive Output," *Journal of Political Economy*, Vol. 72, August 1964.

_____. "Innovation and Technical Change in the Railroad Industry," in *Transportation Economics* (National Bureau of Economic Research). New York: Columbia University Press, 1965.

_____. "Intrafirm Rates of Diffusion of an Innovation," *Review of Economics and Statistics*, Vol. 45, November 1963.

_____. "The Process of Technical Change," in Richard A. Tybout (ed.), *Economics of Research and Development*. Columbus: Ohio State University Press, 1965.

_____. "Rates of Return from Industrial Research and Development," *American Economic Review*, Vol. 55, No. 2, May 1965.

_____. "Size of Firm, Market Structure, and Innovation," *Journal of Political Economy*, Vol. 71, December 1963.

_____. "The Speed of Response of Firms to New Techniques," *Quarterly Journal of Economics*, Vol. 77, May 1963.

_____. "Technical Change and the Rate of Imitation," *Econometrica*, Vol. 29, October 1961.

_____. *Econometric Studies of Industrial Research and Technological Innovation*. New York: W. W. Norton & Co., 1967.

Markham, Jesse W. "Market Structure, Business Conduct, and Innovation," *American Economic Review*, Vol. 55, No. 2, May 1965.

Marschak, Thomas A. "The Role of Project Histories in the Study of R&D." The RAND Corporation, Santa Monica, P-2850, January 1964.

_____. "Strategy and Organization in a System Development Project," in *The Rate and Direction of Inventive Activity* (National Bureau of

Economic Research). Princeton: Princeton University Press, 1962.

Marshall, A. W., and Meckling, W. H. "Predictability of the Costs, Time, and Success of Development," in *The Rate and Direction of Inventive Activity* (National Bureau of Economic Research). Princeton: Princeton University Press, 1962.

McConnell, Campbell R., and Peterson, Wallace C. "Research and Development: Some Evidence for Small Firms," *Southern Economic Journal*, Vol. 31, April 1965.

Mees, Charles E., and Baker, J. R. *The Path of Science.* New York: John Wiley & Sons, Inc., 1946.

Mees, Charles E., and Leermakers, John A. *The Organization of Industrial Scientific Research.* New York: McGraw-Hill Book Co., 1950.

Merton, Robert K. "Fluctuations in the Rate of Industrial Invention," *Quarterly Journal of Economics,* Vol. 49, May 1935.

_____. "Priorities in Scientific Discovery: A Chapter in the Sociology of Science," *American Sociological Review,* Vol. 22, No. 6, December 1957.

Meyerson, Martin, Terrett, Barbara, and Wheaton, William L. C. *Housing, People, and Cities.* New York: McGraw-Hill Book Co., 1962.

Michael, Donald N. *Cybernation: The Silent Conquest.* Santa Barbara: Center for the Study of Democratic Institutions, 1962.

Miernyk, William H. *Inter-Industry Labor Mobility; The Case of the Displaced Textile Worker.* Boston: Northeastern University Press, 1955.

Miller, Ronald, and Sawers, David. *The Development of Civil Aircraft* (forthcoming).

Minasian, Jora R. "The Economics of Research and Development," in *The Rate and Direction of Inventive Activity* (National Bureau of Economic Research). Princeton: Princeton University Press, 1962.

Mishan, Edward J. "Second Thoughts on Second Best," *Oxford Economic Papers,* Vol. 14, No. 3. London: Oxford University Press, October 1962.

Mueller, Willard F. "A Case Study of Product Discovery and Innovation Costs," *Southern Economic Journal,* Vol. 24, July 1957.

_____. "The Origins of the Basic Inventions Underlying Du Pont's Major Product and Process Innovations, 1920 to 1950." in *The Rate and Direction of Inventive Activity* (National Bureau of Economic Research). Princeton: Princeton University Press, 1962.

Myint, Hla. *Theories of Welfare Economics.* London: Longmans, Green & Co., 1948.

National Academy of Sciences—National Research Council. *A Program for Building Research in the United States.* Washington: 1962.

_____. *Current Needs in Research, Relevant to the Interests of the United States Textile Industry.* Washington: 1962.

National Resources Planning Board. *Research, A National Resource, Part II, Industrial Research.* Washington: U.S. Government Printing Office, December 1940.

National Science Foundation. *Basic Research, A National Resource.* Washington: U.S. Government Printing Office, 1957.

_____. *Federal Organization for Scientific Activities, 1962,* NSF 62-37. Washington: U. S. Government Printing Office, 1963.

_____. *Federal Funds for Research, Development, and Other Scientific Activities,* Vol. 14. Washington: U. S. Government Printing Office, 1965.

_____. *Nonprofit Organizations, Expenditures and Manpower.* Washington: U. S. Government Printing Office, 1957.

_____. *Research and Development in Industry 1961,* NSF 64-9. (Surveys of Science Resources Series). Washington: U.S. Government Printing Office, 1964.

_____. *Industrial R&D Funds in Relation to Other Economic Variables.* Washington: U.S. Government Printing Office, 1965.

_____. *Proceedings of a Conference on Academic and Industrial Basic Research.* Washington: U.S. Government Printing Office, 1961.

_____. *Proceedings of a Conference on Research and Development and Its Impact on the Economy* (NSF 58-36). Washington: U.S. Government Printing Office, 1958.

Nelson, Richard R. "Full Employment Policy and Economic Growth," *American Economic Review,* December 1966. Vol. 56.

_____. "The Allocation of Research and Development Resources: Some Problems of Public Policy," in *Economics of Research and Development.* Columbus: Ohio State University Press, 1965.

_____. "The Economics of Invention: A Survey of the Literature," *Journal of Business,* Vol. 32, April 1959.

_____. "The Link Between Science and Invention: The Case of the Transistor," in *The Rate and Direction of Inventive Activity* (National Bureau of Economic Research). Princeton: Princeton University Press, 1962.

_____. "The Simple Economics of Basic Scientific Research—A Theoretical Analysis," *Journal of Political Economy,* Vol. 67, June 1959.

_____. "Uncertainty, Learning and the Economics of Parallel Research and Development Efforts," *Review of Economics and Statistics,* Vol. 43, November 1961.

————. "Aggregate Production Functions and Medium-Range Growth Projections," *American Economic Review,* Vol. 54, September 1964.

Nelson, Richard R., and Phelps, Edmund S. "Investment in Humans, Technological Diffusion, and Economic Growth," *American Economic Review,* Vol. 56, No. 2, May 1966.

Operations Research Office, Johns Hopkins University. Defense Spending and the United States Economy, Johns Hopkins University Press, Baltimore. 1959.

Organisation for Economic Co-operation and Development. *Science, Economic Growth, and Government Policy.* Paris: February 1964.

Peck, Merton J. *Competition in the Aluminum Industry 1945-1958.* Cambridge: Harvard University Press, 1961.

————. "Inventions in the Postwar American Aluminum Industry," in *The Rate and Direction of Inventive Activity* (National Bureau of Economic Research). Princeton: Princeton University Press, 1962.

Peck, Merton J., and Scherer, Frederic M. *The Weapons Acquisition Process: an Economic Analysis.* Boston: Harvard University Graduate School of Business Administration, Division of Research, 1962.

Phillips, Almarin. "Concentration, Scale and Technological Change in Selected Manufacturing Industries, 1899-1939," *Journal of Industrial Economics,* Vol. 4, June 1956.

Plant, Arnold. "The Economic Theory Concerning Patents for Inventions," *Economica,* Vol. 1, New Series, February 1934.

Polanyi, Michael. "Patent Reform," *Review of Economic Studies,* Vol. 11, Summer 1944.

Popper, Karl R. *The Logic of Scientific Discovery.* Toronto: University of Toronto Press, 1959.

Price, Don K. *Government and Science, Their Dynamic Relation in American Democracy.* New York: New York University Press, 1954.

————. *The Scientific Estate.* Cambridge: Harvard University Press, 1965.

Reck, Dickson. *Government Purchasing and Competition.* Berkeley: University of California Press, 1954.

Report of the Administrator of General Services, 1964. Washington: U.S. Government Printing Office, 1964.

Report of the Committee on the Economic Impact of Defense and Disarmament, July 1965. Washington: U.S. Government Printing Office, 1965.

Report of the National Commission on Technology, Automation, and Economic Progress. *Technology and the American Economy,* Vol. 1, Washington: U.S. Government Printing Office, 1966.

Resek, Robert W. "Neutrality of Technical Progress," *Review of Economics and Statistics,* Vol. 45, February 1963.

Rogers, Everett M. *The Diffusion of Innovations.* New York: The Free Press of Glencoe, Inc., 1962.

Rosenblum, Richard S. "Utilization of Technological By-Products of Military and Space R&D." Unpublished draft of a report to the Carmrand Committee of National Planning Association, Washington, D.C., March 1965.

Rossman, M. Joseph. *The Psychology of the Inventor: A Study of the Patentee.* Washington: Inventors Publishing Co., 1931.

Rubenstein, Albert H. "Setting Criteria for R&D," *Harvard Business Review,* Vol. 35, No. 1, January-February 1957.

Ruttan, Vernon W. "The Contribution of Technological Progress to Farm Output: 1950-75," *Review of Economics and Statistics,* Vol. 38, February 1956.

_____. "Research on the Economics of Technological Change in American Agriculture," *Journal of Farm Economics,* Vol. 42, November 1960.

Ryan, Bryce. "A Study of Technological Diffusion," *Rural Sociology,* September 1948.

Ryan, Bryce and Gross, Neal C. "The Diffusion of Hybrid Seed Corn in Two Iowa Communities," *Rural Sociology,* March 1943.

Salter, W. E. G. *Productivity and Technical Change.* Cambridge: Cambridge University Department of Applied Economics, 1960.

Samuelson, Paul A. "A New Theorem on Non Substitution," in Hugo Hegeland (ed.), *Money, Growth, and Methodology, and Other Essays in Economics in Honor of Johan Akerman* (Lund Social Science Studies No. 20). Lund, Sweden: C. W. K. Gleerup Publishers, 1961.

_____. "A Theory of Induced Innovation Along Kennedy-Weisäcker Lines," *Review of Economics and Statistics,* Vol. 47, November 1965.

Sanders, Barkev S. "The Course of Invention," *Journal of the Patent Office Society,* October 1936.

Scherer, Frederic M. "Firm Size, Market Structure, Opportunity, and the Output of Patented Inventions," *American Economic Review,* Vol. 55, December 1965.

_____. "Size of Firm, Oligopoly, and Research: A Comment," *Canadian Journal of Economics and Political Science,* May 1965.

_____. "The Watt-Boulton Steam Engine: A Case Study in the Economics of Technological Change." Unpublished manuscript.

Scherer, Frederic M., et al. *Patents and the Corporation.* Boston: J. J. Galvin, 1958.

Schlaifer, Robert O. and Heron, S. D. *The Development of Aircraft Engines and Fuels.* Boston: Harvard University Graduate School of Business Administration, Division of Research, 1950.

Schmookler, Jacob. "Bigness, Fewness, and Research," *Journal of Political Economy,* Vol. 67, December 1959.

————. "Changes in Industry and in the State of Knowledge as Determinants of Industrial Invention," in *The Rate and Direction of Inventive Activity* (National Bureau of Economic Research). Princeton: Princeton University Press, 1962.

————. "Economic Sources of Inventive Activity," *Journal of Economic History,* Vol. 22, March 1962.

————. *Invention and Economic Growth.* Cambridge: Harvard University Press, 1966.

————. Invention, Innovation and Competition," *Southern Economic Journal,* Vol. 20, April 1954.

————. "Inventors Past and Present," *Review of Economics and Statistics,* Vol. 39, August 1957.

————. "Technological Progress and the Modern American Corporation," in Edward S. Mason (ed.), *The Corporation in Modern Society.* Cambridge: Harvard University Press, 1960.

————. "The Level of Inventive Activity," *Review of Economics and Statistics,* Vol. 36, May 1954.

————. "The Utility of Patent Statistics," *Journal of the Patent Office Society,* June 1953.

Schmookler, Jacob, and Brownlee, Oswald. "Determinants of Inventive Activity," *American Economic Review,* Vol. 52, May 1962.

Schon, Donald A. *Displacement of Concepts.* New York: Humanities Press, Inc., 1964.

Schrier, Elliot. "Toward Technology Transfer," *Technology and Culture,* Vol. 3, No. 3, Summer 1964.

Schultz, Theodore W. *Transforming Traditional Agriculture.* New Haven: Yale University Press, 1964.

Schumpeter, Joseph A. *Capitalism, Socialism, and Democracy.* New York: Harper and Row, 1950.

————. *The Theory of Economic Development.* Cambridge: Harvard University Press, 1934.

Silk, Leonard S. *The Research Revolution*. New York: McGraw-Hill Book Co., 1960.

Simon, Herbert A., and Newell, Allen. "The Simulation of Human Thought." The RAND Corporation, Santa Monica, P-1734, June 1959.

Solo, Robert A. *Synthetic Rubber: A Case Study in Technological Development Under Government Direction*, Study of the Committee on the Judiciary, U.S. Senate, 85 Cong. 2 sess. Washington: 1959.

Solow, Robert M. "Investment and Technical Progress," in *Mathematical Methods in the Social Sciences, 1959*. Stanford: Stanford University Press, 1960.

_____. "Technical Change and the Aggregate Production Function," *Review of Economics and Statistics*, Vol. 39, August 1957.

_____. "Technical Progress, Capital Formation, and Economic Growth," *American Economic Review*, Vol. 52, No. 2, May 1962.

Stafford, Alfred B. "Is the Rate of Invention Declining?," *American Journal of Sociology*, May 1952.

Stein, M. I. "Creativity and the Scientist," in *The Direction of Research Establishments*. New York: Philosophical Library, 1957.

Stigler, George. "Industrial Organization and Economic Progress," in L. D. White (ed.), *The State of the Social Sciences*. Chicago: University of Chicago Press, 1956.

_____. *Capital and Rates of Return in Manufacturing Industries* (National Bureau of Economic Research). Princeton: Princeton University Press, 1963.

Stoikov, Vladimir. "The Allocation of Scientific Effort: Some Important Aspects," *Quarterly Journal of Economics*, Vol. 78, May 1964.

Strassmann, W. Paul. "Interrelated Industries and the Rate of Technological Change," *Review of Economic Studies*, Vol. 27, October 1959.

_____. *Risk and Technological Innovation: American Manufacturing Methods During the Nineteenth Century*. Ithaca: Cornell University Press, 1959.

Summers, Robert. *Cost Estimates as Predictors of Actual Weapons Costs: A Study of Major Hardware Articles*. The RAND Corporation, Santa Monica, RM-3061-PR, March 1965.

Taussig, Frank W. *Inventors and Money Makers*. New York: The Macmillan Company, 1915.

Terleckyj, Nestor E., Assisted by Halper, Harriet J. *Research and Development: Its Growth and Composition*. New York: National Industrial Conference Board, 1963.

_____. "Sources of Productivity Change. A Pilot Study Based on the

Experience of American Manufacturing Industries, 1899-1953." Unpublished doctoral dissertation, Columbia University, New York, 1959.

True, Alfred Charles. *A History of Agricultural Experimentation and Research in the United States, 1607-1925.* U.S. Department of Agriculture, Misc. Publication No. 251. Washington: 1937.

_____. *A History of Agricultural Extension Work in the United States, 1785-1923.* U.S. Department of Agriculture, Misc. Publication No. 15. Washington: U.S. Government Printing Office, 1928.

Tybout, Richard A. (ed). *Economics of Research and Development.* Columbus: Ohio State University Press, 1965.

U.S. Bureau of the Census. Report prepared for the Subcommittee on Antitrust and Monopoly of the Committee on' the Judiciary, U.S. Senate. *Concentration Ratios in Manufacturing Industry, 1958.* Washington: U.S. Government Printing Office, 1962.

U.S. Congress, Joint Committee on Atomic Energy. *Scientific Research in Great Britain.* Washington: U.S. Government Printing Office, 1960.

_____, Subcommittee on Economic Statistics of the Joint Economic Committee, 87 Cong. 1 sess. *Higher Unemployment Rates, 1957-60: Structural Transformation or Inadequate Demand.* Washington: U.S. Government Printing Office, 1961.

U.S. Department of Agriculture. *State Agricultural Experiment Stations.* Misc. Publication No. 904. Washington: U.S. Government Printing Office, 1962.

U.S. Department of Commerce, Area Redevelopment Administration. *Economic Redevelopment Research: The Geographic Mobility of Labor, Summary Report.* September 1964.

U.S. Department of Commerce, National Bureau of Standards. "Improving the National Climate for Invention and Innovation," Washington, November 16, 1964, Sec. 4, mimeographed.

U.S. Department of Labor, Bureau of Labor Statistics. *Impact of Automation.* A collection of 20 articles about technological change from the *Monthly Labor Review.* Bulletin No. 1287. Washington: Government Printing Office, 1960.

_____. *Manpower Report of the President and a Report on Manpower Requirements, Resources, Utilization, and Training, March 1965.* Washington: U.S. Government Printing Office.

Usher, Abbott P. *A History of Mechanical Inventions.* Cambridge: Harvard University Press, 1954.

Usher, Dan. "The Welfare Economics of Invention," *Economica,* Vol. 31, August 1964.

Van Deusen, E. L. "The Inventor in Eclipse," *Fortune,* December 1954.

Villard, Henry. "Competition, Oligopoly, and Research," *Journal of Political Economy*, Vol. 66, December 1958.

Weber, Arnold R. "The Interplant Transfer of Displaced Employees," in Gerald G. Somers, Edwin L. Cushman, and Nat Weinberg (eds.), *Adjusting to Technological Change*. New York: Harper and Row, 1963.

Weidenbaum, Murray L. "Government Encouragement of Private Sector Research and Development," *Studies in Comparative International Development*, Vol. I, No. 9. St. Louis: Washington University, 1965.

Weinberg, Alvin M. "Criteria for Scientific Choice," *Minerva*, Vol. 1, Winter 1963, and Vol. III, Autumn 1964.

Wiener, Norbert. *The Human Use of Human Beings*. Boston: Houghton Mifflin Co., 1950.

Williamson, Oliver E. "Innovation and Market Structure," *Journal of Political Economy*, Vol. 73, February 1965.

Wolfle, Dael. *America's Resources of Specialized Talent*. New York: Harper & Brothers, 1954.

Yeh, K. C. "Soviet and Communist Chinese Industrialization Strategies." The RAND Corporation, Santa Monica, P-3150, May 1965.

Index

A. D. Little, Inc., 54, 57, 62
Adams, Leonard P., 121*n*
Adjustments to technological advance, 2-3, 99-107, 109, 113-48
Administrative changes, difficulty of, 175
Advance notice of layoffs, need for, 126, 127*n*
Advertising, in technology diffusion, 103-04, 204
Aerojet General, 71, 84*n*
Aerospace. *See* Space research.
Agriculture: Employment in, 116, 120; research in, 56, 60, 88, 164, 166-67
Agriculture, Department of, 152; experiment stations, 41, 59, 76, 78; extension service, 104, 205-06; R&D in, 41, 159, 189, 191, 197, 203*n*; research support programs, 178, 180; training programs, 151
Air Force, U.S., 83, 94, 152, 165, 187
Aircraft, development of, 24-28, 42-43, 83, 94*n*, 105, 186
Aircraft industry: Employment in, 115-16; R&D in, 48-53, 55, 63, 67-73, 79, 164-65
Aluminum, 20, 81
American Research and Development Corp., 63

Applied research, 55-56, 59-61, 85, 87-88, 157, 164
Area Redevelopment Act, 123*n*
Army, U.S., 83, 152, 155, 157, 163
Aronson, Robert L., 121*n*
Arrow, Kenneth J., 18*n*
Asher, Harold, 105
Ashton, T. S., 29*n*
Atomic energy, R&D in, 52
Atomic Energy Commission (AEC), 165; civilian applications programs, 159, 164; R&D in, 153-54; sponsoring of research, 61, 158, 178; training programs, 151
Attrition: In employment reduction, 117-19, 122*n*, 124; in product development, 97
Automation, 113, 118*n*
Automobiles (*see also* Transportation industry), 31, 131, 146-48
Aviation (*see also* Aircraft industry), 42, 76, 164-65, 178

Bain, A. D., 99*n*
Bain, Joe S., 194*n*
Baldwin, William, 62*n*
Bancroft, Gertrude, 117*n*, 119*n*
Basic research, 55-56, 59-61, 76, 85-88, 158, 164-67, 177-81

229